DRAWING
THE HEAD
FOR ARTISTS

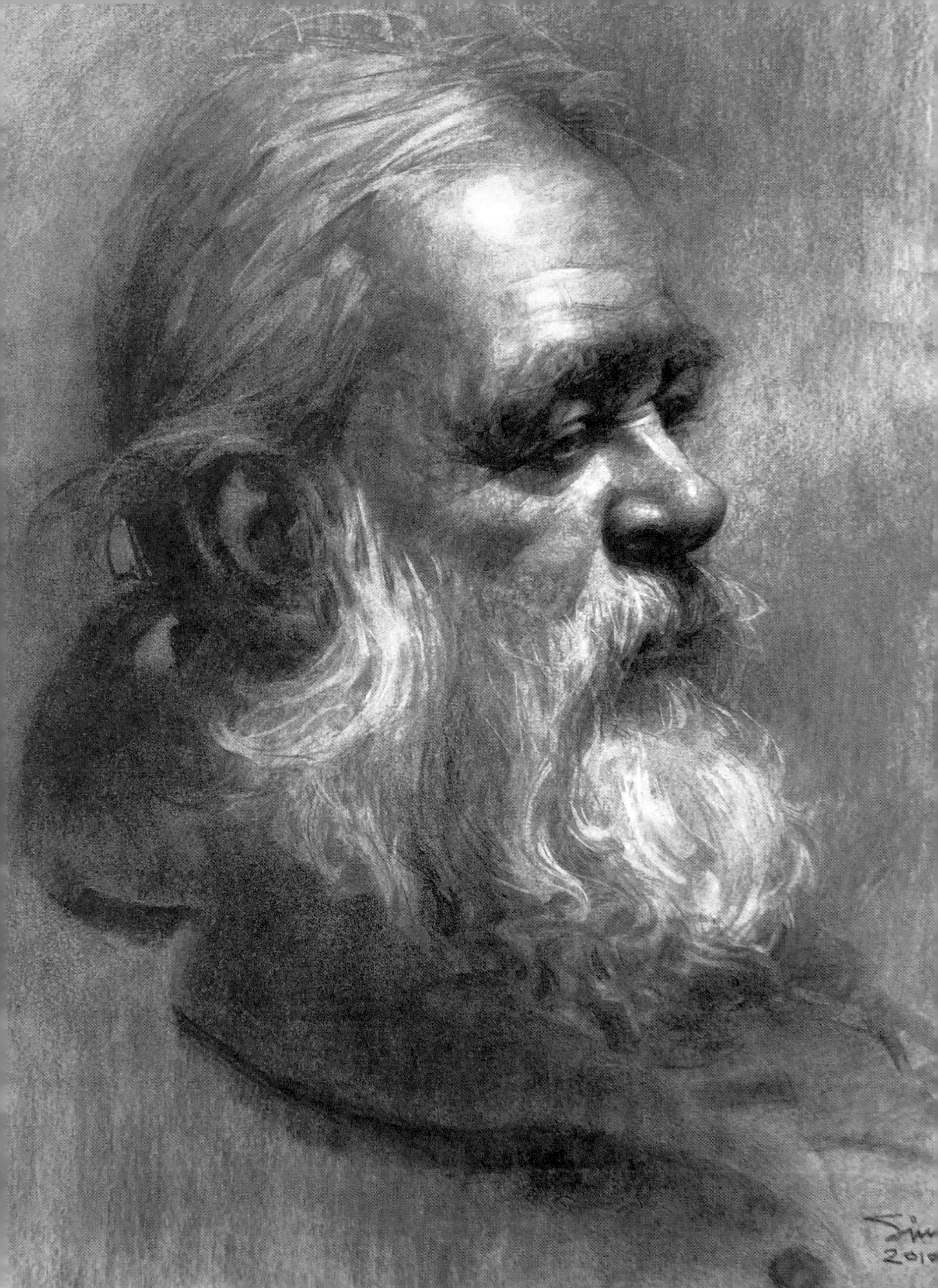

DRAWING THE HEAD
FOR ARTISTS

Techniques for Mastering
Expressive Portraiture

OLIVER SIN

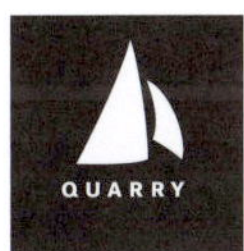

Quarto.com

Design and presentation © 2019 Quarto Publishing Group USA Inc.
Text and artwork © 2019 Oliver Sin

First published in 2019 by Quarry Books, an imprint of The Quarto Group,
100 Cummings Center, Suite 265-D, Beverly, MA 01915, USA.
T (978) 282-9590 F (978) 283-2742

EEA Representation, WTS Tax d.o.o.,
Žanova ulica 3, 4000 Kranj, Slovenia.
www.wts-tax.si

Quarry Books titles are also available at discount for retail, wholesale, promotional, and bulk purchase.
For details, contact the Special Sales Manager by email at specialsales@quarto.com or by mail at
The Quarto Group, Attn: Special Sales Manager, 100 Cummings Center, Suite 265-D, Beverly, MA 01915, USA.

12

ISBN: 978-1-63159-692-6

Digital edition published in 2019
eISBN: 978-1-63159-693-3

Library of Congress Cataloging-in-Publication Data

Sin, Oliver, author.
Drawing the head for artists : techniques for mastering expressive
   portraiture / Oliver Sin.
ISBN 9781631596933 (ebook) | ISBN 9781631596926 (pbk. with flaps)
1. Portrait drawing--Technique. 2. Head in art.
LCC NC773 (ebook) | LCC NC773 .S53 2019 (print)
DDC 743.4/2--dc23

LCCN 2019011790 (print) | LCCN 2019012443 (ebook)

Design and page layout: Allison Meierding

Page 2: *Bob*. Vine charcoal on paper, 14" × 17" (36 × 43 cm). Recognized for Exceptional Merit at the 2019
International Portrait Competition by the Portrait Society of America.

Printed in Huizhou City, Guangdong, China TT032026

This book is dedicated to
the many students whom I have
taught but also have learned from.
I have tried to teach you what I know,
but you have opened my eyes to what
I wouldn't have otherwise seen.

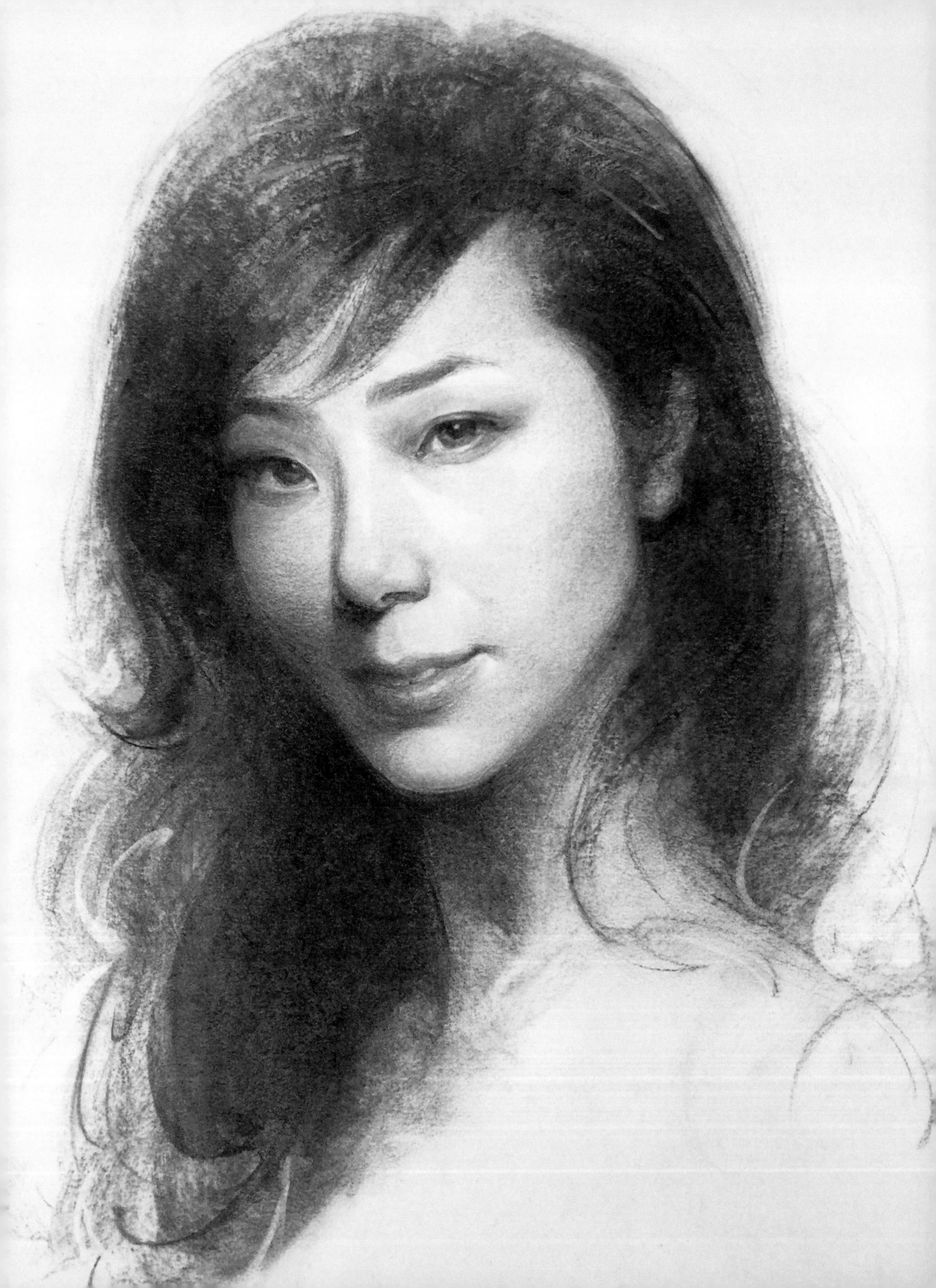

CONTENTS

PREFACE:
CREATING A PORTRAIT WITH SPIRIT

There is a difference between head drawing and portrait drawing. Head drawing focuses on shapes, plane changes, anatomy, form, and perspective. Portrait drawing is an artistic representation of a person's spirit—their expression, likeness, personality, and mood.

The "form" of the head refers only to the external appearance of the face, expression, and position. "Spirit" refers to the character, personality, and energy. Working from live models is important, not only to develop drawing skills but also to gain a better understanding of the subject's character and personality. When there is interaction, the artist and subject develop some level of connection and share a humanistic moment, and the quality of the portrait benefits from this.

It's easy to become absorbed in the technical aspects of drawing and miss the purpose. Technique without spirit is meaningless, but feeling cannot be conveyed without technique—the two must be united.

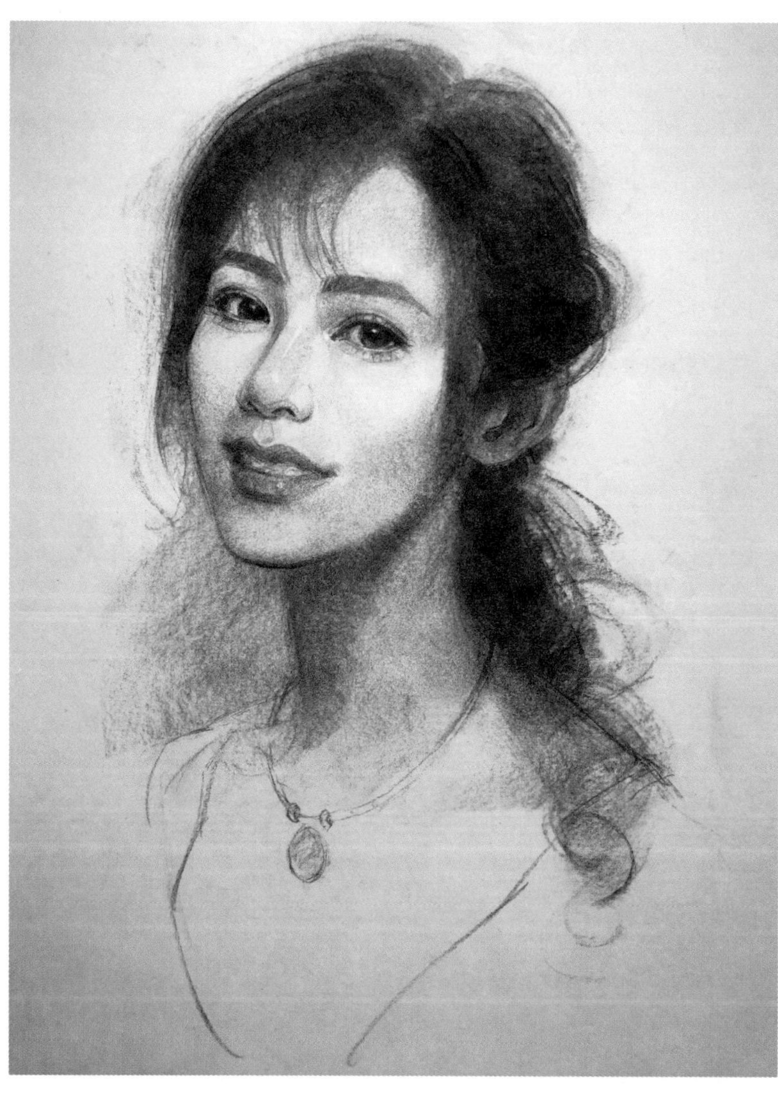

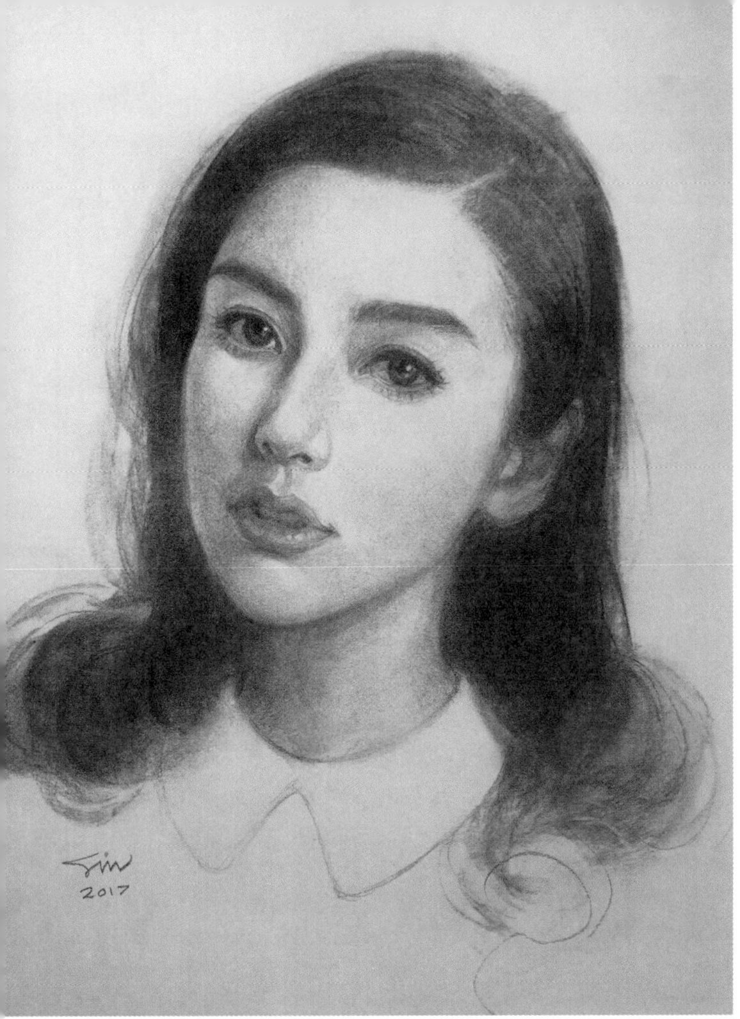 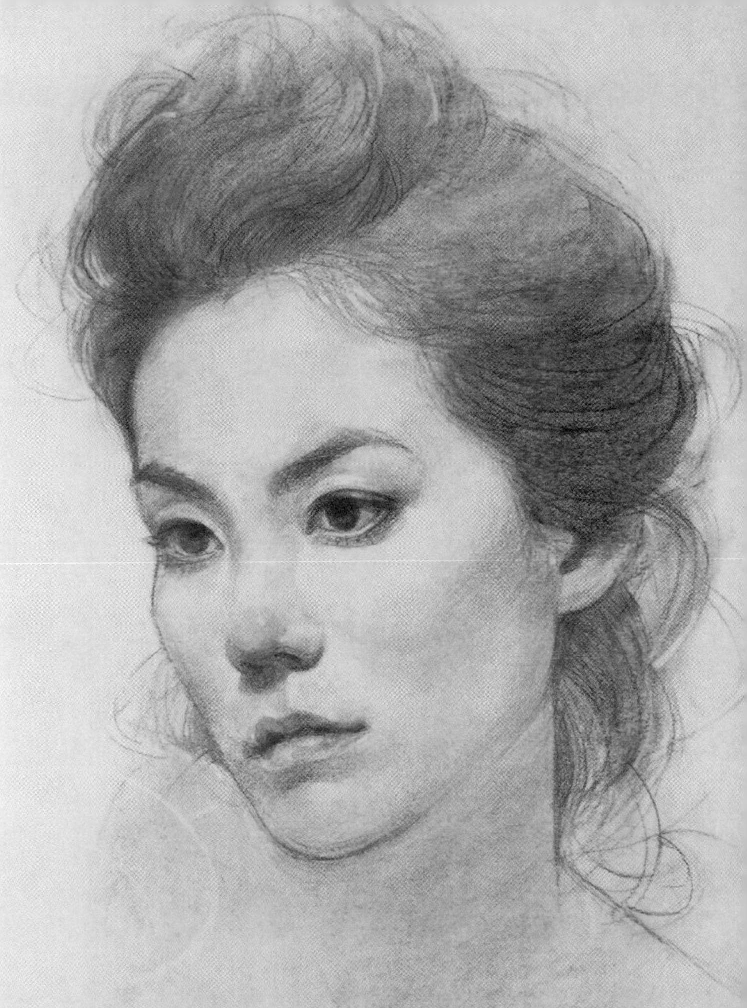

To draw spirited portraits, you must consider what message, or perception, a portrait will communicate. The artist's personal perspective is the common denominator of every work of art he or she creates. Each artwork reflects the unique perspective of the artist, no matter the style or subject. This is the element of a good drawing that only comes from within the artist.

What catches your attention at the first impression of a model who is a stranger? If your model is a young woman smiling sweetly, keep the line qualities light, fluid, and minimal. Focus on the twinkle in her eyes or the simple curves in her full lips. Aim for a lighthearted rendition, nothing overworked.

These portraits are of my mother and father, drawn from life in 2016 and 2018, respectively. Since moving to the United States almost three decades ago from my native city, Hong Kong, China, I haven't spent much time with my parents. Drawing them was an unforgettable and priceless experience and a time of reconnection. Both drawings express an impromptu mood, compelling the viewer to observe two real personalities. These are two of the most representative works in my art career, so I touch on them a couple of times in this book.

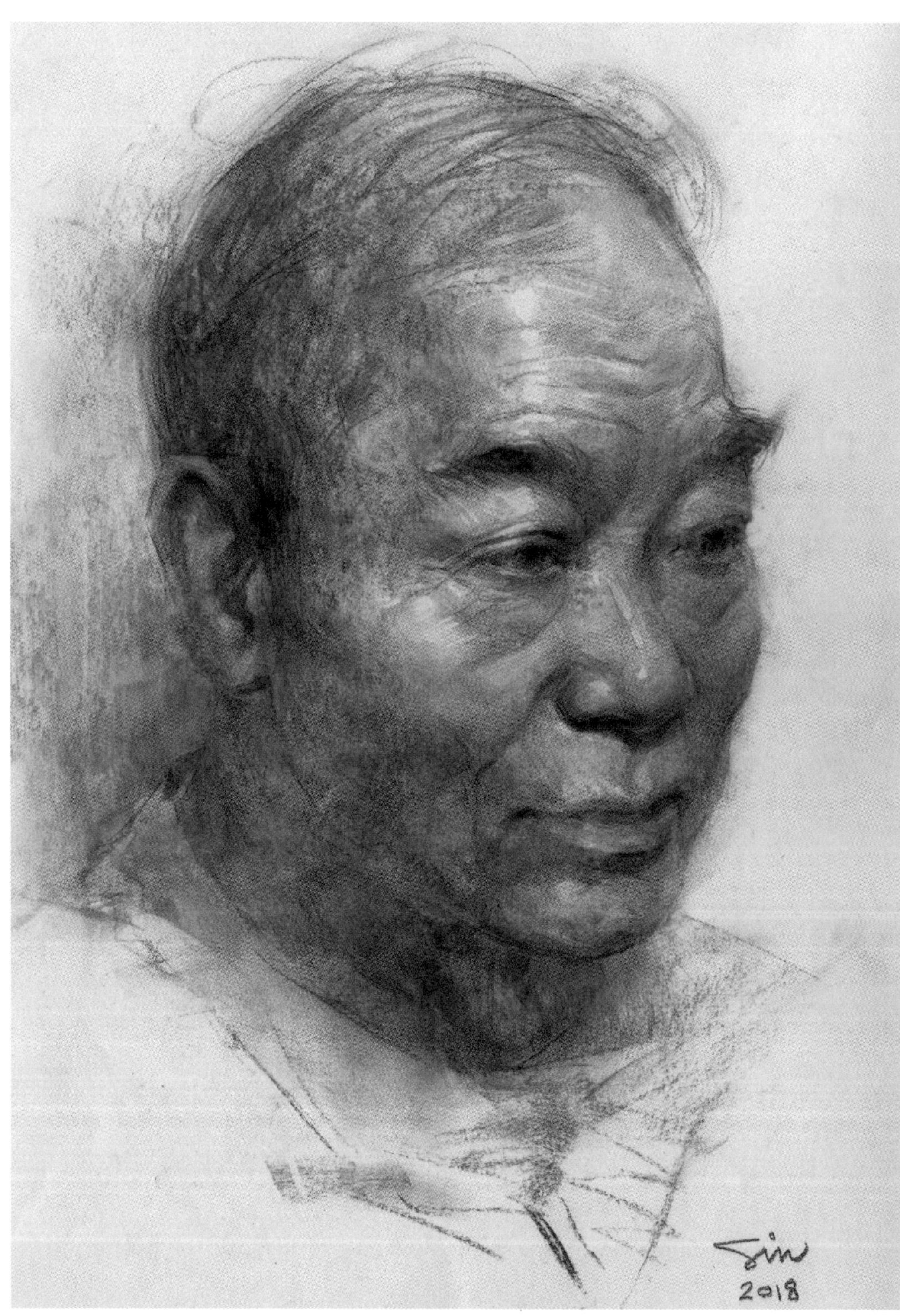

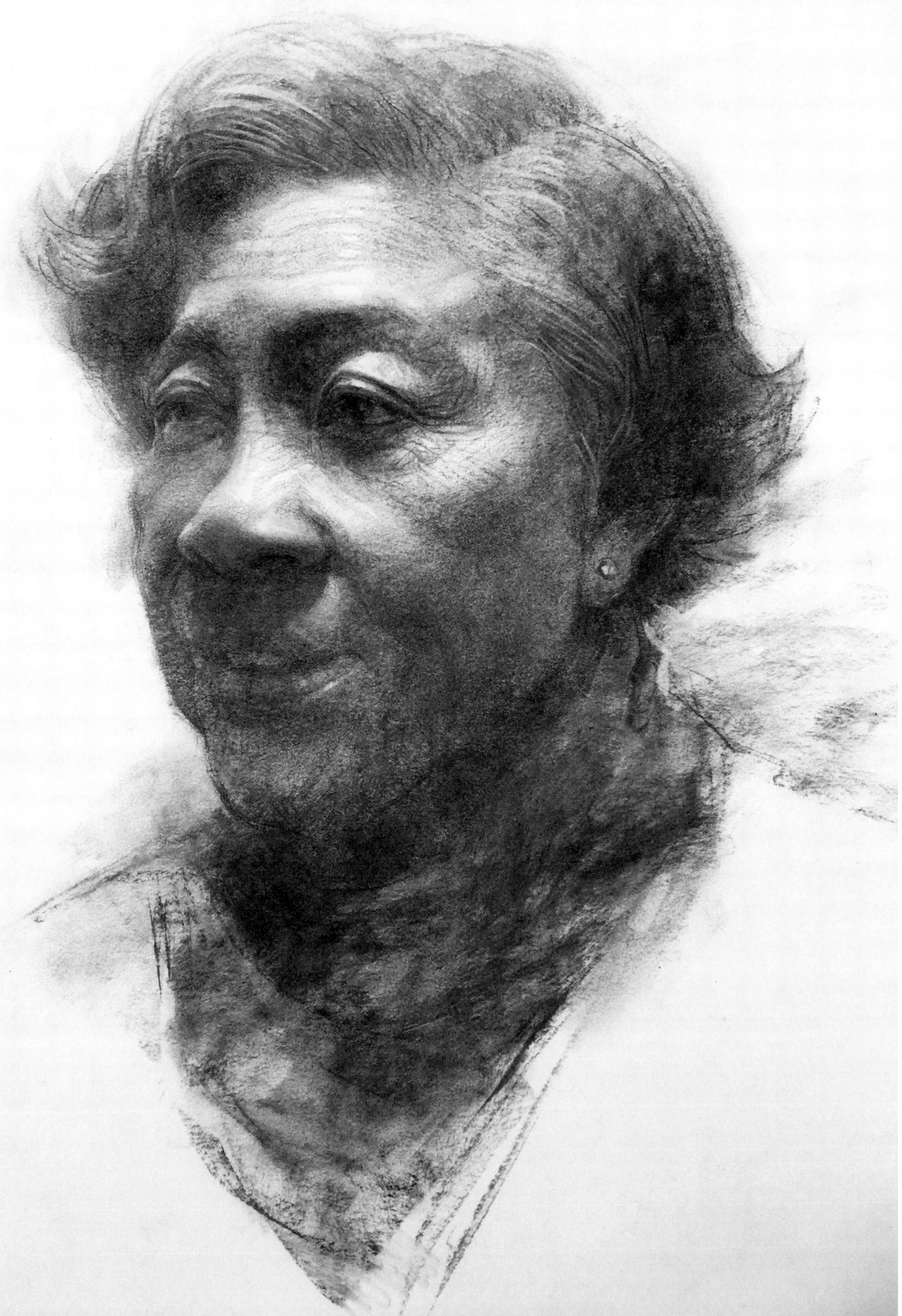

The model in these portraits is Vivian Chow Wai-Man, one of the most renowned singers and actresses in Asia. I grew up listening to her music in the 1980s and have always been a faithful fan. I have rendered more than ten portraits of Vivian Chow throughout the years. She happened to see them on Instagram, through which we connected and have been friends ever since. I returned to Hong Kong, China, in 2017 to attend her concert, during which she was gracious enough to display my portraits of her on the concert screen and acknowledge our friendship through interaction in art. I was so blown away by her graceful gesture in including our acquaintance along her rich, glamorous journey as a great celebrity.

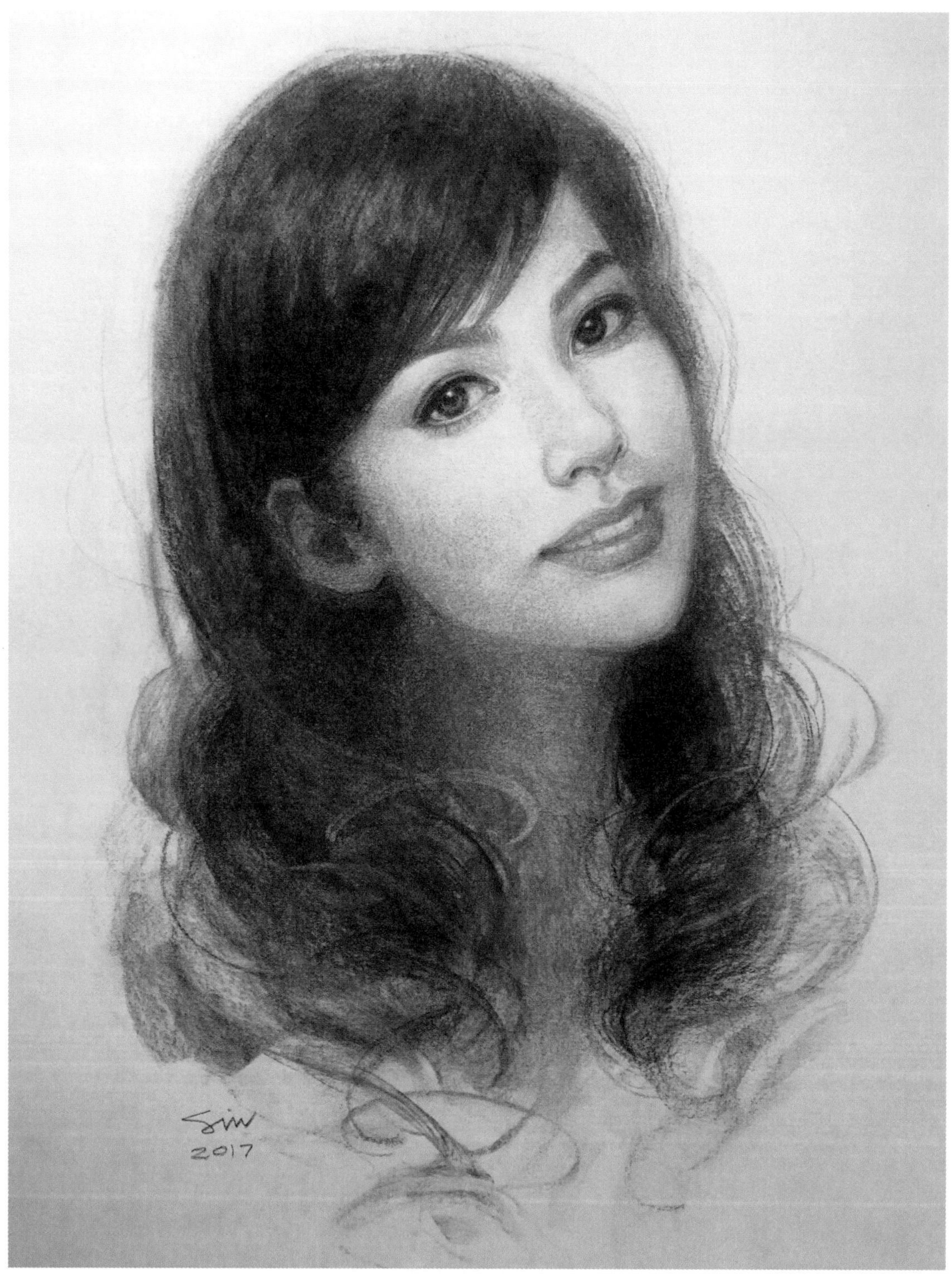

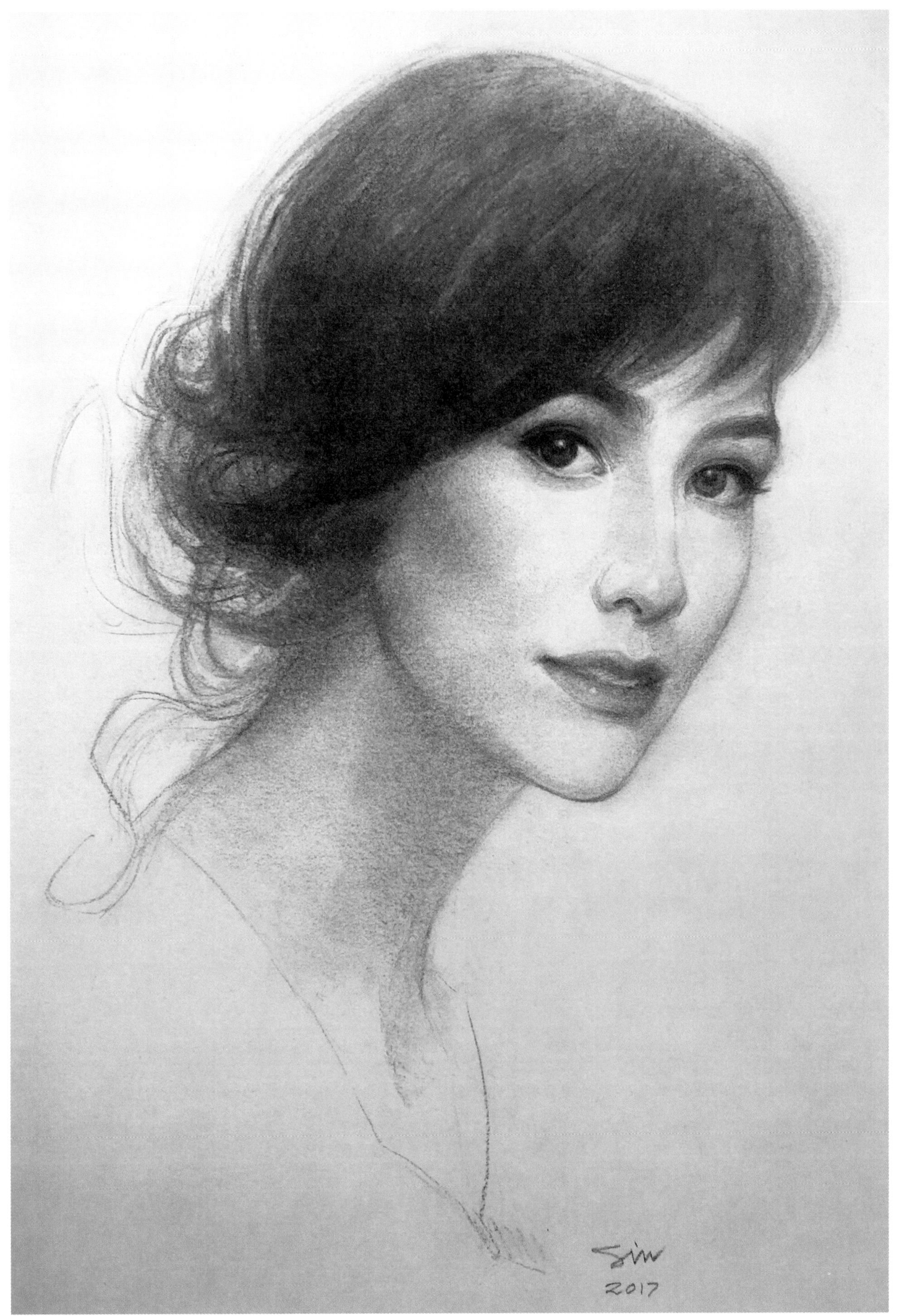

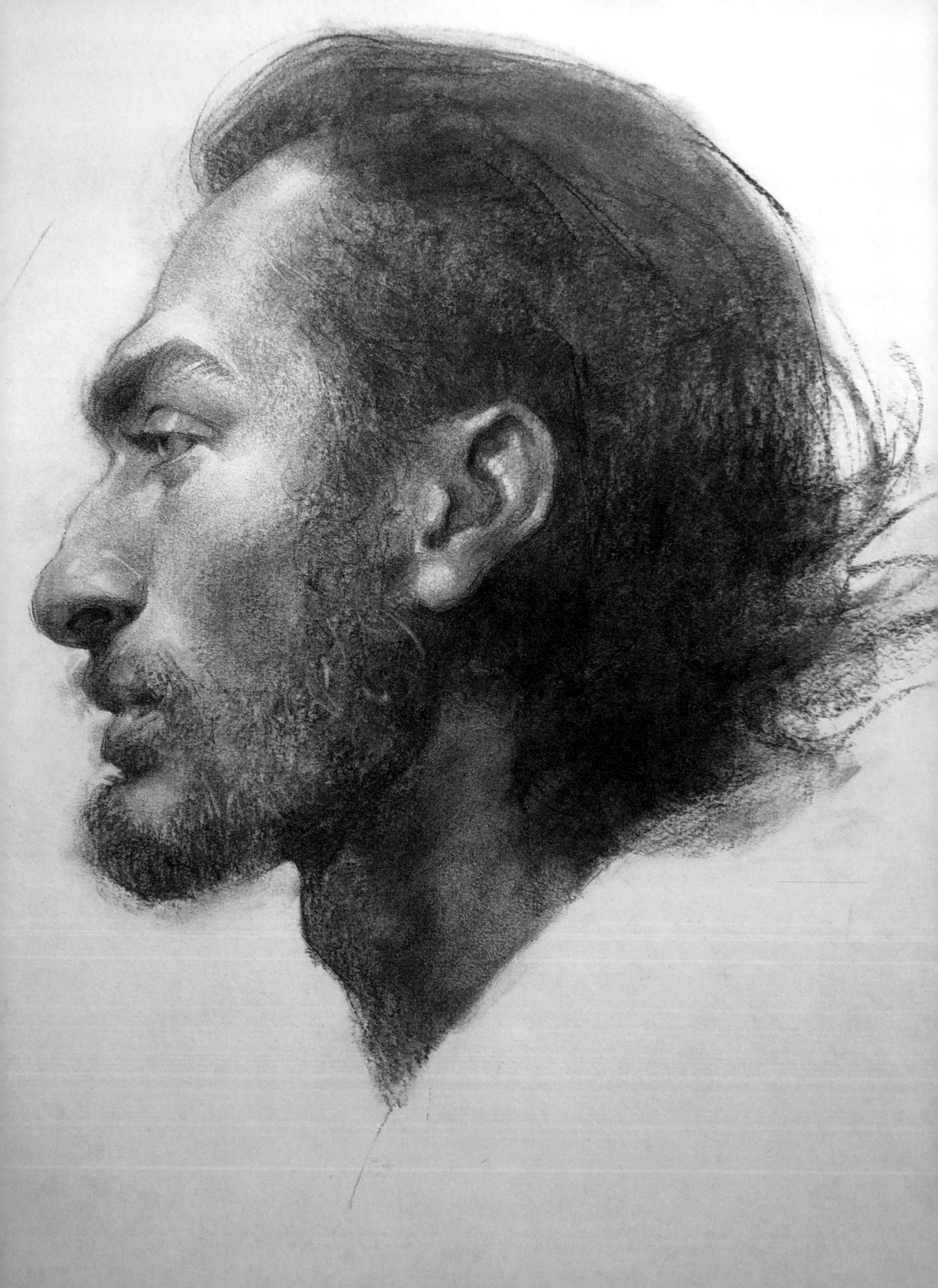

1

PORTRAIT DRAWING MATERIALS

KEY MEDIUMS & TOOLS

Vine Charcoal and Willow Charcoal

I use vine and willow charcoal sticks for my portrait drawings to achieve the chiaroscuro technique. *Chiaroscuro*, an Italian term meaning light (*chiaro*) and dark (*oscuro*), is used to enhance the dimensionality of drawings by creating smooth, subtle transitions among values.

Artists use vine and willow charcoal, which are made by burning vines or branches in a kiln, for their versatile properties. Sticks of vine and willow charcoal, which are fragile and break easily, are available in a variety of lengths, thicknesses, and densities or degrees of hardness. These mediums produce marks in a wide range of values, from very light to intensely dark, which suits them perfectly to the chiaroscuro technique.

Willow charcoal is black, while vine charcoal is dark gray. Vine charcoal's lighter tone and ease of removal make it a favorite of artists for creating initial sketches or preliminary compositions, but it is less suitable for creating detailed artworks because it has a tendency to fade. Darker values can be achieved by applying willow charcoal over vine charcoal, or applying the two together. Vine charcoal can also be combined with other charcoal mediums, such as compressed charcoal.

> ### Safety Note
> Both workable and final fixatives are toxic, so only use them outdoors.

Kneaded Eraser

When working with vine and willow charcoal, I use a kneaded eraser to remove, lift, and redistribute values.

Because kneaded erasers can be easily stretched and shaped, they're excellent for subtractive work, to shape form, refine linework, and create highlights.

Other helpful tools for subtracting and manipulating values are retractable erasers, gum erasers, extra-soft erasers, single-edged razor blades, and bristle brushes. The narrow head of a retractable eraser allows for greater control in adjusting details.

Fixative

Unfixed charcoal drawings are extremely vulnerable to surface damage. The slightest movement or an accidental touch can leave a noticeable smudge, reduce the intensity of value, and muddy highlights. Fixative can actually strengthen a drawing, allowing for additional layering by acting as a "glue" for a new application of medium, and ensuring that fine dustings are not lost.

Use a workable fixative while a drawing is in process. Note that fixative will change the appearance of a charcoal drawing by

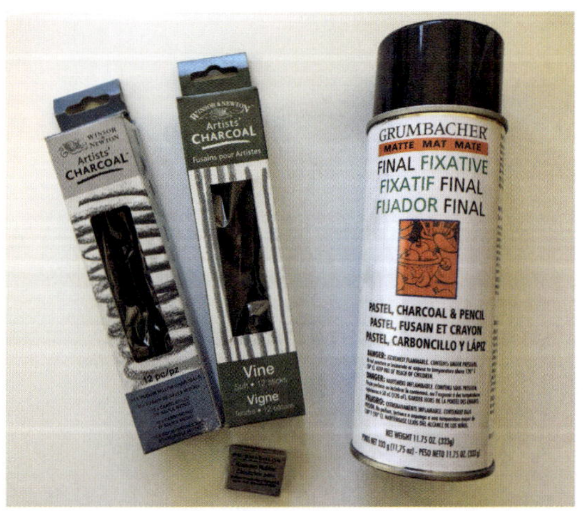

▶ *From left:* Willow charcoal, a kneaded eraser, vine charcoal, and a spray can of final fixative

darkening its values slightly, and that a heavy coat of fixative will cause charcoal particles to float into the saturated paper's grain, thus compromising the drawing's finer details.

The number of layers of workable fixative you use will depend on the number of layers of charcoal in a drawing. Typically three to five layers of fixative are sufficient.

To finish a charcoal drawing, use a final fixative in a matte sheen.

WORKING WITH VINE AND WILLOW CHARCOAL

1 | Break a charcoal stick into smaller pieces about 1 inch (2.5 cm) long. To hold the charcoal correctly, position it between the thumb and the first two fingers, and draw with the broad side rather than the tip to create an extremely soft-value stroke. If you hold a piece of charcoal as if to write with it, that angle will produce a hard line, which is undesirable. Value is the most basic element in my portrait drawings, and I use line minimally, usually only in conjunction with massing to clarify edges and details.

2 | Practice changing strokes from value to hard line, then from hard line to value, applying soft pressure as if you're caressing the drawing surface, so that you may use your finger to blend the charcoal into the paper.

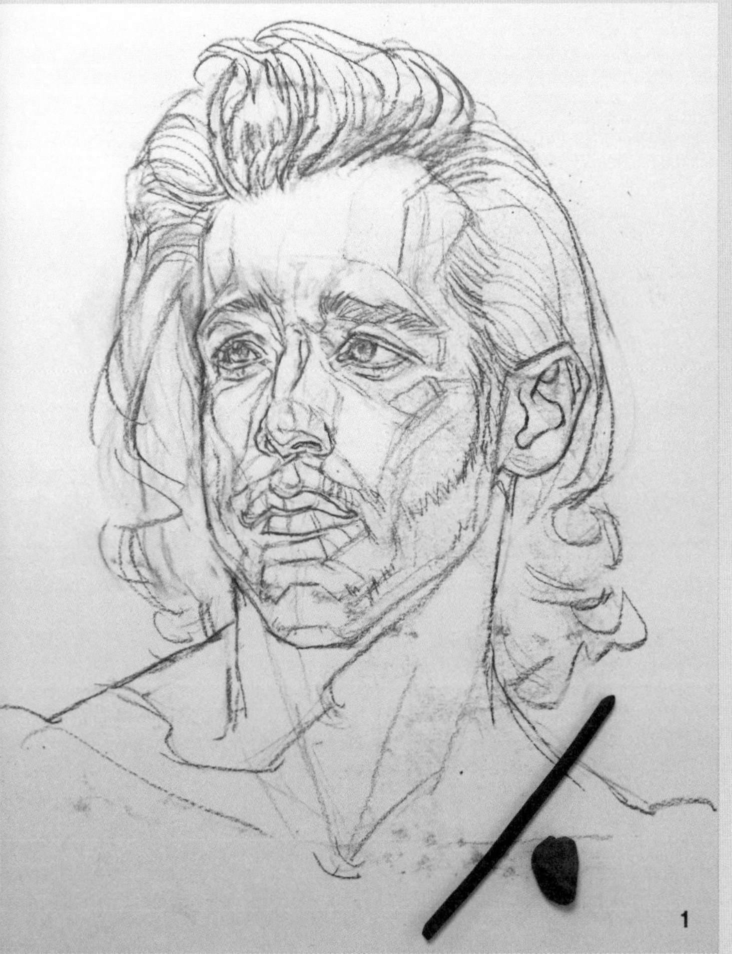

1

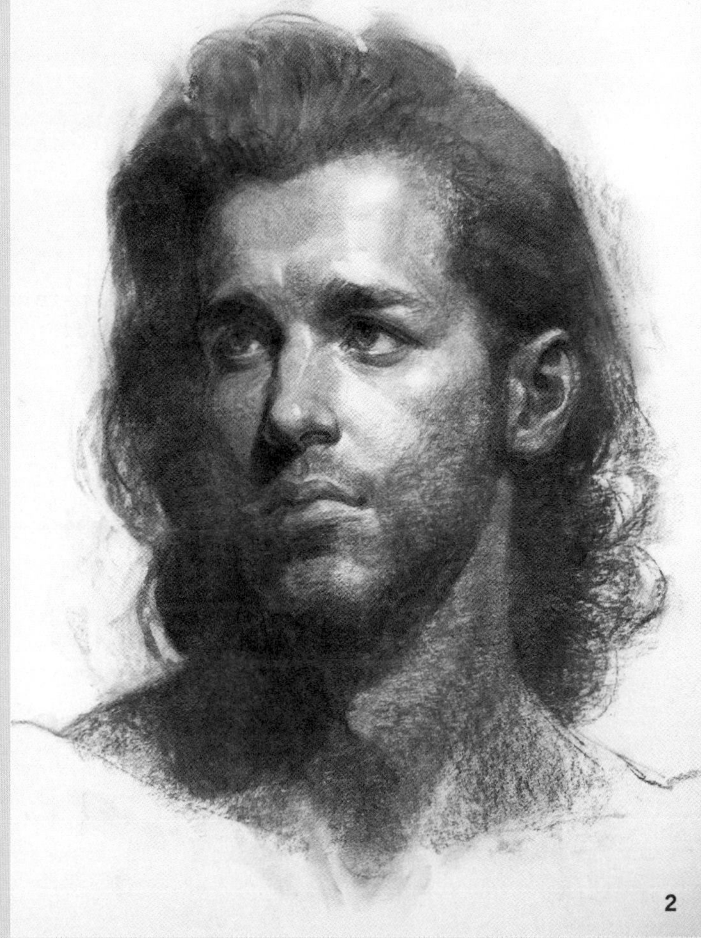

2

Compressed Charcoal

Compressed charcoal, which is harder than both vine and willow charcoal, is sold as sticks and pencils. I use this tool sparingly, and usually only to finish a drawing, to help create visual emphasis by defining hard edges (see page 96).

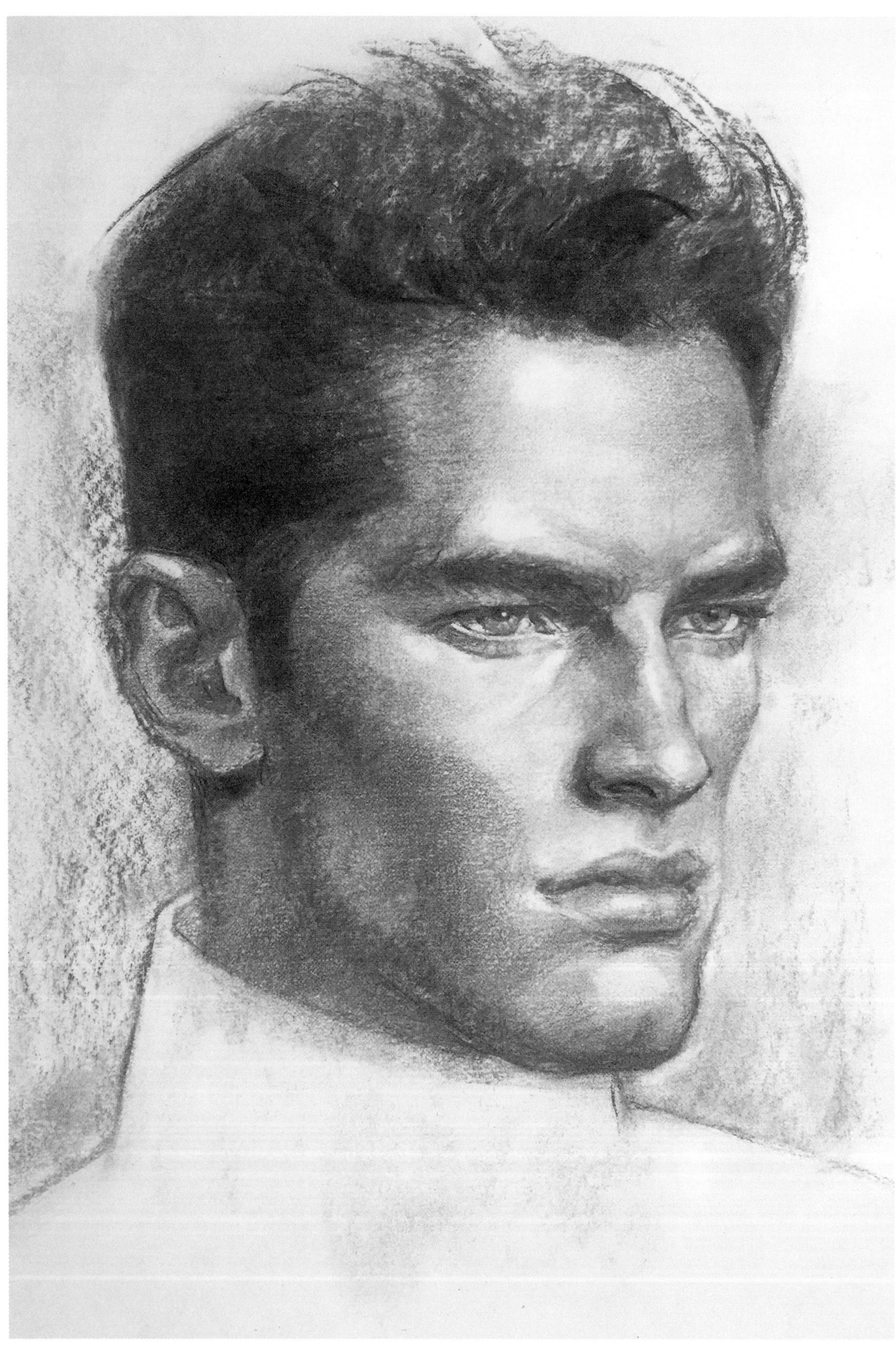

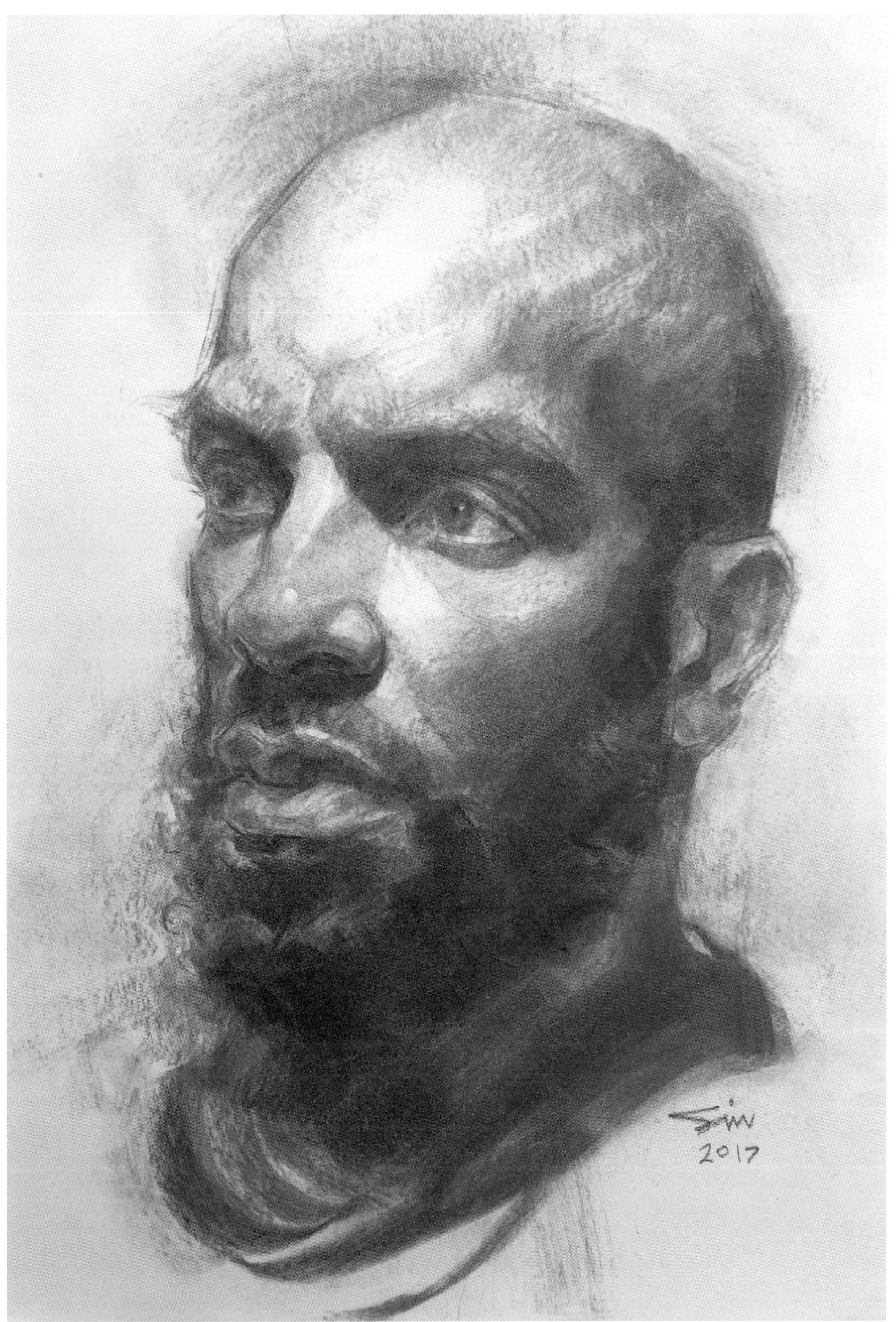

2017

Paper

Paper is as important to your artwork as the charcoal you make your marks with. Good paper can make or break a drawing; it can also make the drawing process easier or more difficult.

The paper I use and recommend is Strathmore 400 Series Drawing (18 x 24 inches/46 x 61 cm), which has a durable surface with a medium tooth; and 500 Series Drawing, Medium Surface (23 x 29 inches/ 58 x 74 cm), which is professional grade.

Another aspect to consider is whether a paper is of archival quality, which can also affect its durability as well as the value of the finished artwork.

With the exception of the textured and toned papers I use in two alternate techniques (see page 131), in my experience papers made specifically for charcoal are too textured, and Bristol papers are too smooth, flawless, and nonabsorbent. Regardless, I strongly recommend that you experiment with different surfaces to explore a range of results.

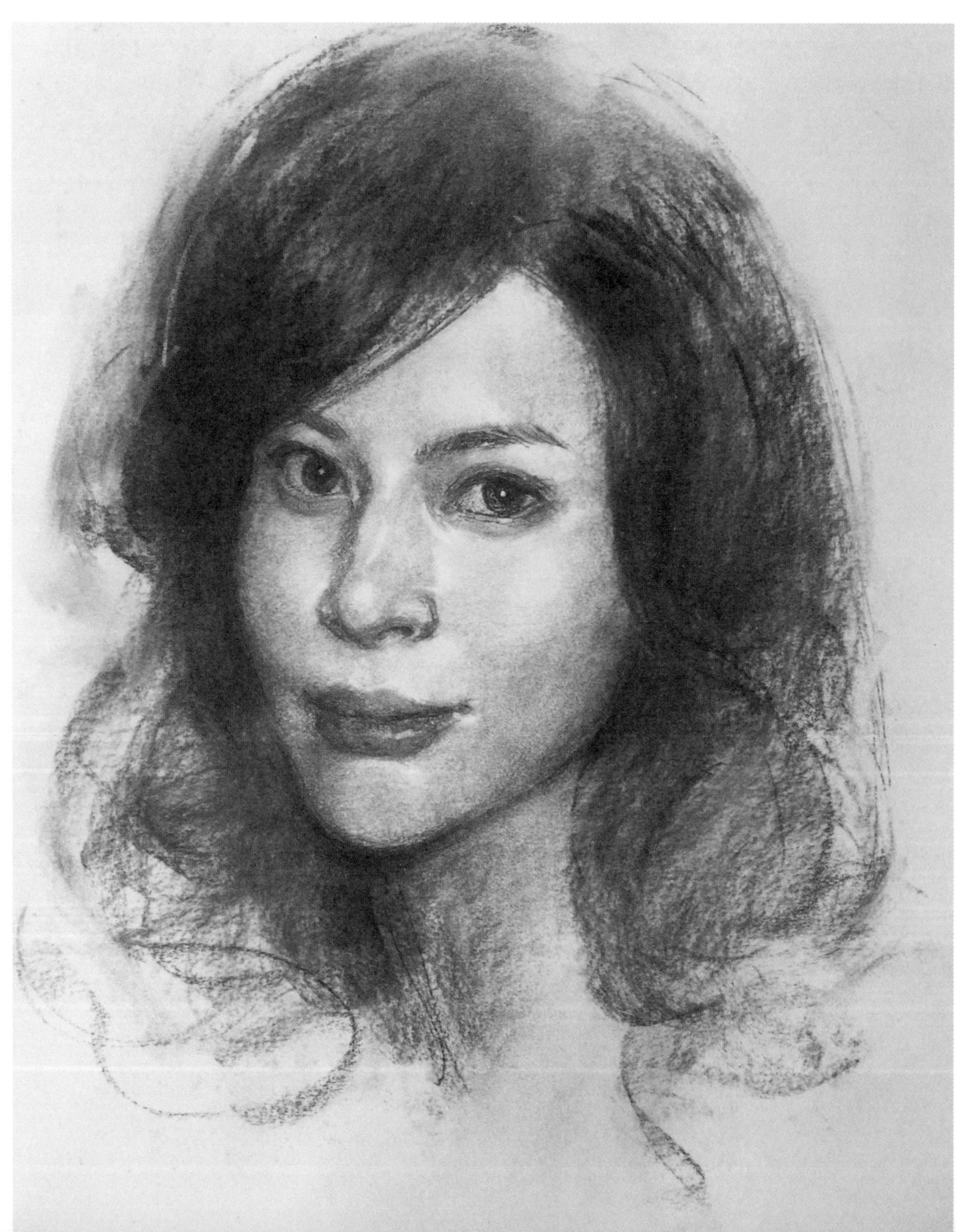

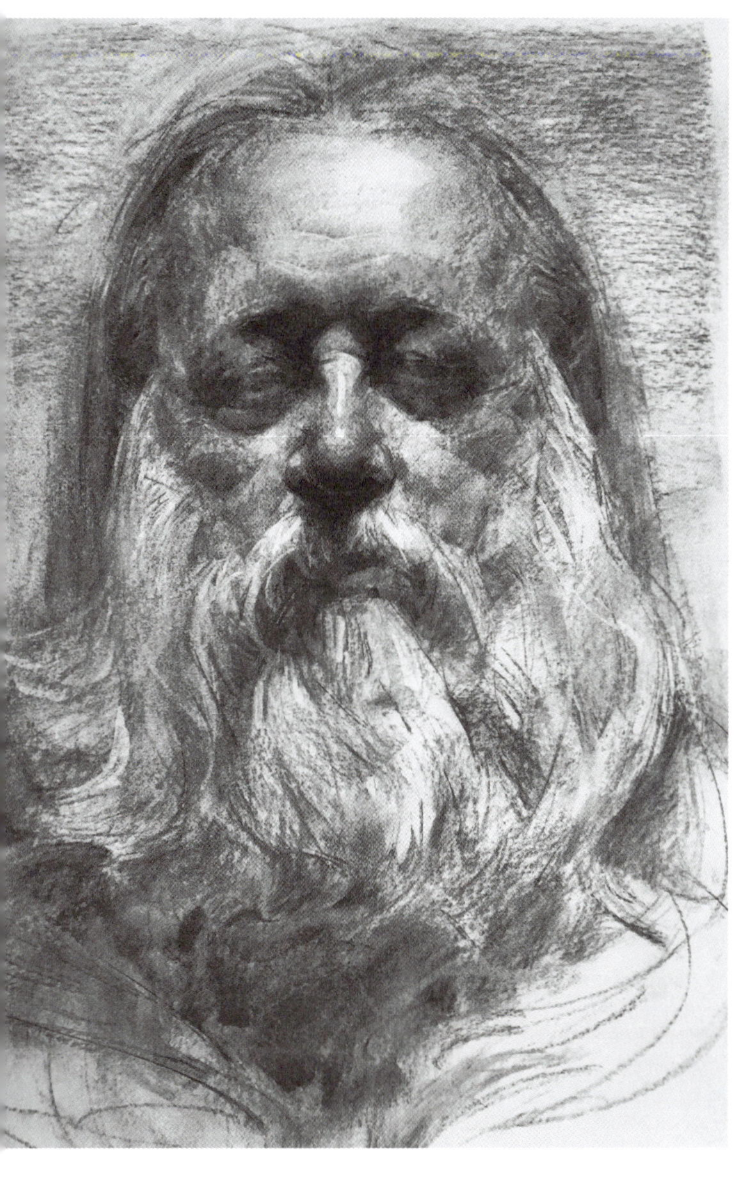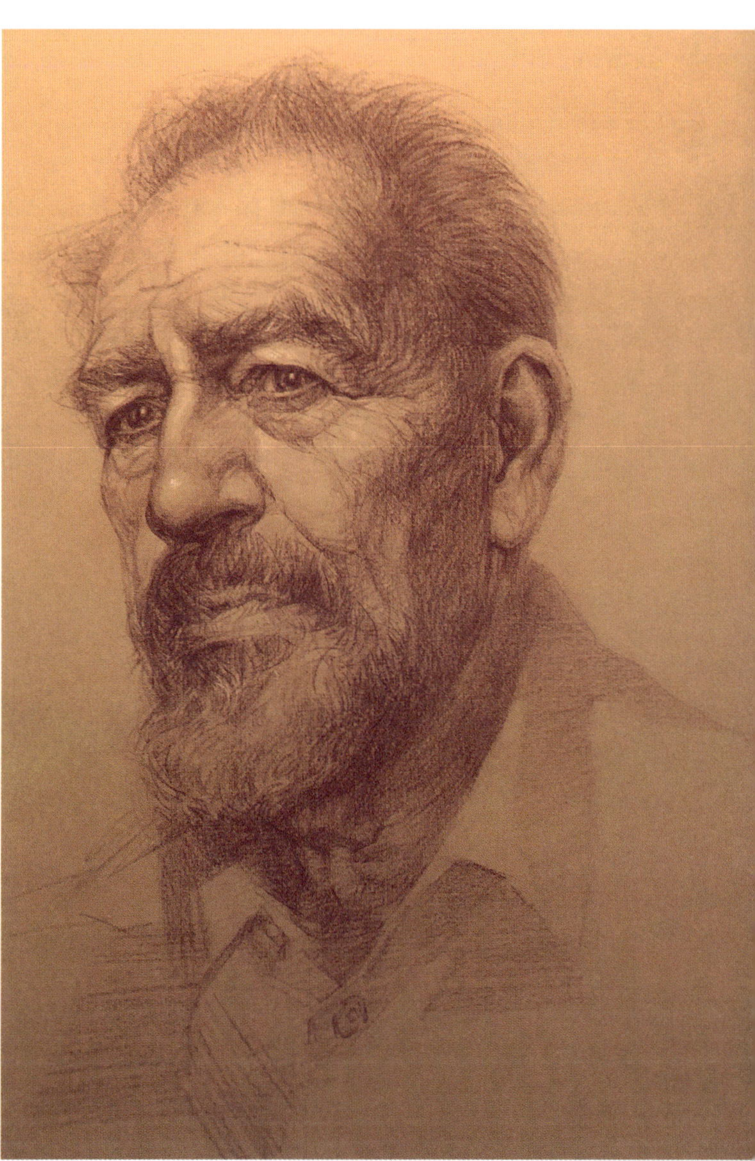

▲ The papers used for the portraits shown above and opposite are representative of the choices I make based on the technique I use: smoother paper for working light to dark, the primary technique shown in this book (opposite), and toothier papers for dark-to-light work (above left) and work on toned paper (above right). For the portrait on toned paper, I used CarbOthello pastel pencil in Caput Mortuum Red (#645) on Strathmore 500 Series charcoal paper in Golden Brown.

SKETCHBOOKS

Sketchbooks are great tools for collecting information, forming creative ideas, and keeping a creative journal of exploration. I use sketchbooks predominately for drawing from life. The purpose of a sketch is to observe and capture interesting details and the general pose and gesture of the subject. The more you can observe and appreciate at a glance, the faster you can draw and the more you can capture.

A sketchbook is an avenue for free-flowing creativity. There are no deadlines to meet, no rules, and no client expectations. You can sketch anything or anyone who interests you. Don't worry about finishing any one drawing or perfecting a sketch. The goal of sketching is observation. It's okay to make mistakes. Try to simply have fun, and let your sketchbook become a small passion project.

Sketchbooks are available in a variety of sizes and paper types. I always carry a small, 5- x 8-inch (12.5 x 20 cm) Moleskine sketchbook so I can record anything that appeals to me.

You can sketch with any drawing medium, including pen. Although the permanence of the lines may be intimidating, it motivates artists to observe more carefully before sketching, making it a great learning tool. Try different tools and combinations. With experimentation, you will discover what you prefer.

Sketching is an "anytime, anywhere" pursuit for me, especially when traveling. You may find time to draw while waiting in line, riding public transportation, or sitting in a café, at the airport, or on an airplane.

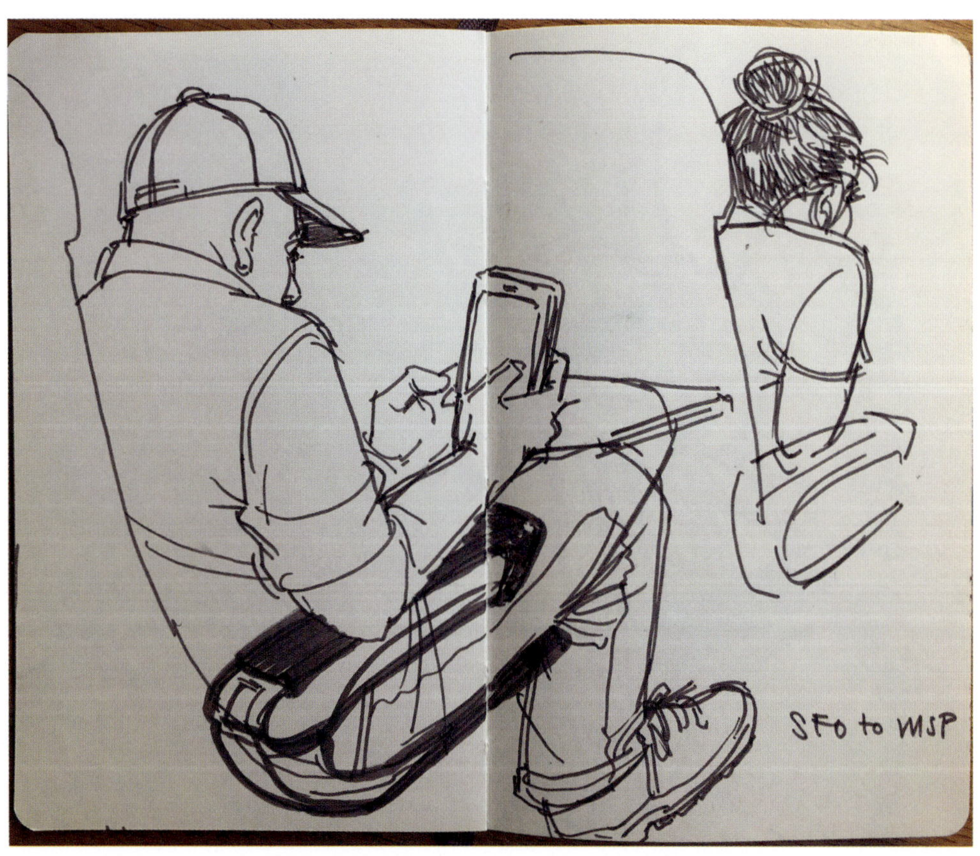

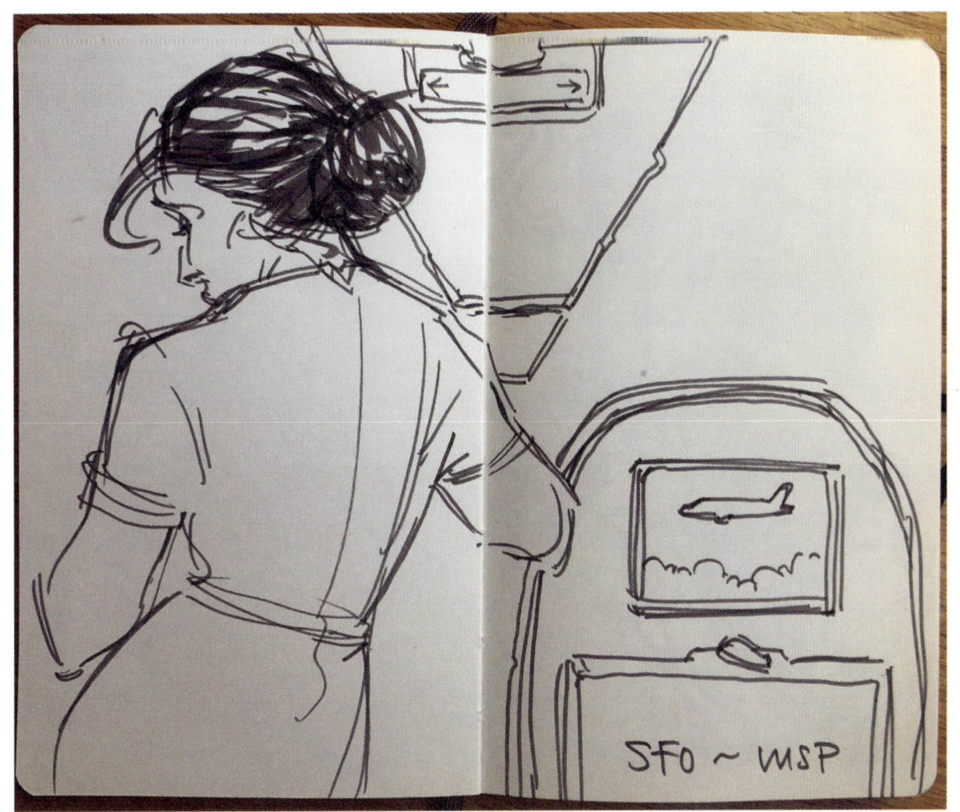

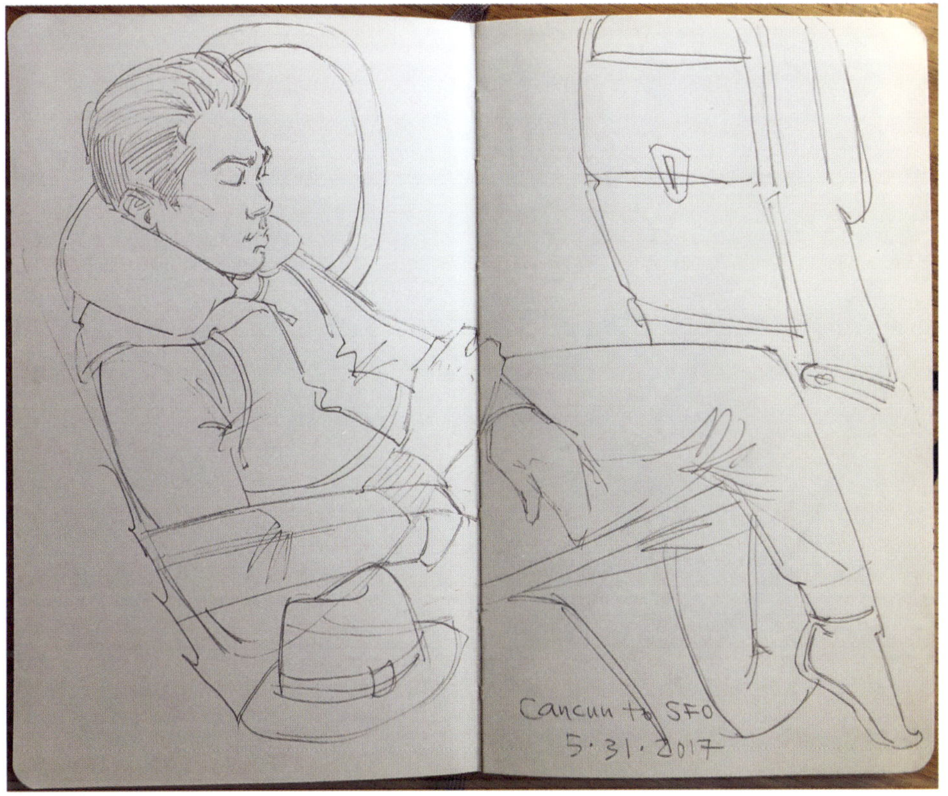

I created these sketches while flying on airplanes, using ink marker and pen in a 5- x 8-inch (12.5 x 20 cm) Moleskine sketchbook. If sketching in public makes you feel self-conscious, working with a small sketchbook like this draws little attention.

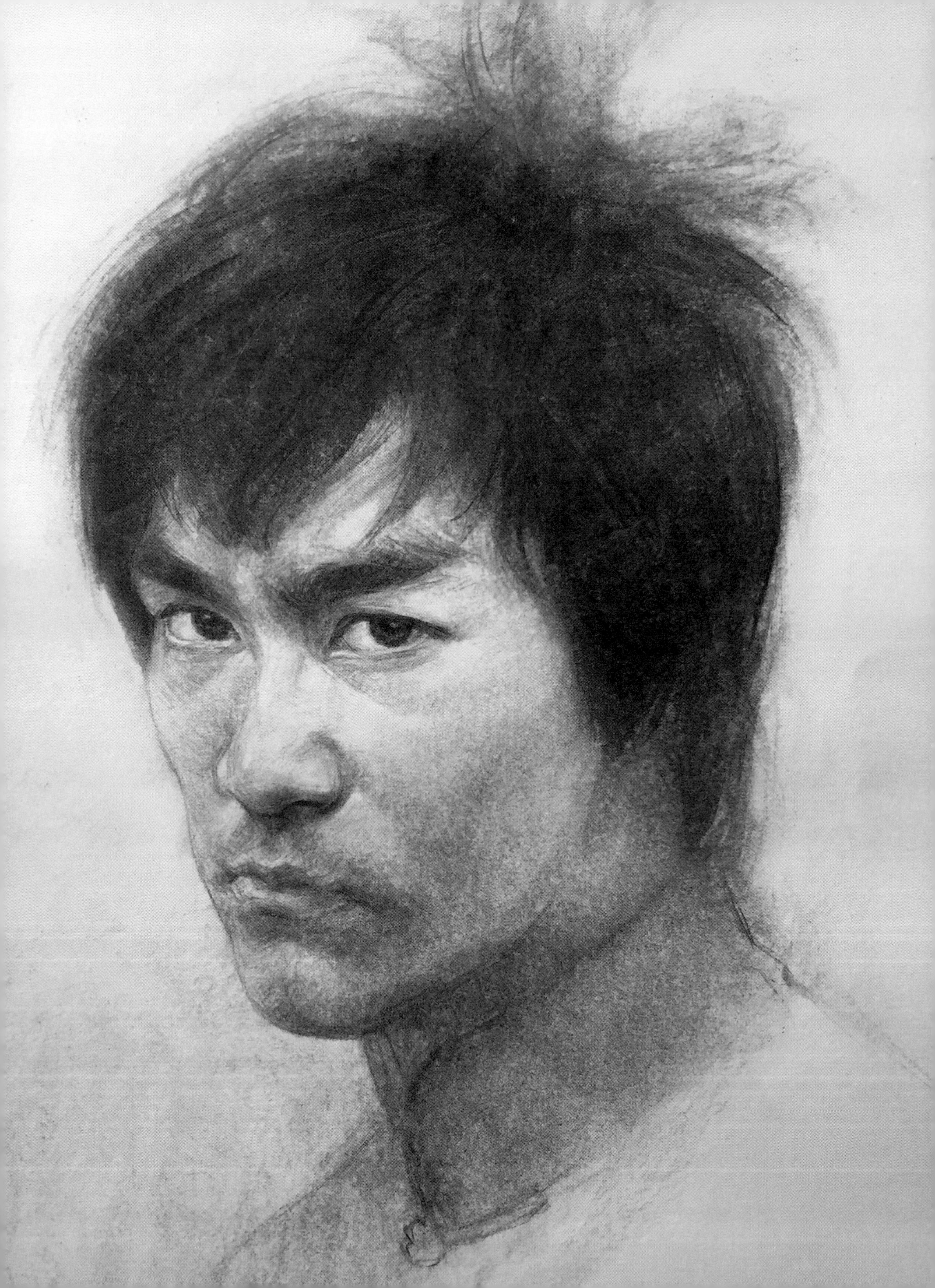

2

—

ESSENTIAL CONCEPTS & TECHNIQUES

BASIC DRAWING TECHNIQUES

The possibilities for using drawing materials are limitless, but there are some traditional methods of application you should know.

Hatching

Hatching is the application of tone, or shading, by drawing closely spaced parallel lines. The closer the lines are together, the darker the shading appears. Artists adjust the length, angle, closeness, and quality of the lines to create variation.

Crosshatching

Crosshatching is the application of single hatch marks at an angle to existing hatch marks to darken the tone. Hatching and crosshatching are often used together to add dimension and shading.

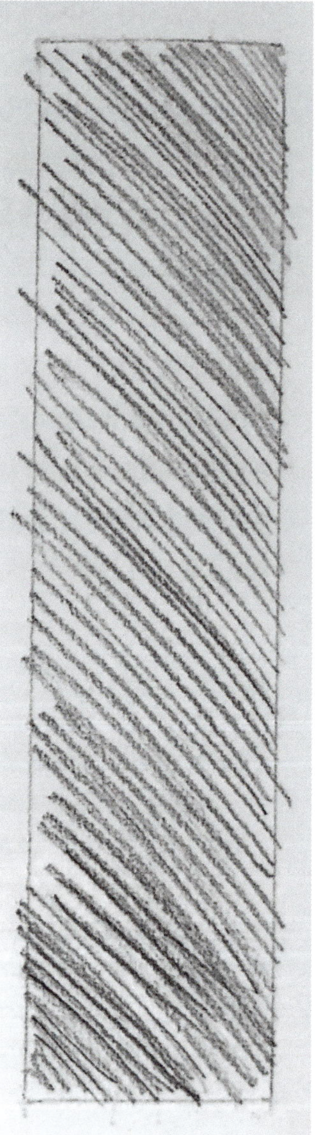

Hatching

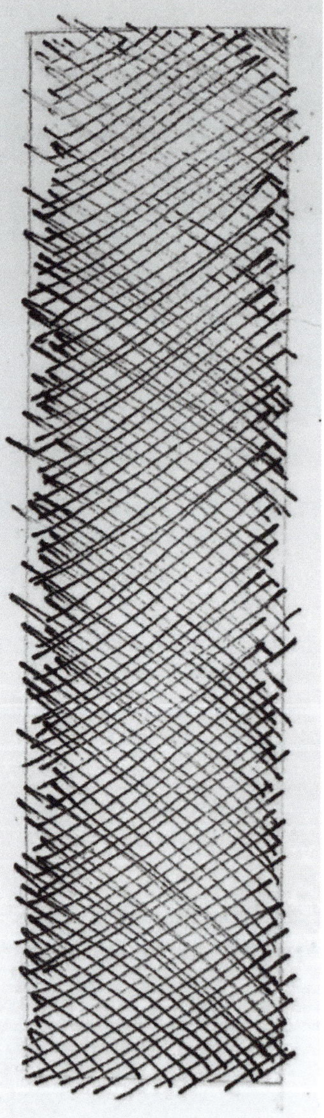

Crosshatching

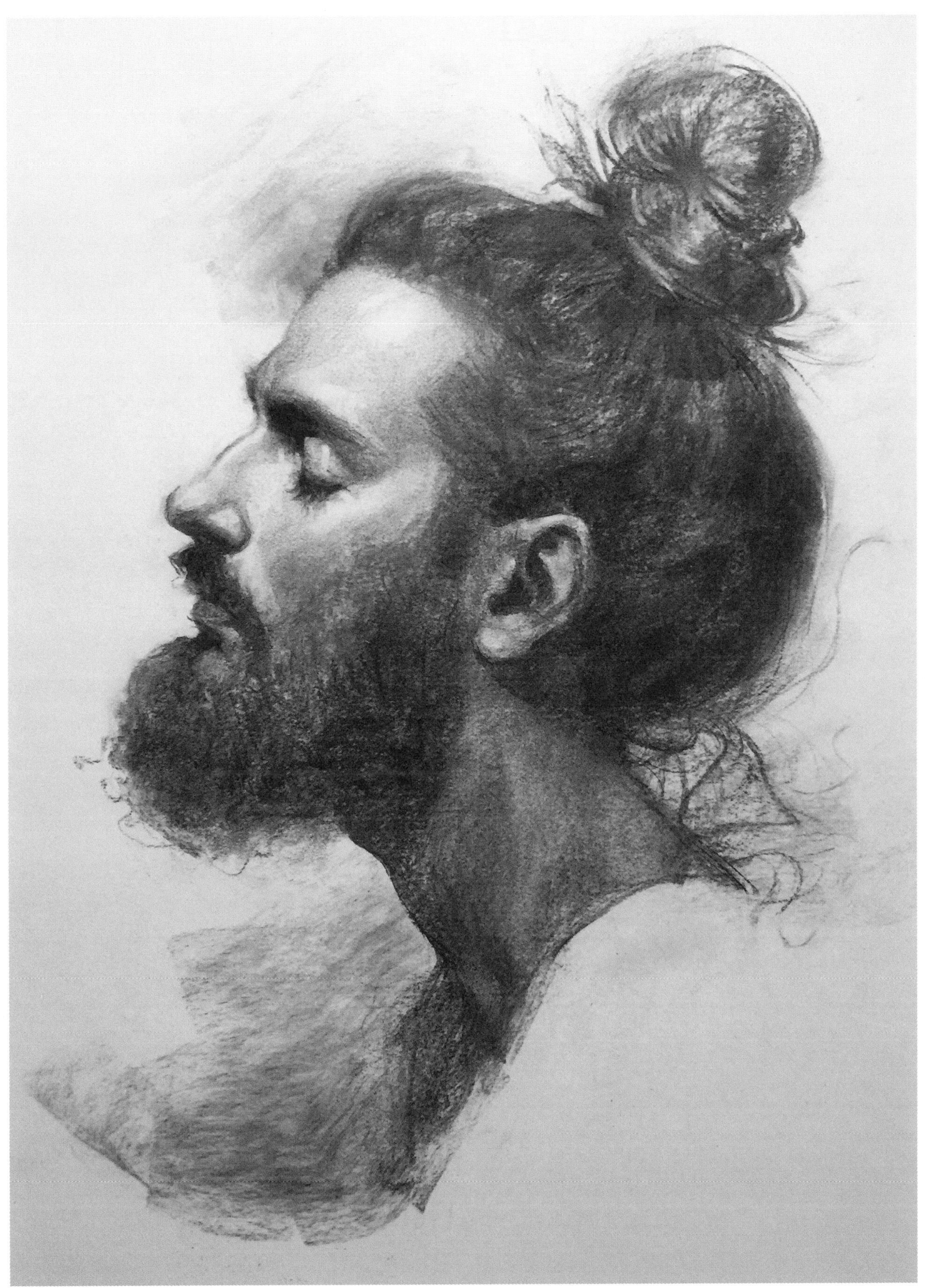

▲ Hatch marks and crosshatch marks can be curved to define and suggest shape, as well as shadow and texture. Curved hatch marks in this man's topknot suggest strands of hair and also define the rounded shape of the bun.

Side Strokes

Artists draw side strokes (or broad strokes) by using the side of vine or willow charcoal to achieve a wide mark. The appearance varies, depending on the surface texture of the paper.

Blending

The blending technique is used to soften lines and gently intermingle values to create a gradual transition among them.

You may use your finger, a cotton swab, or an old rag as tools for blending. You may also use a blending stump, also called a *tortillon*, which is a long stick of tightly twisted paper. The big advantage to using a stump is its fine tip, which allows for precise control when blending even the smallest details.

Blending can destroy the integrity of a drawing, so it's important to avoid overusing it. This skill doesn't come naturally to many artists, so you'll want to hone it. Be patient and practice until you're comfortable with various blending tools and methods.

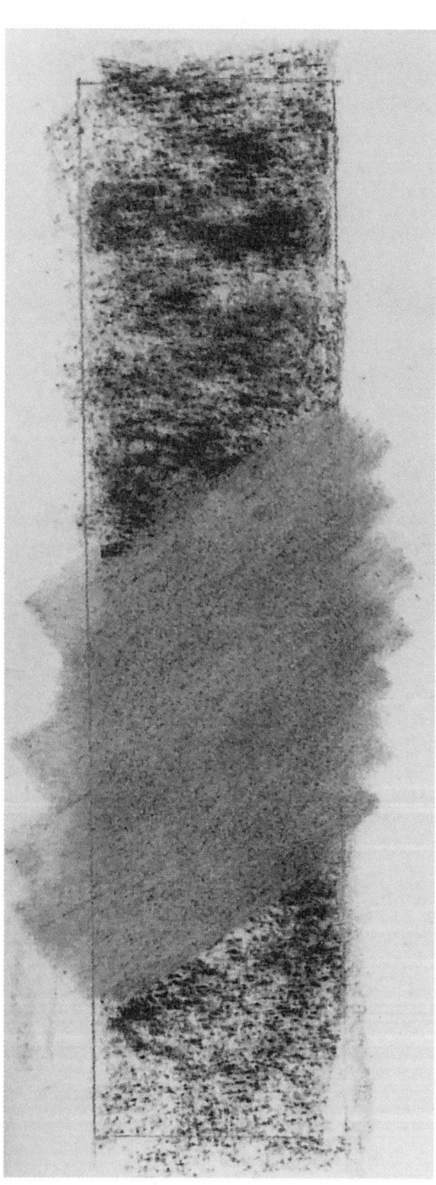

Side strokes with stump blending

Broad strokes with stump blending

◀ These blended textures are created with the side of a vine or willow charcoal stick to achieve a wide mark or tone. The result will vary, depending on the width of the charcoal stick, the surface texture of the paper, and the tool used to blend the marks.

The subject of this portrait, Adja Kaba, is a fashion model whose expressive face and long, graceful neck inspired me to draw her.

At this stage of the drawing—after doing the careful work of mapping the position of the head and neck, the gesture line of the neck, and the masses of the composition—I added blocks of middle to dark values to establish shading and shadows.

1 | Note the heavier bone and muscle construction of the planes of the cheekbones (top right), which means everything under the cheekbone is in an area of shadow. Try to unify these shadow areas, at this point ignoring such details as the highlights within them. Think of drawing a portrait like sculpting a piece of marble, where details can only be revealed once the form has been established.

2 | If you're concerned about a lack of detail, keep in mind that there are many details to each part of the head that can be developed as you continue working. Rendering detail can be confusing or challenging to a beginning artist, but it's neither possible nor necessary to include every single detail. Use your critical thinking to carefully choose which details to include, instead of blindly re-creating every detail in an attempt to achieve a photographic likeness.

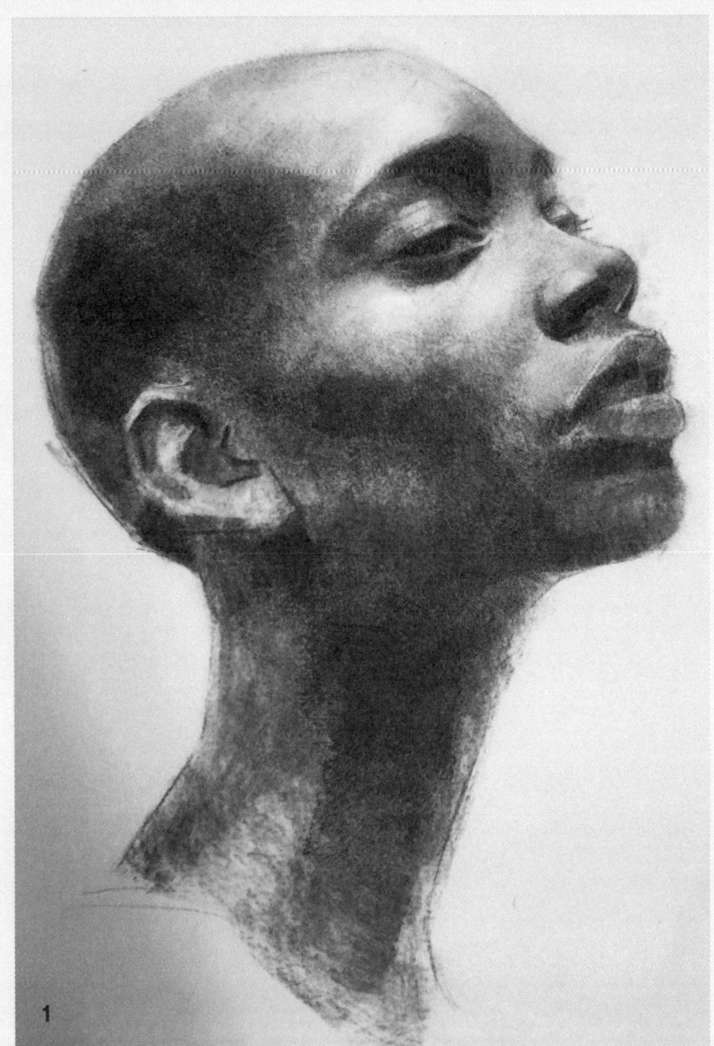

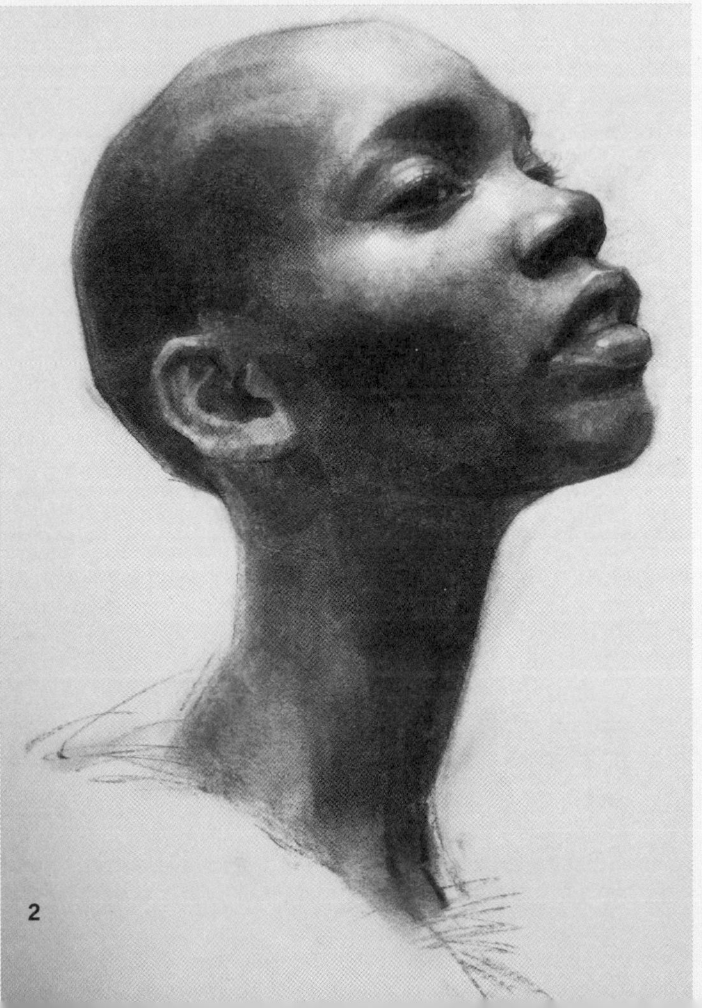

THE ELEMENTS OF ART

Line

Shape

Form

Value

Space/Depth

Texture

Color

Line

It's been said that a line is a moving dot, or a point in motion. Line can guide a viewer's eye by defining edges and outlining shapes. Lines used to outline a shape are called contours or contour lines.

Artists can create the illusion of form in a drawing by varying a line's quality, or thickness. (See also "Using Edges to Convey Form," on page 96.)

Line can also be used to indicate shadow. Shadow areas have thicker contour lines, while lighter areas have thinner ones.

The five types of line, simply defined:

Vertical lines are positioned vertically, or up and down, on the picture plane, without slanting.

Horizontal lines are parallel to the horizon.

Diagonal lines are slanted relative to the picture plane.

Zigzag lines are made from a combination of diagonal lines.

Curved lines gradually change direction.

Shape

Shapes play an important role in the creation of art. A shape is a closed contour, created when a line is enclosed, or when a line's ends meet. All shapes are two-dimensional, meaning that they have both length and width.

There are two types of shapes: geometric and organic.

Geometric shapes, which can be described using mathematical formulas, include circles, triangles, squares, trapezoids, pentagons, pentagrams, hexagons, and octagons.

Organic shapes are those irregular, uneven shapes that seem to follow no rules. These expressive shapes are typically not man-made.

Form

The world we live in is made up almost entirely of forms. Form and shape are related. I like to think of forms as three-dimensional shapes. In art, the term *form* refers to an object that has three dimensions—that is, it has length, width, and height.

I encourage my students to develop their understanding of form, and how to create the illusion of form in drawings, by studying the effect of light on objects.

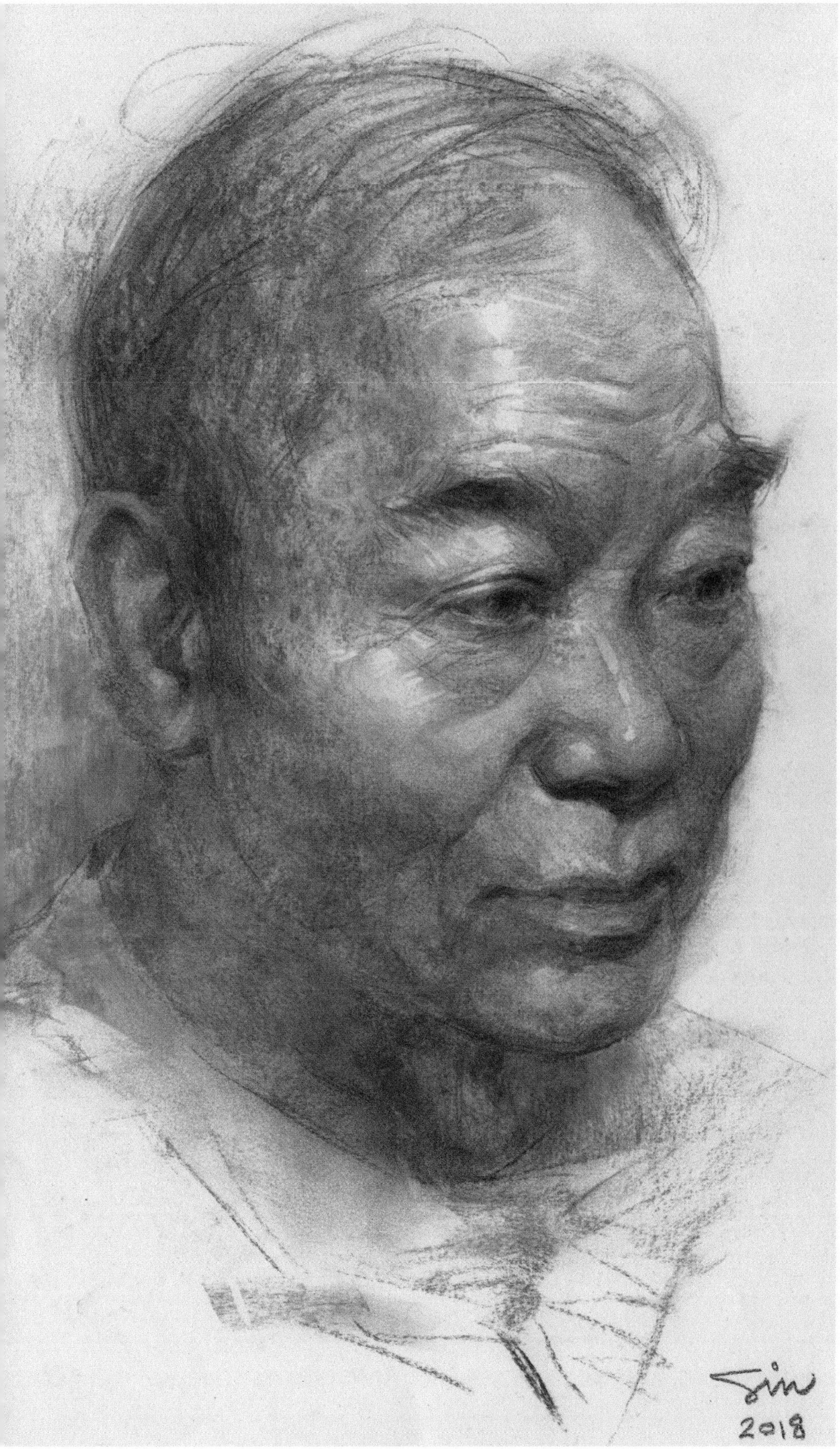

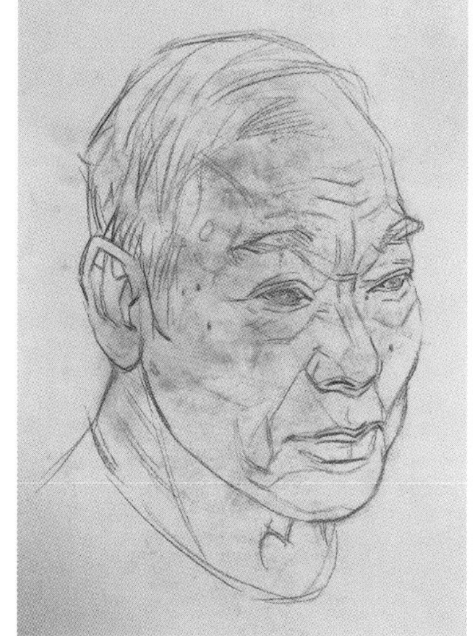

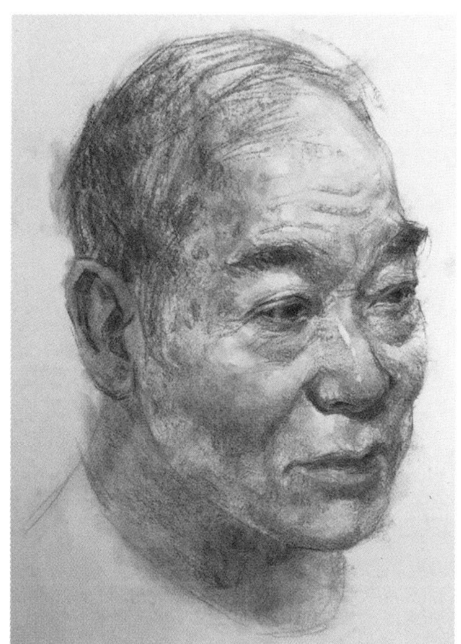

▲ Soft lines are used to define the head's basic shapes (*top right*), which can then be expressed as value masses (*bottom right*), then further refined to capture the effect of light on form (*left*).

I drew these portraits with expressive lines by using only the tip of the vine charcoal, without blending with the flat side. I use contour lines to depict the form of the head. Vine charcoal is available in a variety of soft and hard options. It is very lightweight and moves easily on the page. Because vine charcoal is so light and soft, don't smear or blend it with your fingers. Instead, use tissue or a blending stump.

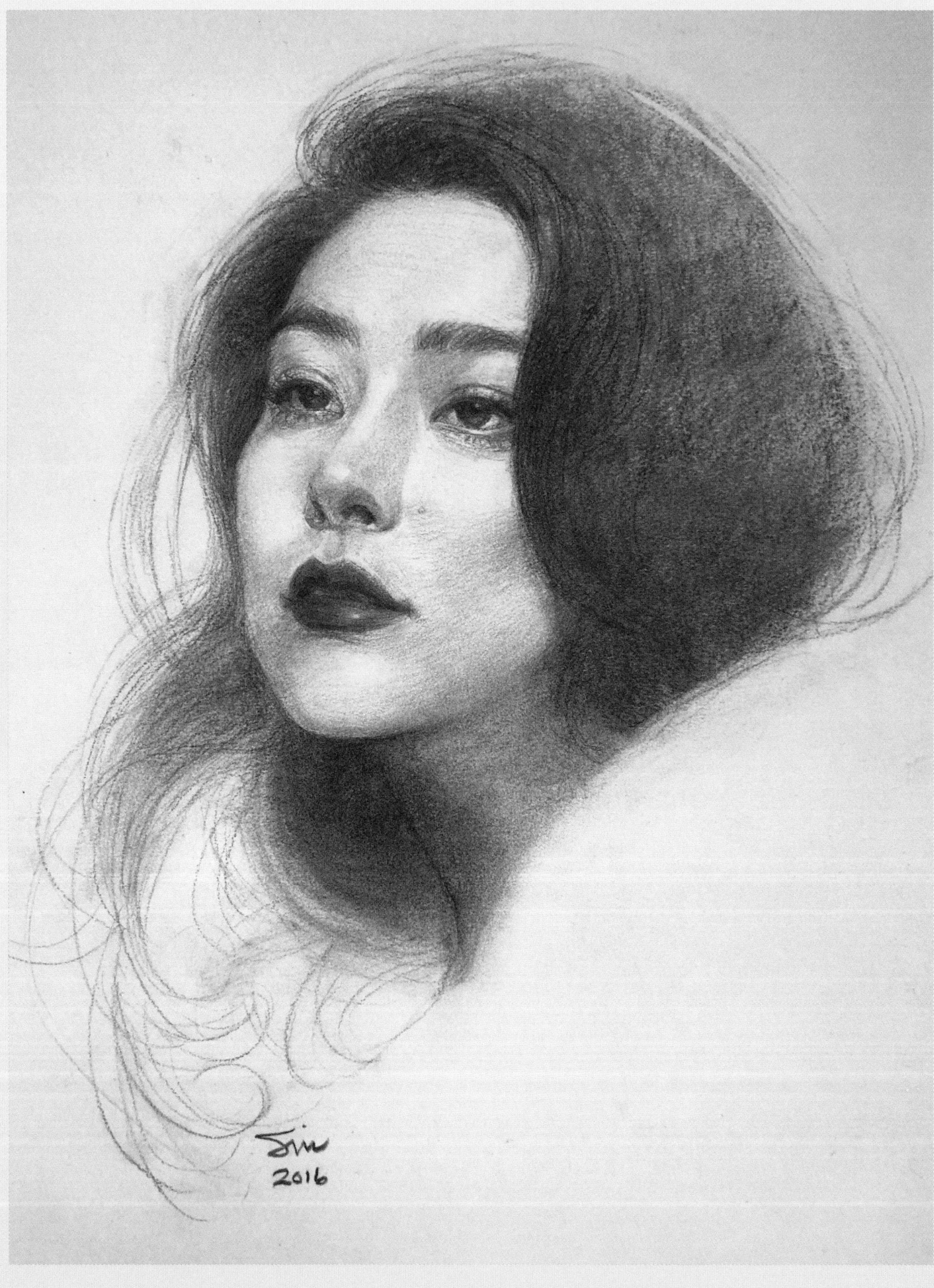

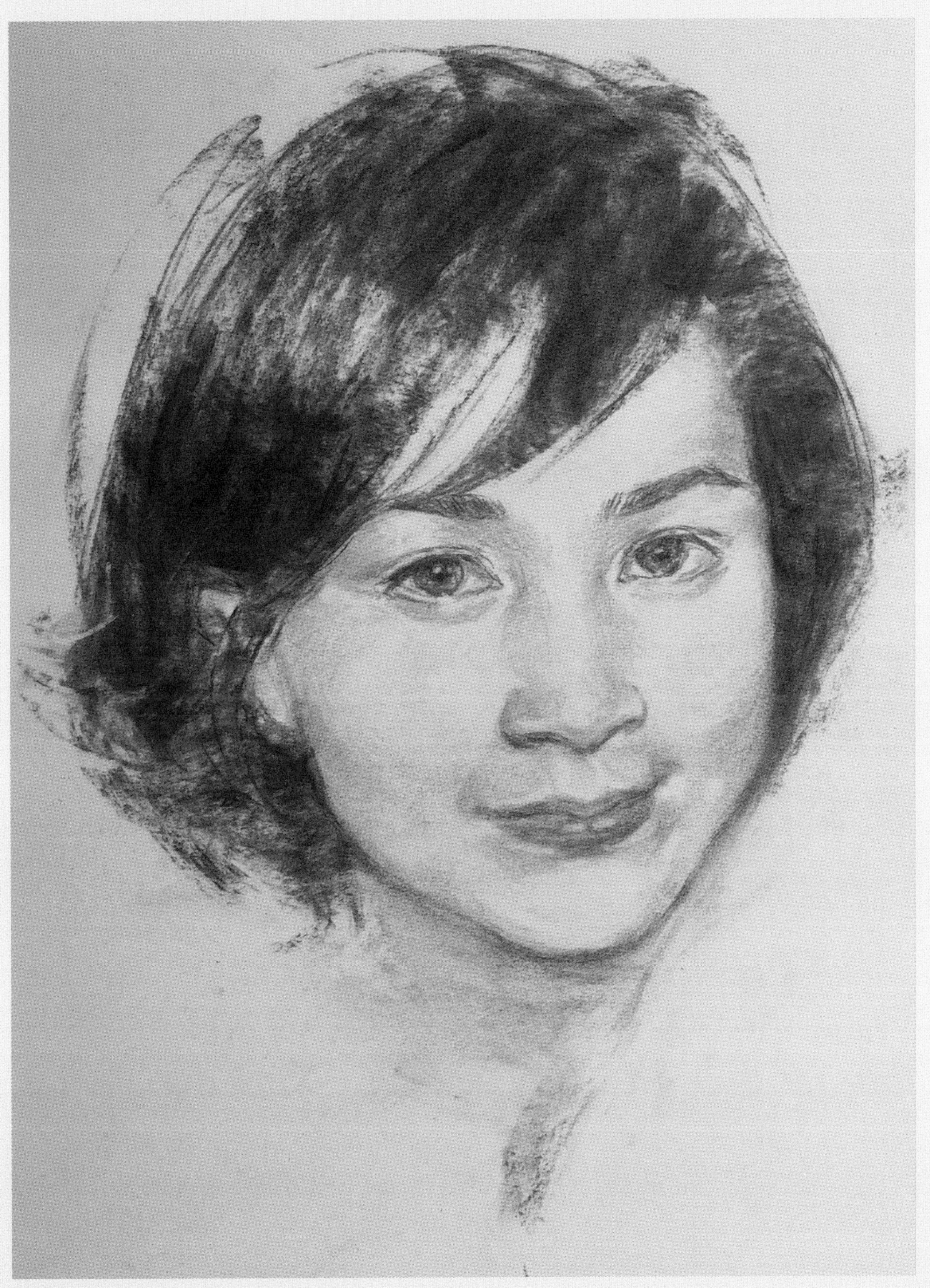

Value

Value refers to the lightness or darkness of a color or tone. Value is incredibly important in a drawing because light and dark values describe the form of an object. All objects have light, middle, and dark values when exposed to light.

Value relates directly to light—we see things because of light on objects, or illumination.

Light reflects off the object into our eyes and our mind processes that light and rationalizes what we see. Value is the key to the illusion of light, and a good realistic drawing depends on a range of values. The effects of light on form are described in the diagram below.

When drawing portraits, light and shadow translate from simple planes and shapes into detailed variation of value and line.

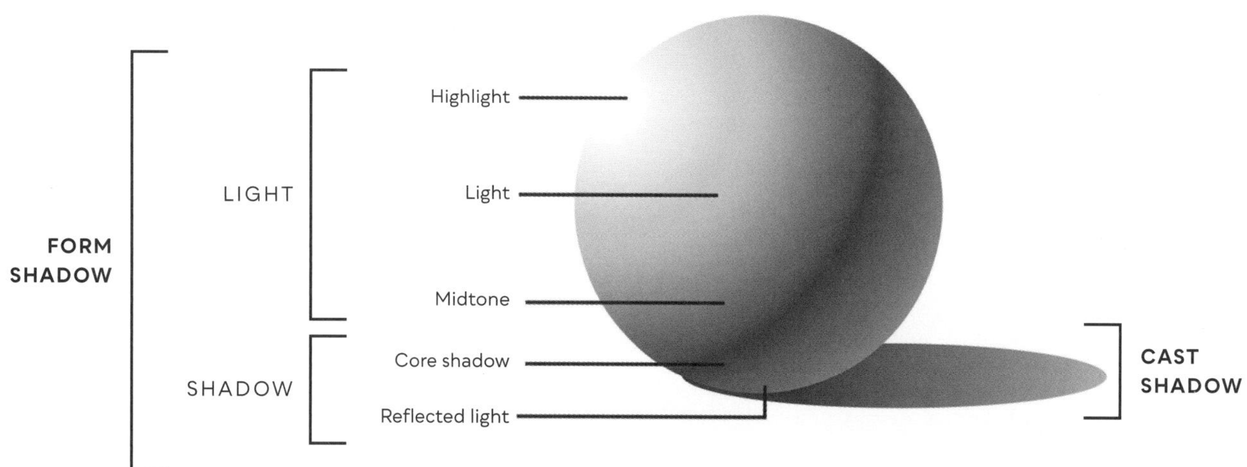

I apply a five-value system to my portrait work.

FORM SHADOW		A shadow created on a figure or object as its surface turns away from the light source. It has soft edges that transition gradually from light to dark.
LIGHT	**Highlight**	The brightest area on an object. It directly faces the light source.
	Light	The area next to the highlight that is somewhat oblique (at an angle) to the light source.
	Midtone	Also known as the halftone, the area of an object that begins to turn away from the light source. The midtone is the transition value between the area in light and the core shadow.
SHADOW	**Core shadow**	The darkest area. It receives no light from the light source and has no reflected light.
	Reflected light	The part of the shadow that received light from surrounding surfaces. It is never as light as any of the areas on the light side.
CAST SHADOW		A shadow created when light is blocked from an object or surface. It has hard edges with an abrupt change from light to dark.

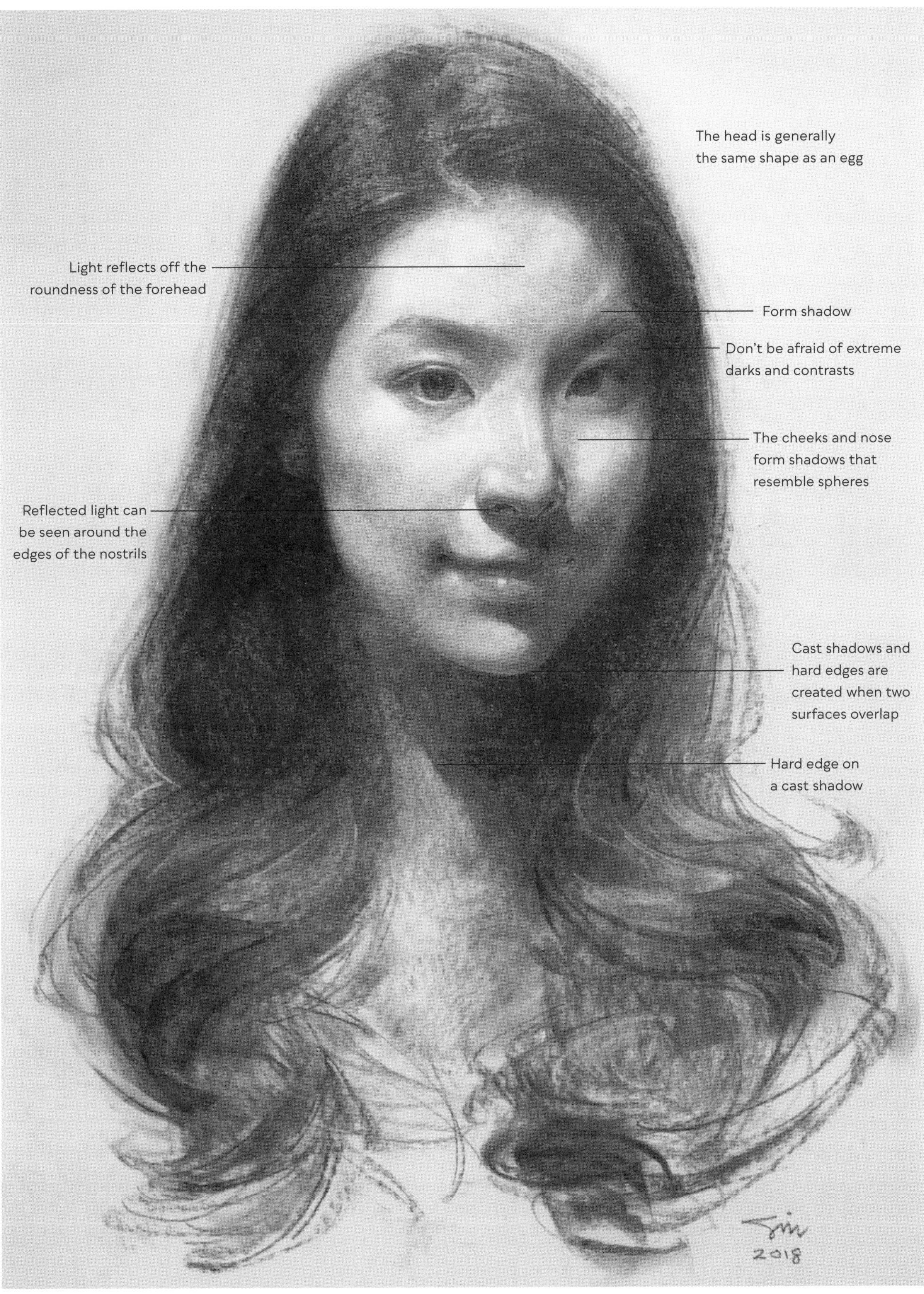

▲ Geometric shapes can be found throughout the face and upper body: an egg shape for the head; spheres in facial features such as the cheek and nose; a cylinder for the neck.

Line and value work together to create a likeness of the subject. Drawing areas of value alone makes the artist aware of masses, forms, and light. Drawing lines encourages the artist to study, judge, and plan before drawing. The knowledge gained from line drawing helps the artist make decisions about the edges of each area of tone as they develop the values.

I drew this portrait of celebrated Hong Kong, China, singer Sandy Lam with a stick of vine charcoal on charcoal drawing paper, which has a medium textured surface on which the charcoal blends smoothly. At this stage of the drawing—after mapping the position of the head and identifying the proportions and relationships between the shapes and features of the face—I constructed the actual shape of the head and hair.

1 | Define the curves of the cheeks, the square shape of the jaw, and the rounded chin. With long, curving lines, draw the sweep of the hair that surrounds the head and neck as a solid, overall shape in your line drawing. The details of the hair will be built up slowly in layers of value. Indicate the facial features, which are slightly tilted with the angle of the head.

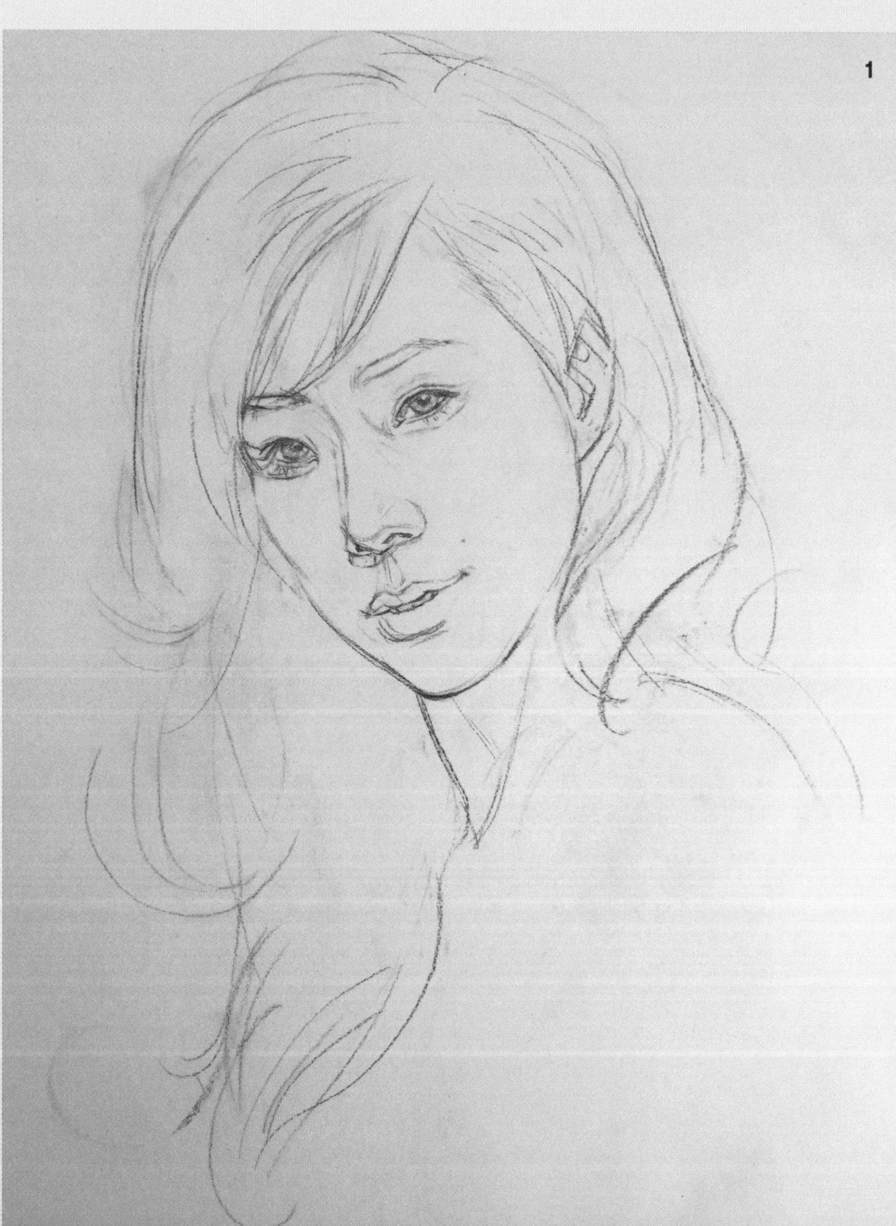

2 | The eyes express much emotion and personality. For that reason, I often render the eyes first to capture the spirit of the subject right away. Use the broad side of vine charcoal to apply long, free strokes for the dark tones of the hair, following the direction of hair growth. A single curving stroke on the shadow side of the nose and a few more short strokes suggest the cast shadow around the nostrils and beneath the tip of the nose. Use short, broad strokes to place the shadows in the outer corners of the eyes, along the cheeks and jaw, and at the pit of the neck. Notice how the strokes wrap around the corners of the eye sockets to define their shape and slant diagonally down the sides of the nose. Fill the lips with tone. At this stage, you're merely indicating areas of value that will be developed in later steps.

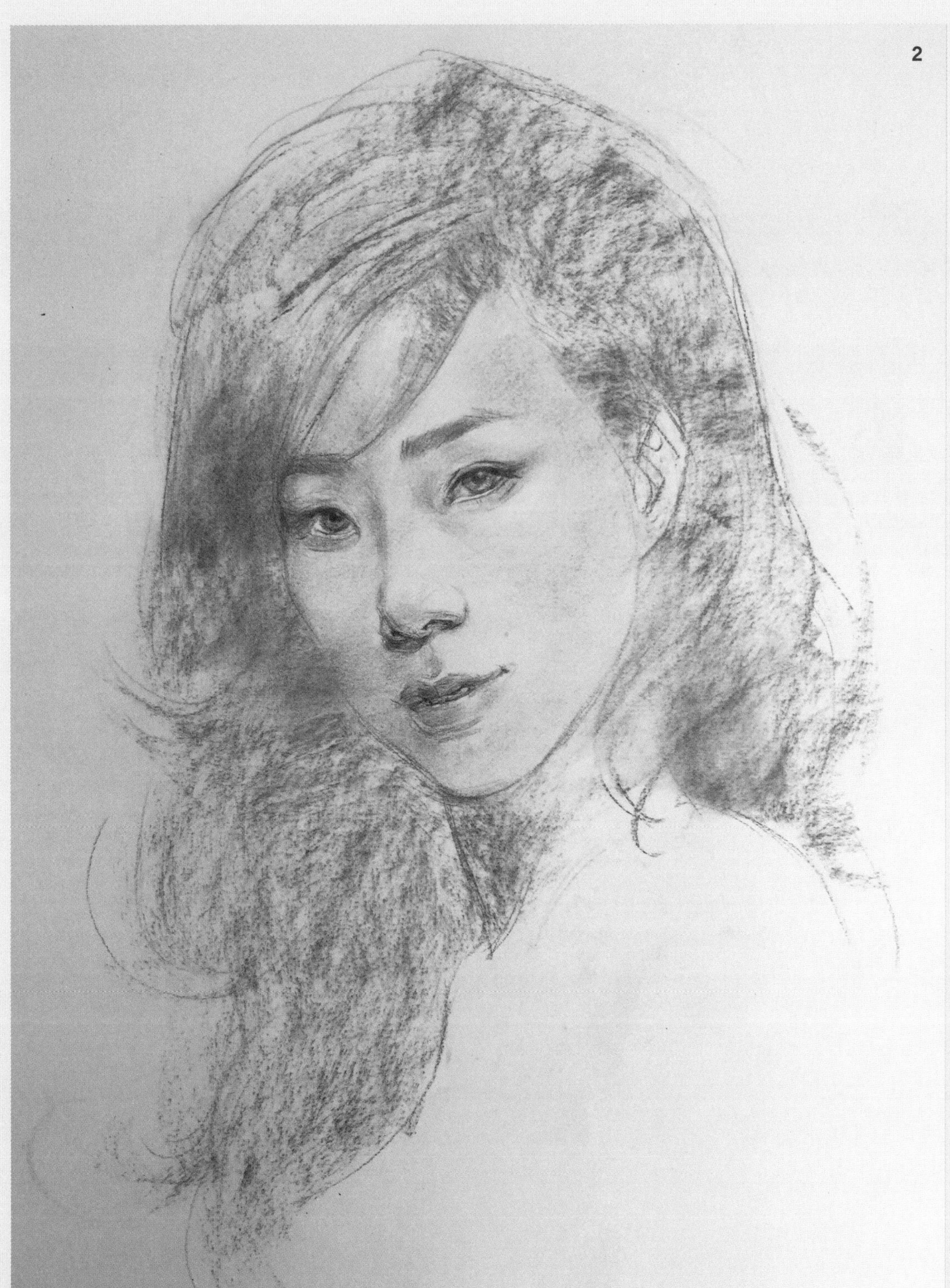

3 | Darken the hair with broad strokes, using the flat side of the vine charcoal and pressing harder. Begin to smudge the strokes in the eye sockets, beneath the nose, and along the sides of the cheeks. With the flat side of a short chunk of vine charcoal, darken the hair and blend the area, carrying some of the tone into the shadows beneath the right cheek. Blend the neck and hair shadows together as well. I sometimes use my fingers like a brush to spread the tone onto the sides of the forehead, blending this area into the hair. Don't delineate the hairline from the forehead with a contour line, which looks unnatural; this area should be soft and blended, with both hair and scalp visible, as can be seen above the temple.

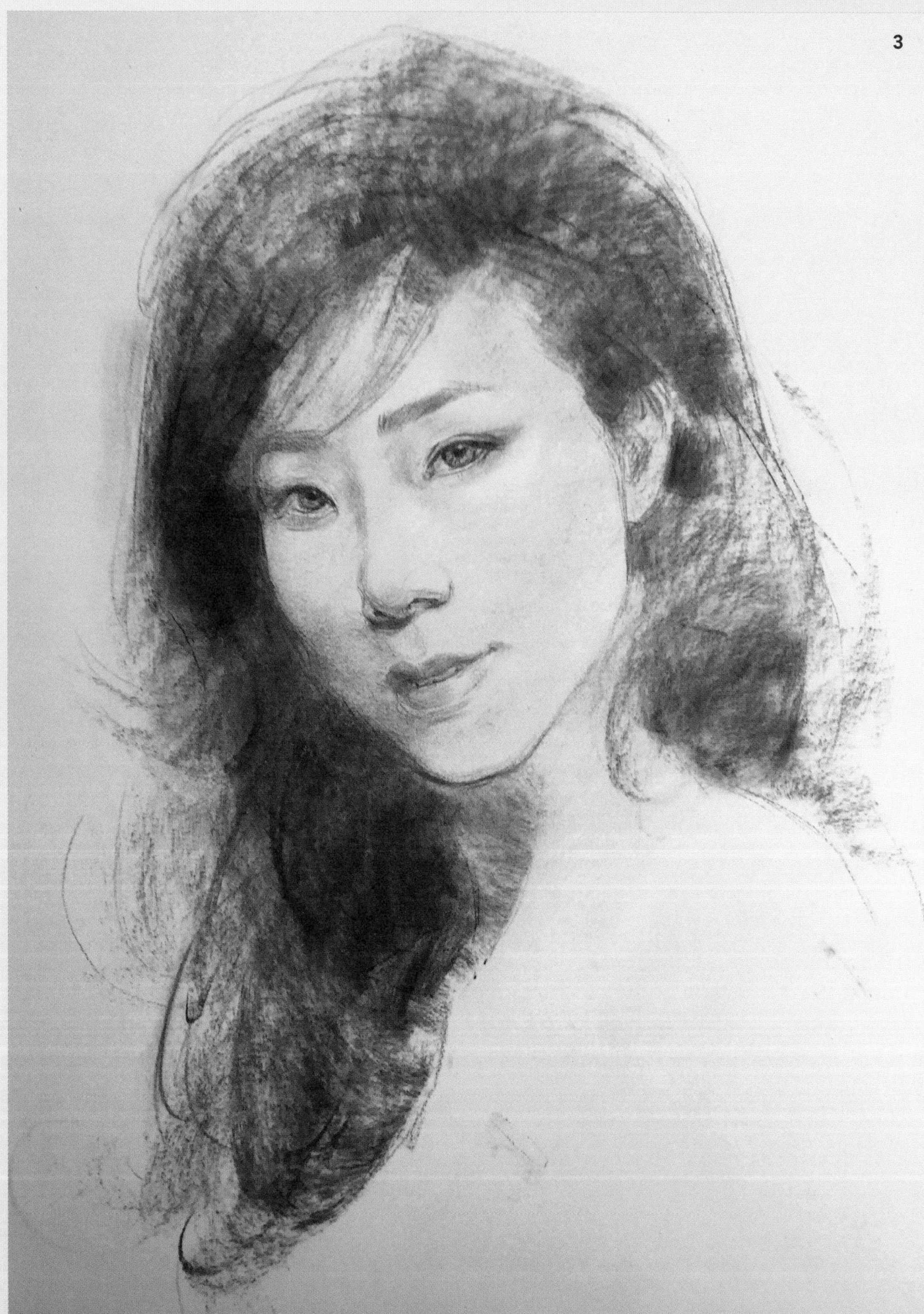

4 | Use your fingertips to blend the hair, blurring the contours and adding a few strokes to suggest detail. Then lift the highlights out with an eraser. Finally, soften the outside edges all the way around the hair with your fingers. Treat both the inside and the outside contours of the hair as if there is no definable edge, so that the hair remains soft and out of focus.

Use the point of a kneaded eraser to pick out highlights on the pupils, eyelids, and tip of the nose, as well as to brighten the whites of the eyes, clean the edges of the lips, and highlight the lower lip. Use the sharp corner of the vine charcoal to strengthen the upper eyelids and add a few eyelashes.

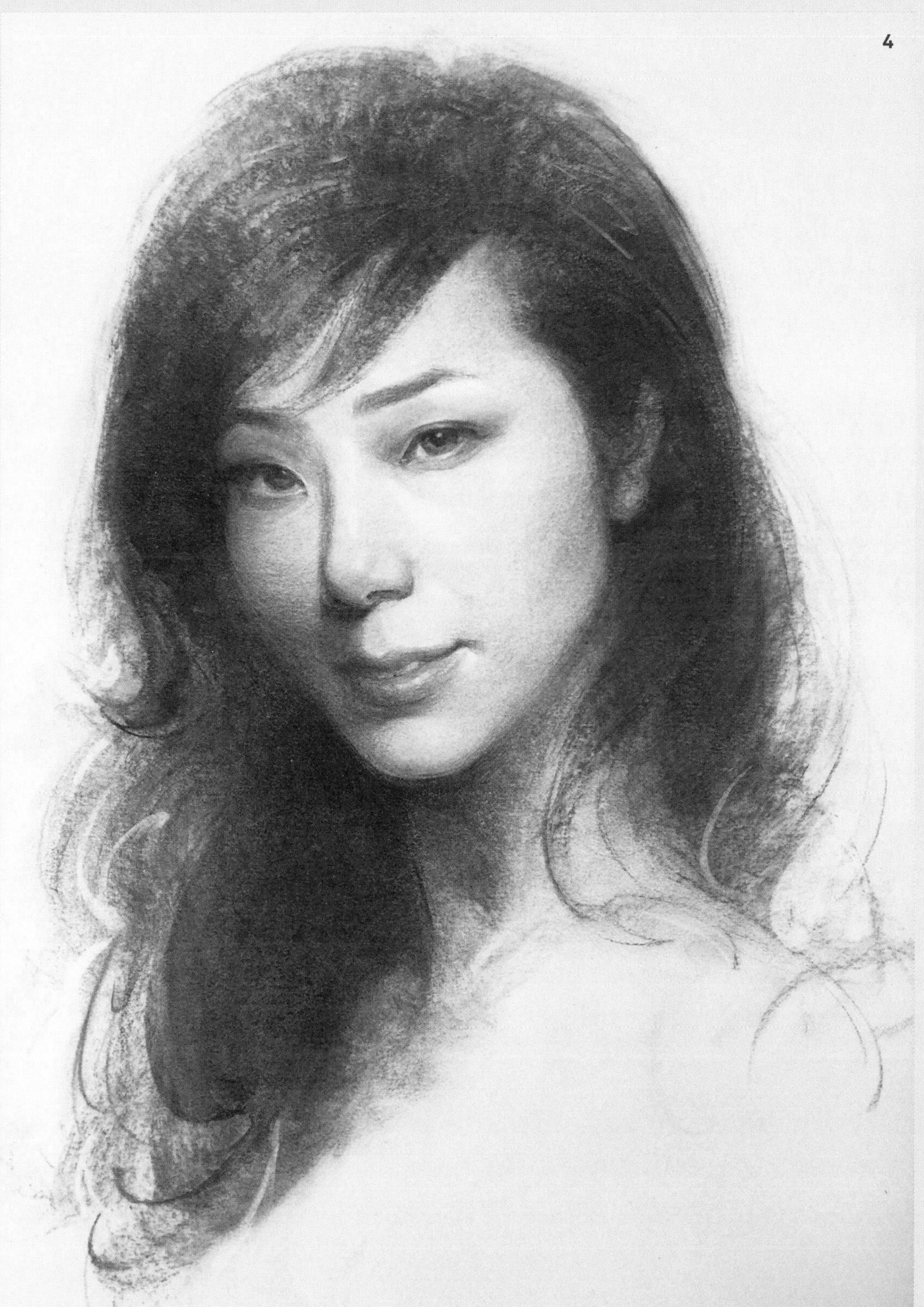

4

Space/Depth

In art and design, space generally refers to the sense of depth in a work of art. When drawing on a two-dimensional surface (paper), the artist creates the illusion of space to give the sense of three-dimensionality. (See also "Atmospheric Perspective," page 98.) Space can also refer to the use of positive and negative space in a work of art. Positive space refers to the object or subject, while negative space refers to the empty areas around and within the subject.

Texture

Texture is an important aspect any work of art, especially portraiture. In two-dimensional artwork, texture can be implied or real. For example, you can achieve the appearance of smooth, delicate skin in a portrait drawn on smooth drawing paper far more easily than on rough drawing paper. Texture can also be implied with drawing techniques such as hatching, crosshatching, and scribbling.

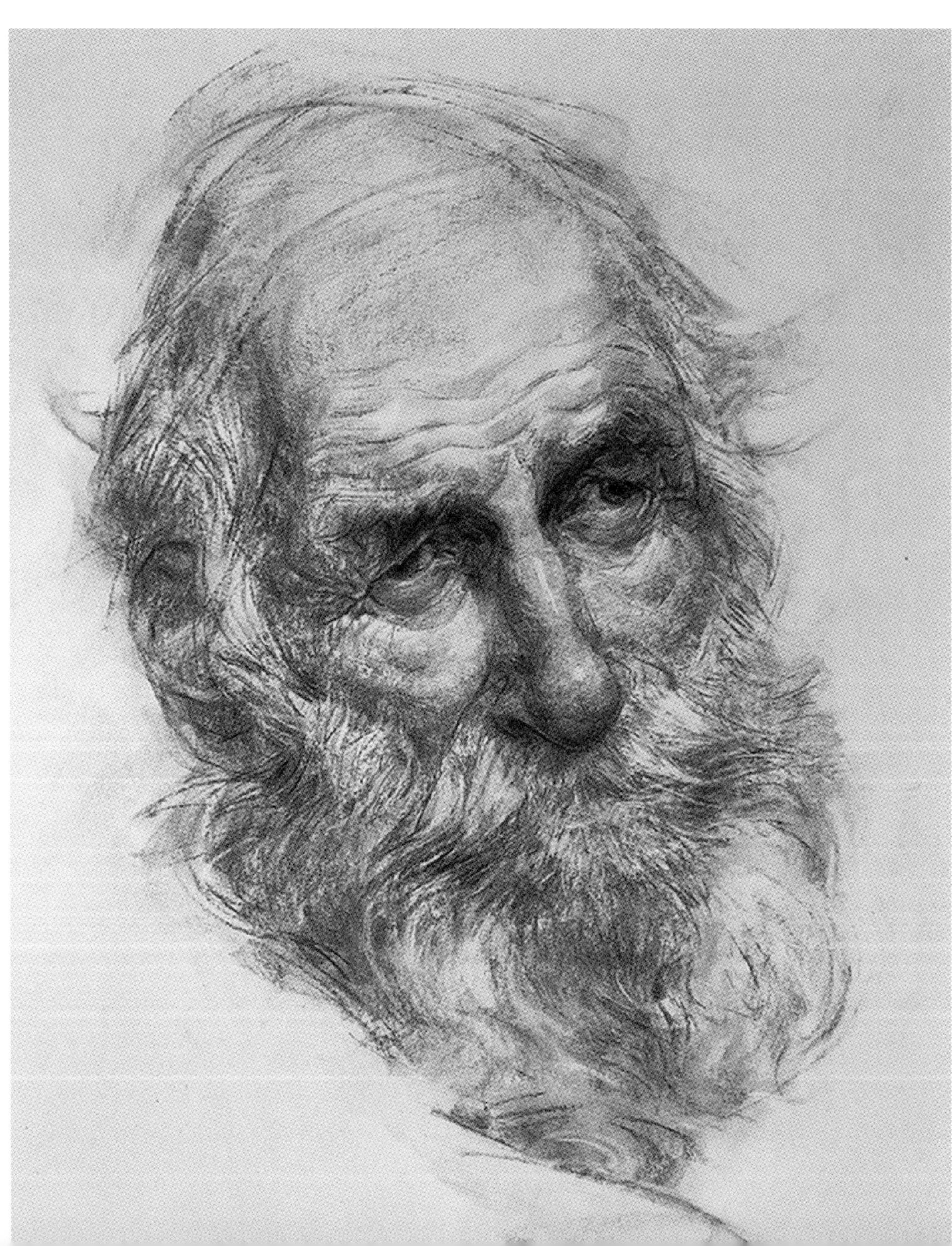

Color

Color can be defined by three properties: hue, value, and intensity. Hue refers to the actual name of a color (e.g., blue). Value refers to that hue's lightness or darkness. Intensity refers to the vividness, or quality, of the hue.

Although the principal technique I explore in this book applies black drawing mediums in varying values to white paper, I also discuss an alternative technique that uses black and white mediums on toned or colored paper (see page 138).

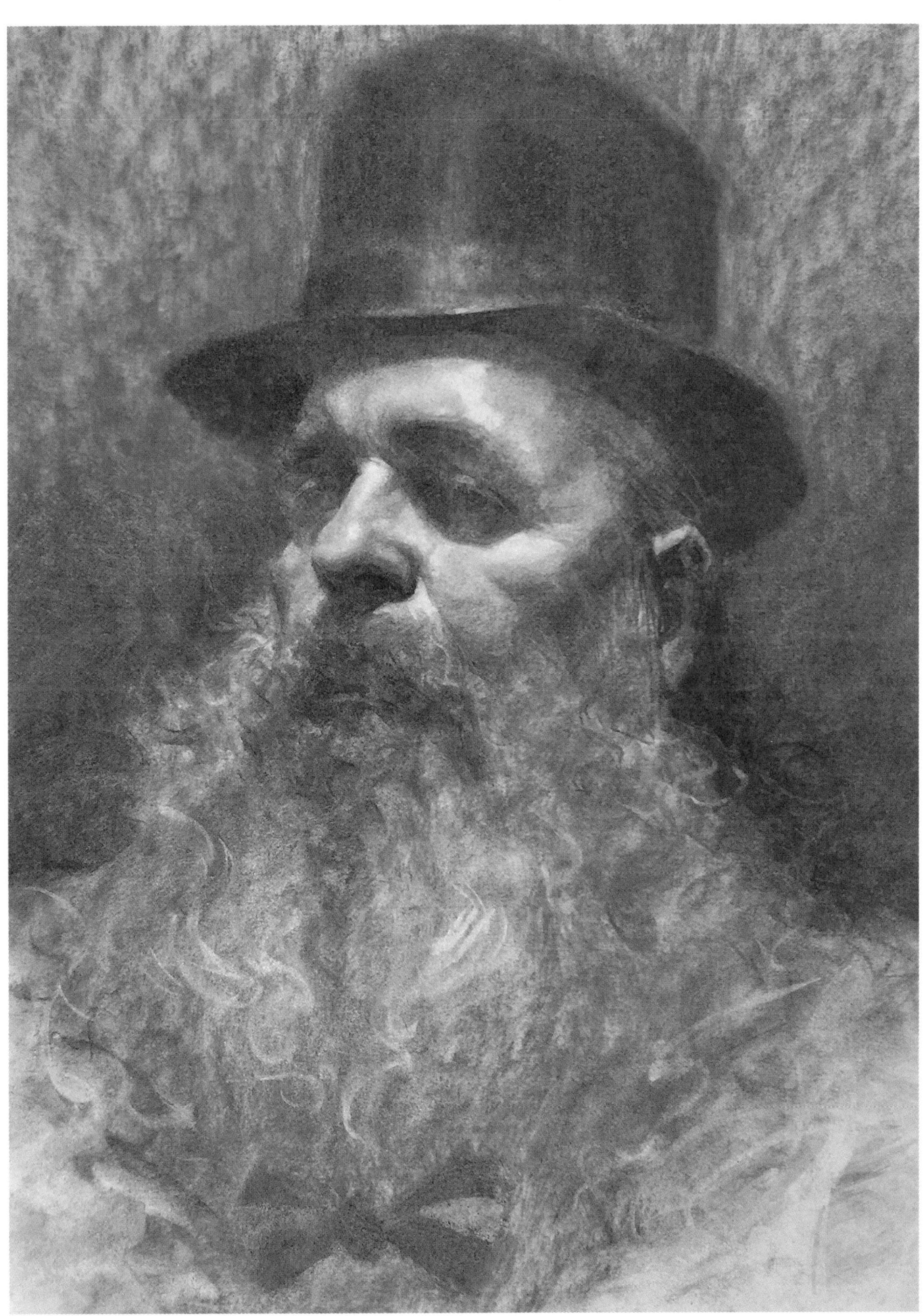

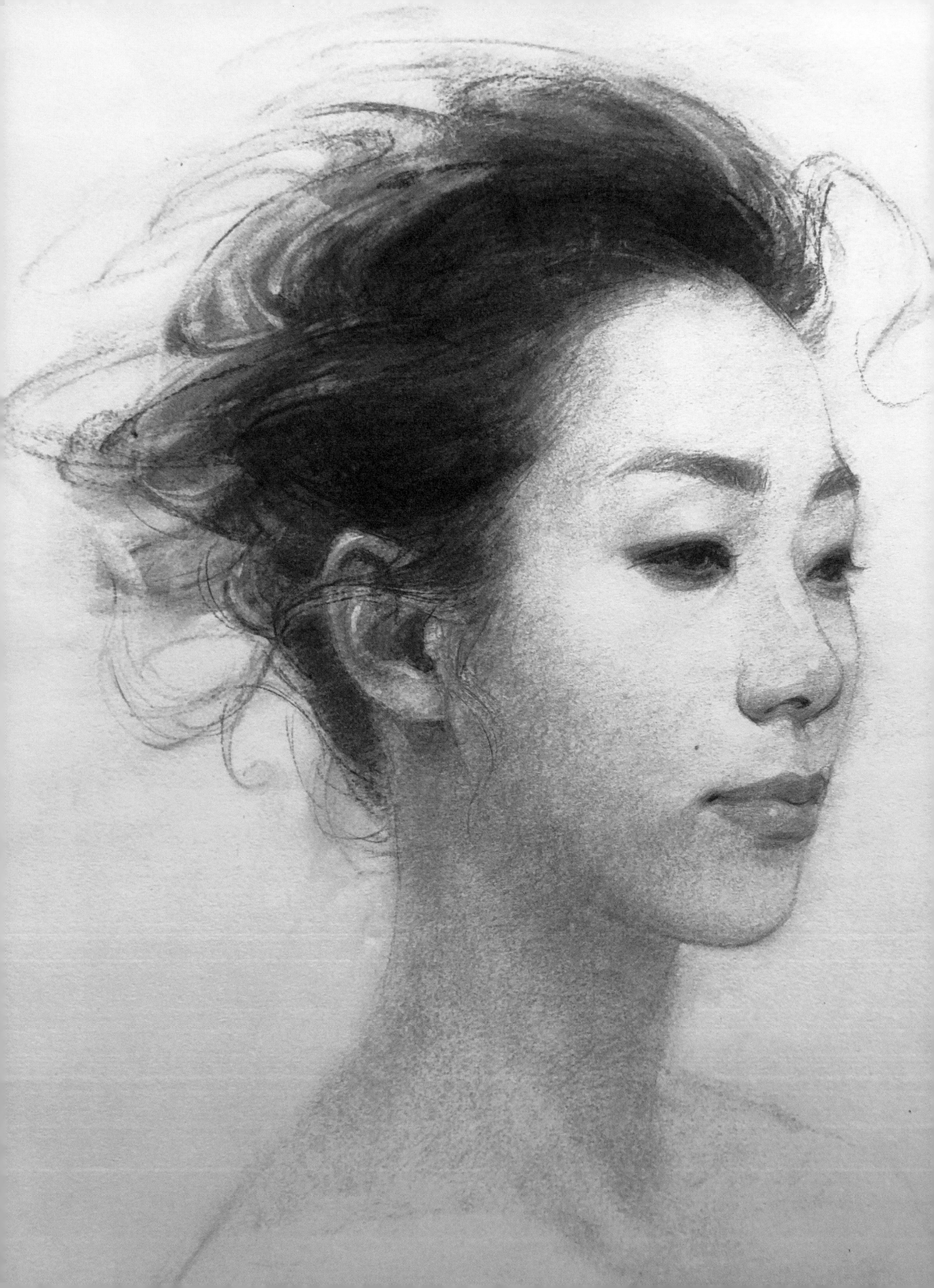

3

POSES & FEATURES

BASIC PROPORTIONS

Artists use a standard set of measurements to create accurate proportions when constructing a head drawing. The following serve as general guidelines. All faces are different, and individuals have varying proportions. Use these guidelines as a starting point, but stay true to the actual proportions of your subject.

The general proportions of the head can be divided into thirds:
One-third from the hairline to the eyebrows
One-third from the eyebrows to the nose
One-third from the nose to the chin

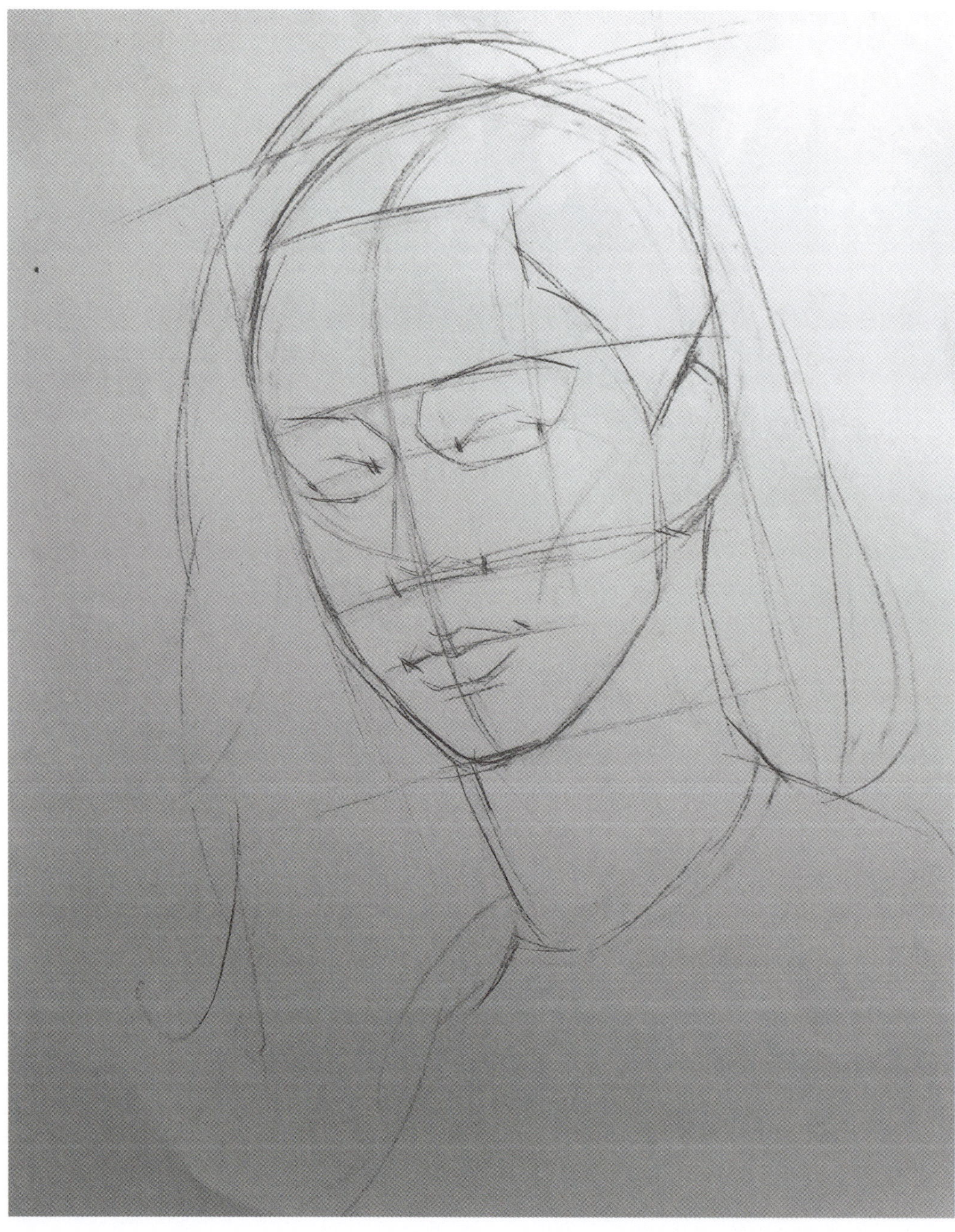

PLANES OF THE HEAD

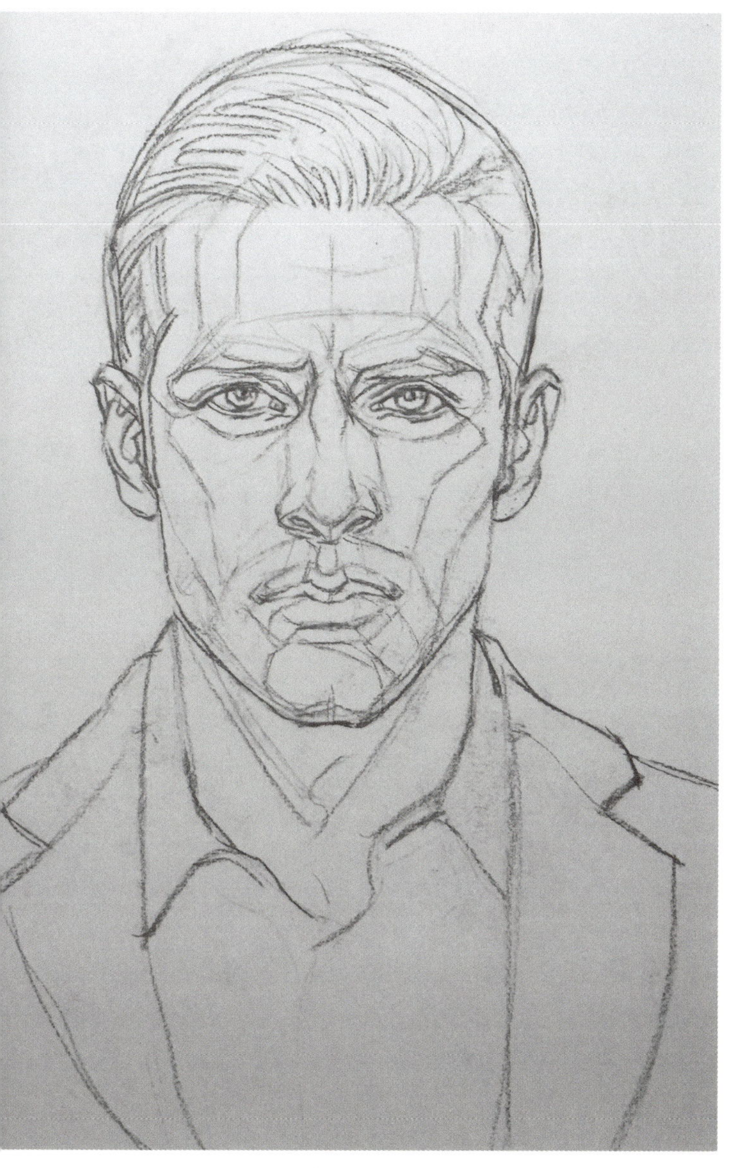

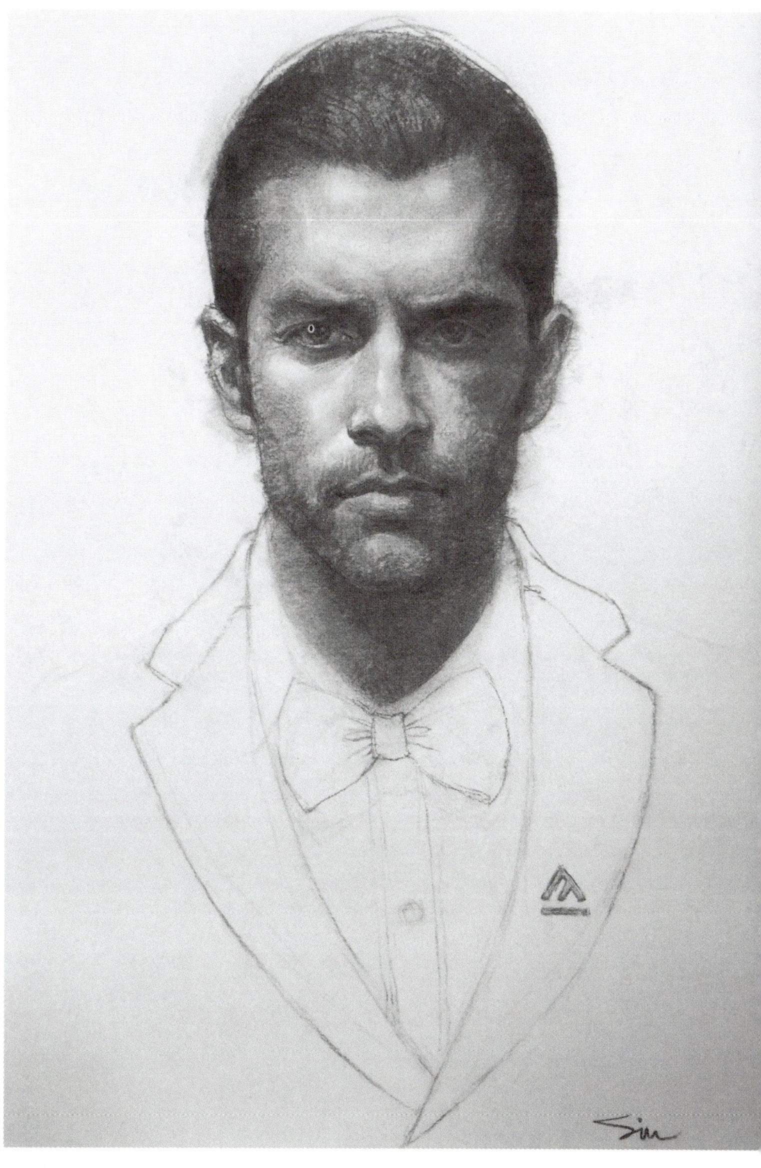

It's important to remember that achieving a likeness is predicated on the artist first depicting the three-dimensional structure of the head, which is often described as the planes of the head.

The shape of the head consists of six planes: top, bottom, front, back, and two sides. Both the front and side planes of the head recede from the viewer's eyes in a three-quarter position, as shown here. The features on the front and side planes diminish in size as they turn from the viewer, under the rules of perspective.

POSING THE SUBJECT

There are three standard viewpoints the artist may choose from when establishing the pose of a portrait: front, profile, and three-quarter. Each viewpoint affects the shapes, shadows, highlights, and proportions of the head and the facial features.

Front Pose

Drawing the face from the front is generally less interesting than drawing a profile or three-quarter view because it lacks depth and shape. However, it can be effective for a dramatic portrait in which the sitter's face is very expressive.

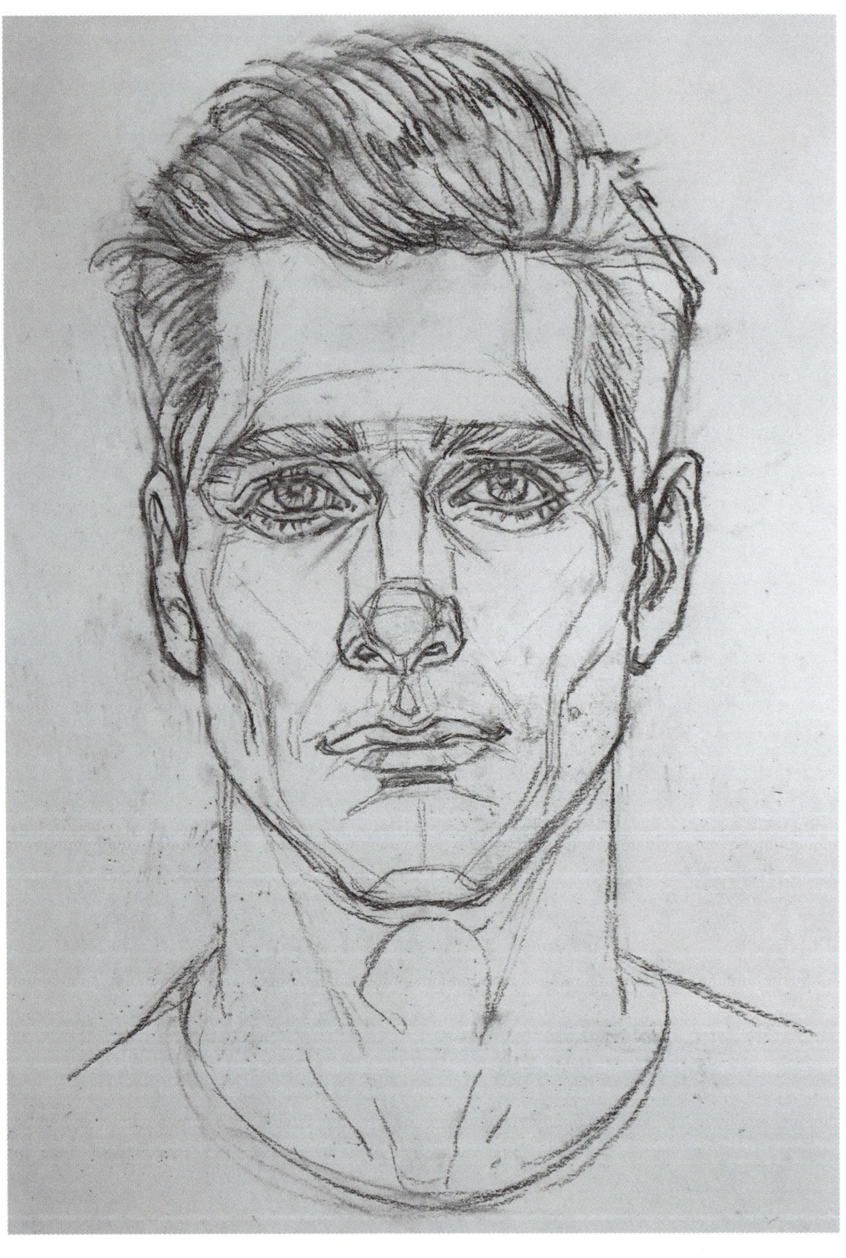

▲ From the front view, notice that the features are symmetrical.

The nose is an excellent subject to practice the elements of shading and blending and how they apply to all the facial features. The nose is important to the overall size and scale of all the other facial features. If you can draw a nose well, you're on your way to very good portrait drawing!

Never outline the nose; instead, use blended tones to give the illusion of form. In general, the nose is a triangular, wedge-shaped block that is narrow and depressed under the brow and broad and prominent at its base. The nose is composed of soft edges where it gently curves and hard edges where the planes overlap. The tip of the nose is similar to a sphere. A common mistake is to make the nostrils too dark, shaped, and noticeable; instead, treat this area lightly. Drawn inaccurately, the nose affects the total outcome of the portrait and ruins the likeness.

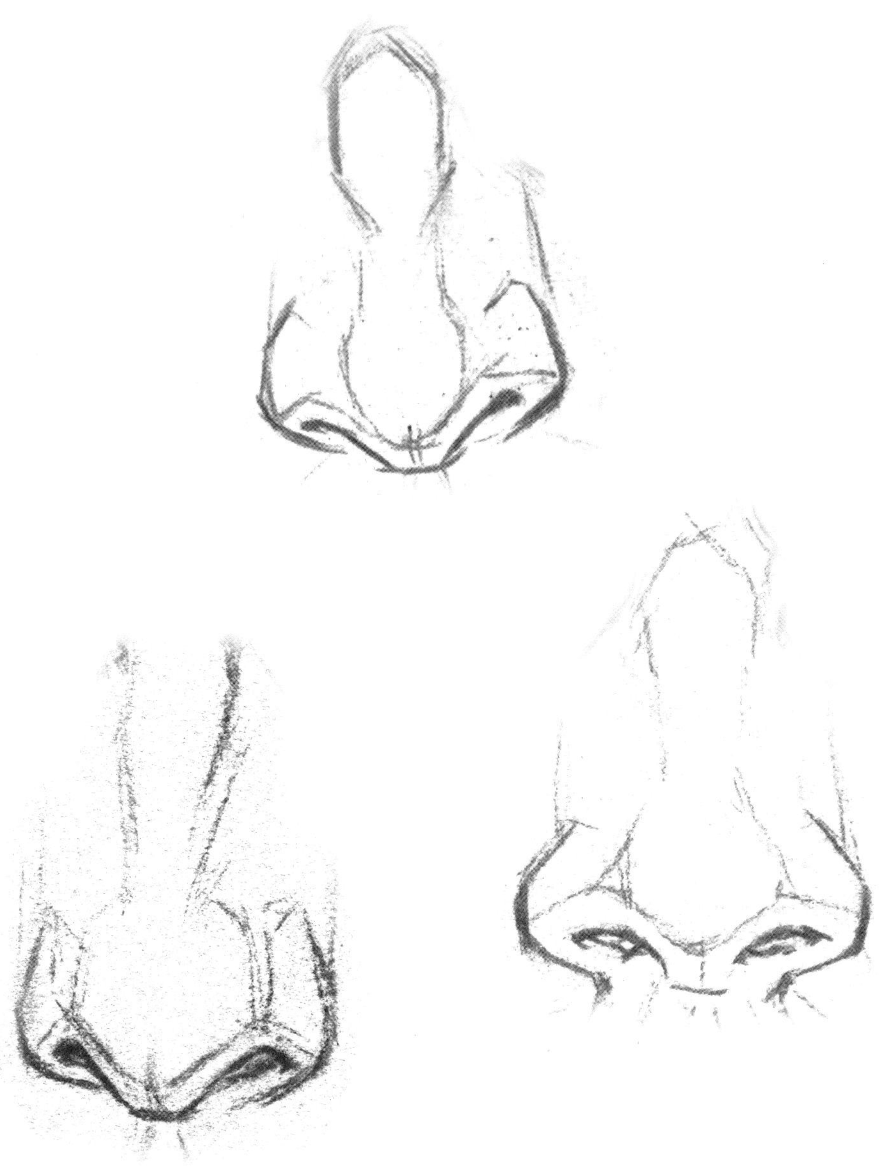

FRONT POSE: THE EAR

The ear comprises many interlocking shapes. Because it is curved, with rounded surfaces, there are many shadow edges and lots of reflected light and highlights to watch for. The ear projects from the head, so there are also cast shadows. The ear is shell-shaped, and the outer contour looks like a top-heavy letter *C*, wider at the top and narrower at the base. In the center is a bowl-like depression.

Approach each ear as though you have never drawn one before. The same ear can be a new challenge each time you draw it, because the angle and shadows change with each new pose.

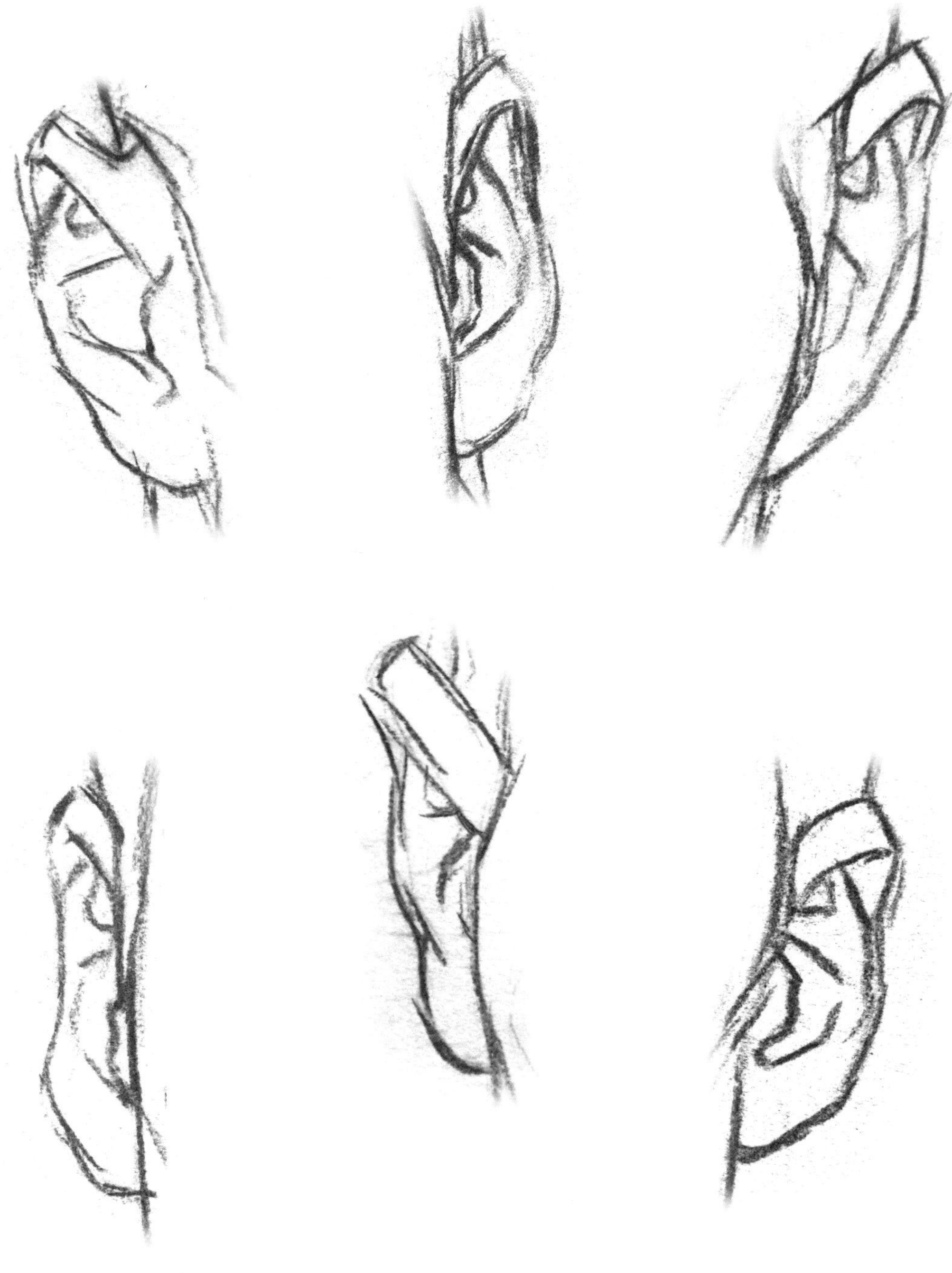

FRONT POSE: THE MOUTH

The mouth, much like the nose, must be viewed as shapes and developed with various values and shading to define it. Because the mouth doesn't project from the face as much as the nose does, the cast shadow is not as dark; the darkest dark is in the corner of the mouth, which is called the pit.

The mouth is very important in conveying the mood or feeling of the individual. Though the expression of the eyes may be subtle, the mouth expresses emotion more obviously.

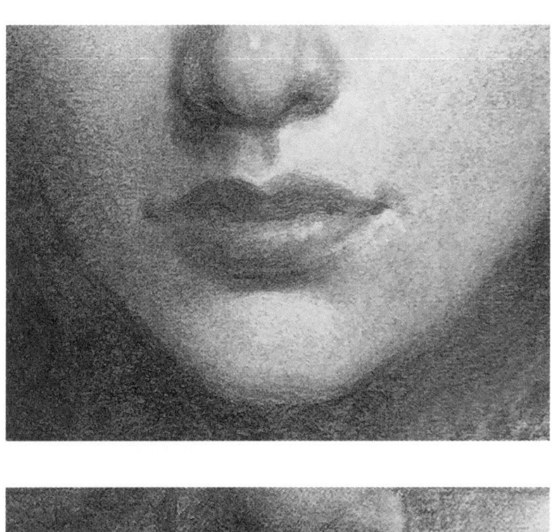

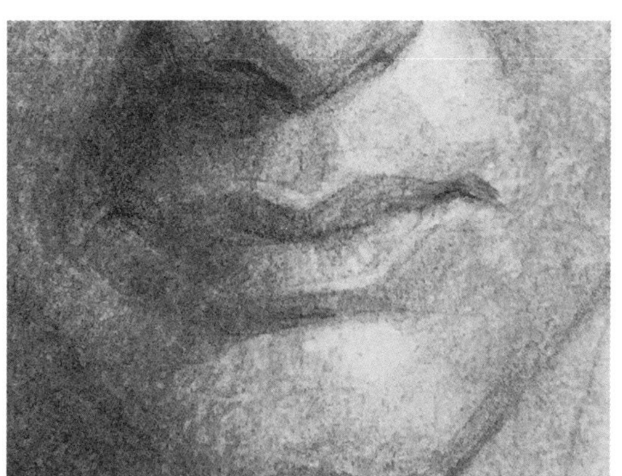

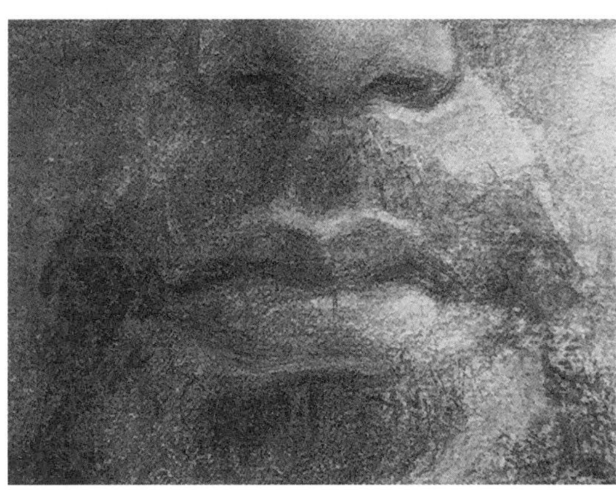

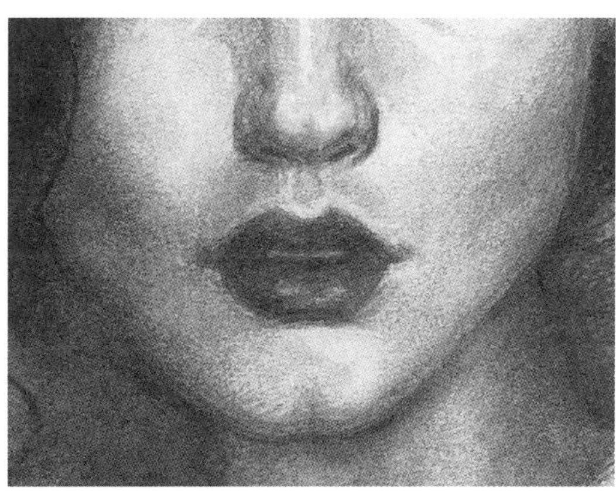

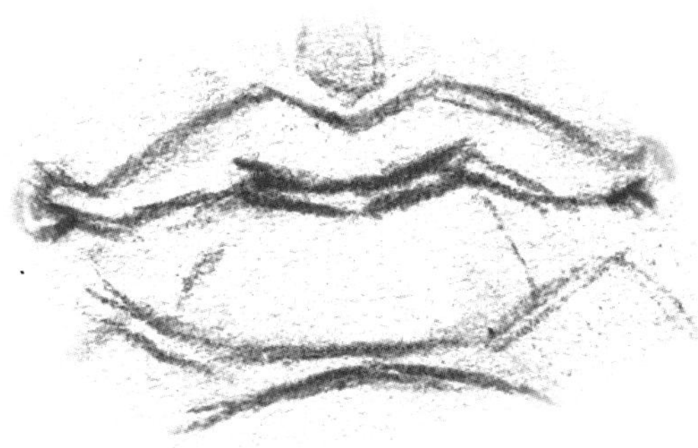

The eyes are often referred to as the "windows to the soul" because they convey so much emotion and personality. This is one of the most important aspects of a good portrait, and I begin all my portraits by rendering the eyes first. In this way, I capture the spirit of the person right away, and I always know early on whether I have missed the personality of the subject in my work.

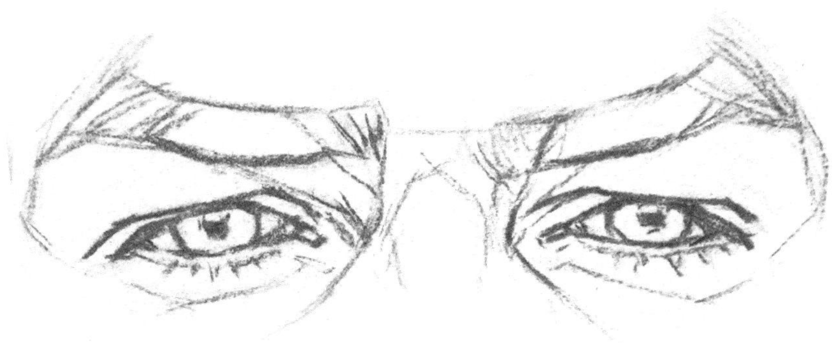

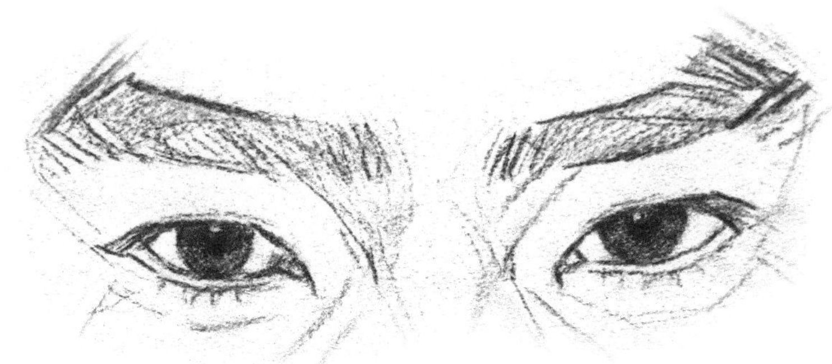

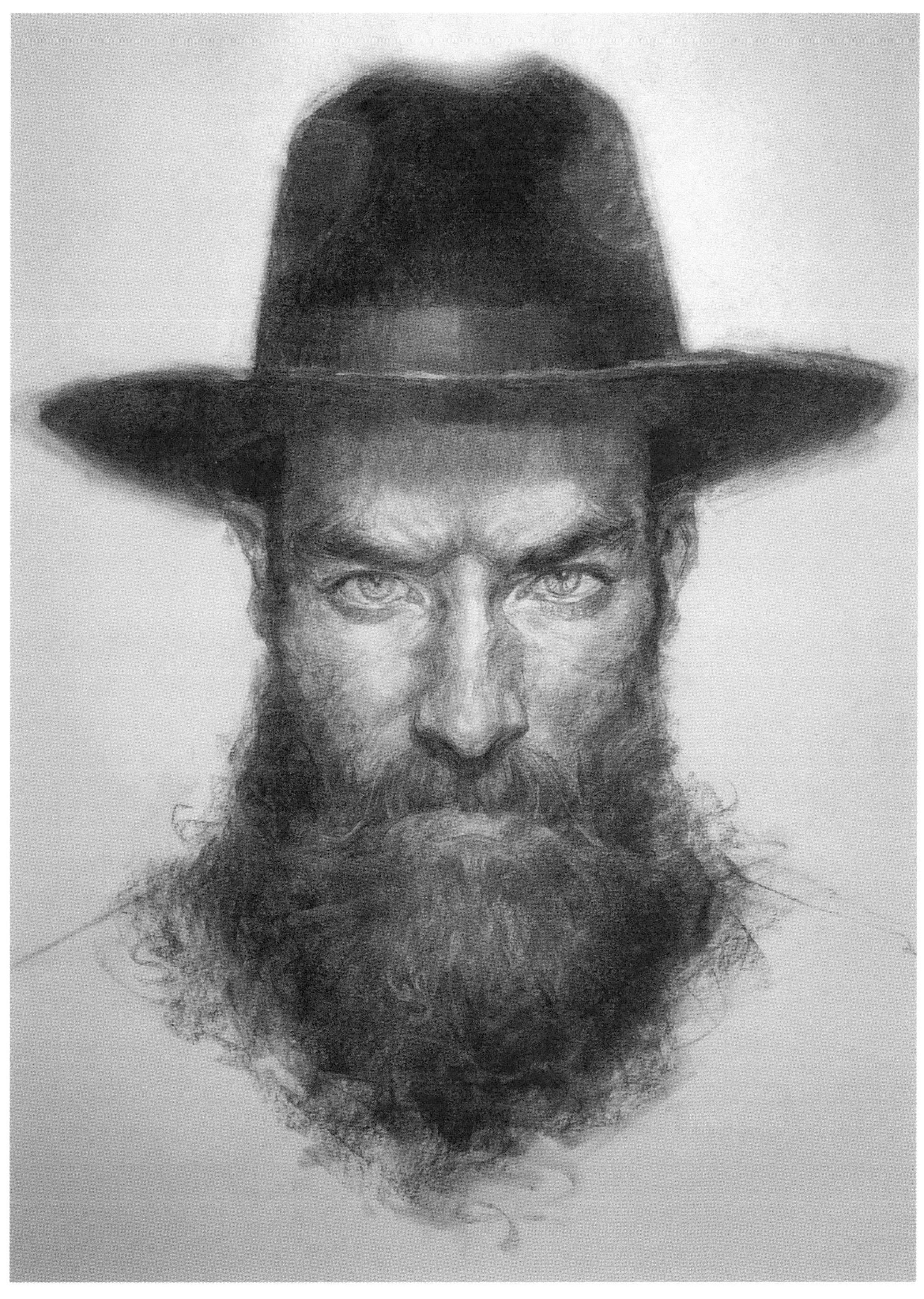

Profile Pose

In this pose, the head is viewed from one side. A masterful profile portrait is always appealing and can be mysterious. Profiles are a good choice for beginning artists because you only draw one half of the face. With practice, you'll internalize the knowledge and be able to visualize without having to draw all the construction lines.

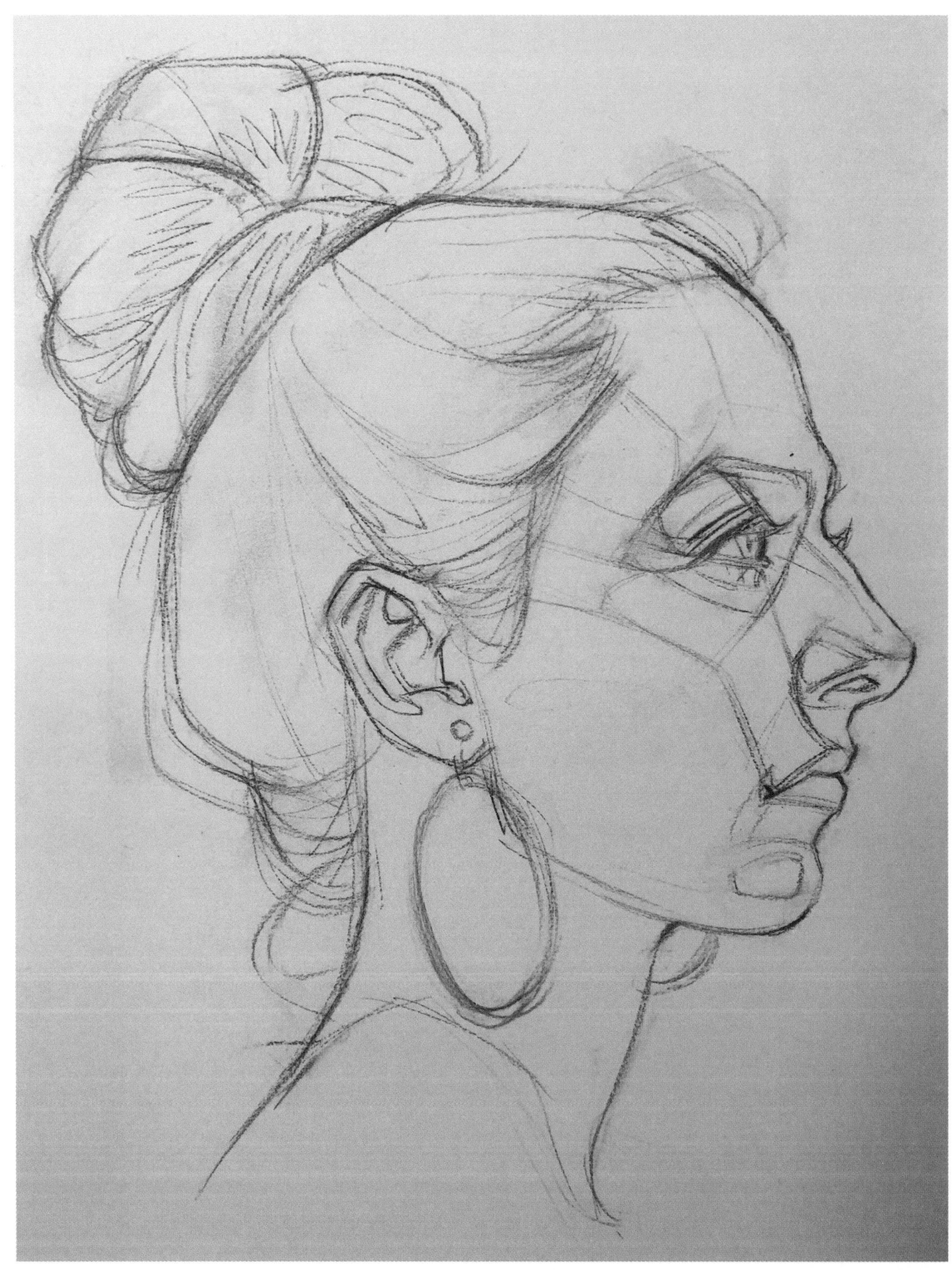

▲ Practice drawing the profile in both directions to perfect your drawing skills. You will likely gravitate toward drawing in one direction, but you should be able to draw both.

PROFILE POSE: THE NOSE

1 | The shape of the nose in profile is triangular; pay attention to the height and width of the nose, and mark the shape with straight lines.

2 | Shape the bottom plane of the nose and the wing.

3 | Building on your guidelines, define the contours more precisely to form the planes of the nose and the nostril wing. Use just a few strokes to divide the tip of the nose and the nostril into separate shapes. Add the shape of the nose's cast shadow.

4 | Begin to block in tone with broad strokes, using the flat side of the vine charcoal. The light is coming from the top, so the top plane of the nose is in the light, while the side and bottom planes are in shadow.

5 | Strengthen the dark tones to form clear distinctions between light, midtone, and shadow on the side and underside of the nose.

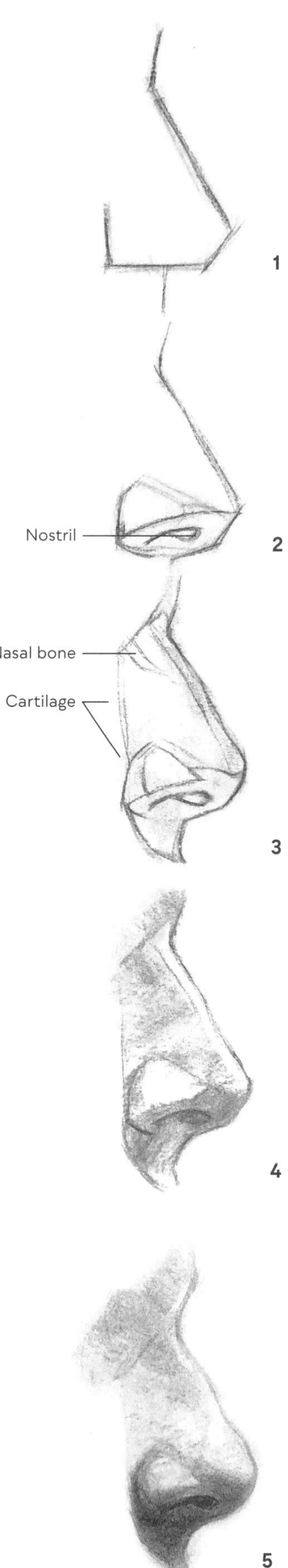

PROFILE POSE: THE EAR

1 | Begin by drawing a diagonal guideline up from the jaw; the ear attaches to this line. Then draw the shape of the ear with angular lines.

2 | Soften and slightly curve the lines to define the outer ear and lobe. Draw the shapes of the inner detail with short, curved strokes.

3 | Over the sketchy lines, draw the contours of the ear with darker, more precise lines and define the inner shape more accurately.

4 | Add the pools of shadow within the ear, darkest just inside the rim. Move around the outer edge of the lobe, adding touches of shadow to make the shape look three-dimensional. Notice the small shadow where the lobe attaches to the jaw.

5 | Darken the shadows within the ear with heavy strokes. Use small parallel strokes to strengthen the tones around the edge of the ear and then brighten the light areas with an eraser. Don't forget the cast shadow on the back of the neck.

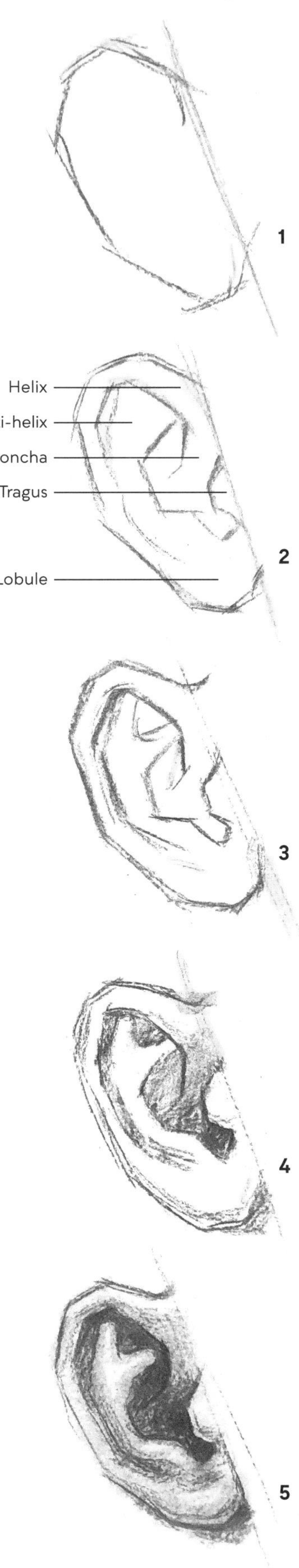

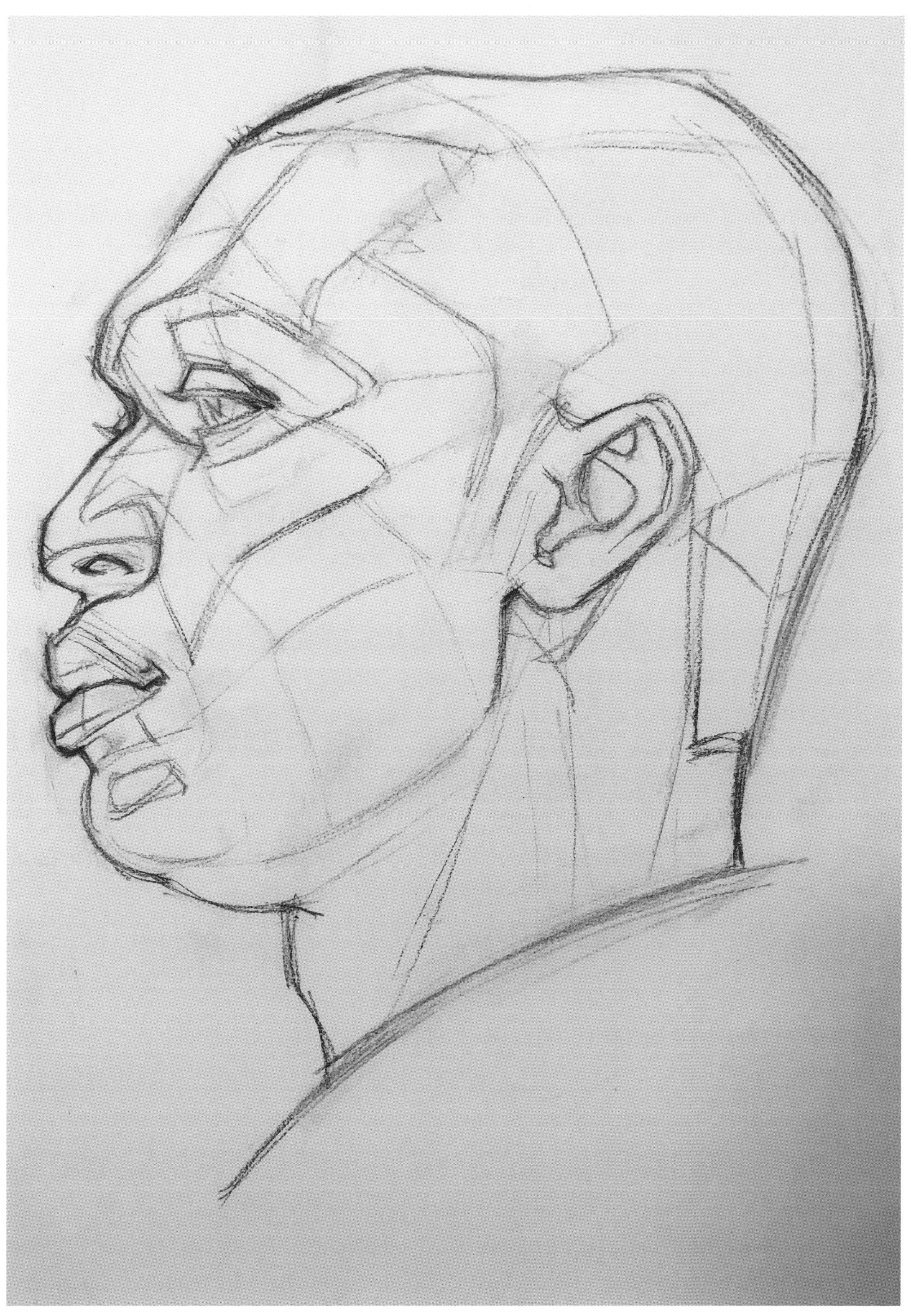

PROFILE POSE: THE MOUTH

1 | From the side, the mouth is triangular. Block in the lips with a few crisp lines and use more curved strokes for the chin. The dividing line between the lips would also be the horizontal guideline for the face.

2 | Soften and curve the lines to more accurately define the shape of the mouth. The slanted line that touches the tips of both the upper and the lower lip indicates the relationship between the lips: the upper lip normally protrudes farther forward.

3 | Working carefully over your guidelines, redefine the shapes of the lips with darker lines. The upper lip turns down and slightly overlaps the lower lip, while the lower lip recedes slightly and is thicker than the upper lip. Strengthen the lines of the chin and accentuate the shadowy corner of the mouth.

4 | Apply broad areas of tone with the flat side of the vine charcoal. The upper lip slants down away from the light and is in shadow, while the lower lip turns up toward the light and is a lighter value. The upper lip casts a hint of shadow across the lower lip. The concave area beneath the lower lip is filled with shadow. Add more shadow at the corner of the mouth and begin to model the chin and jaw.

5 | Darken the upper lip and accentuate the line between the lips, as well as the dark corner of the mouth. Deepen the pool of shadow beneath the lower lip and add more strokes to model the jaw and chin so that it appears rounder and more three-dimensional. Finally, darken the forward edge of the lower lip where the cast shadow of the upper lip overlaps.

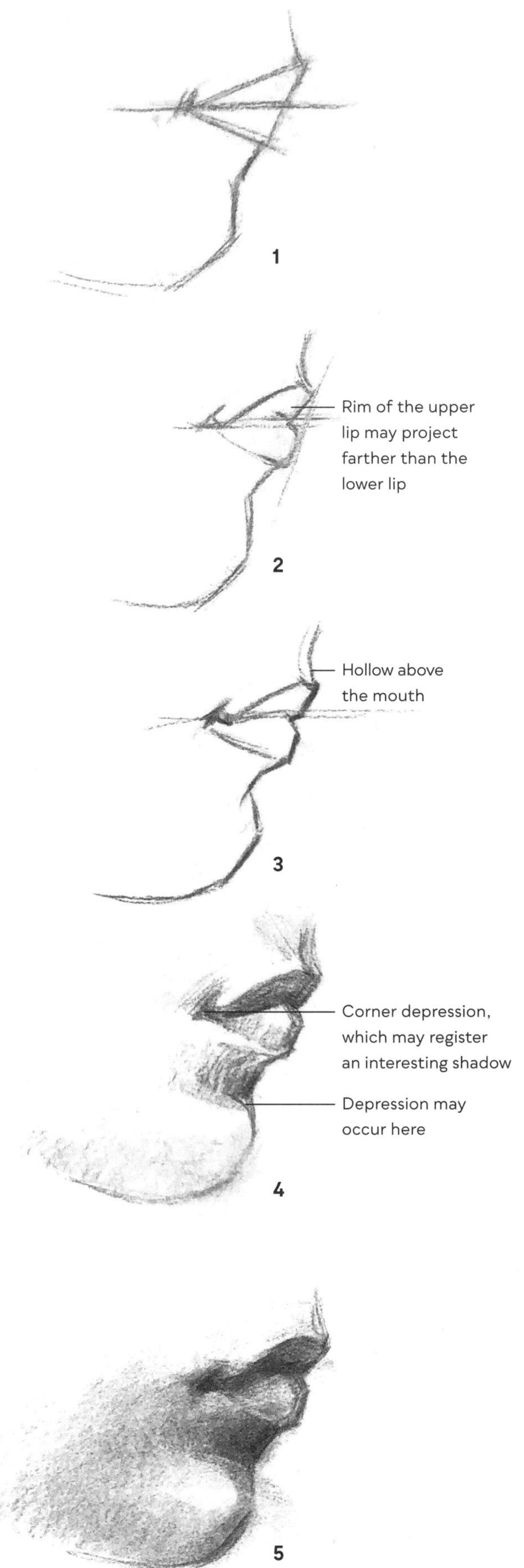

PROFILE POSE: THE EYE

1 | First block in the shapes with vine charcoal, mapping out the geometric shape of the eye socket and the triangular shape of the eye.

2 | The eye is a small sphere in the circular cup of the eye socket. Draw the complete sphere first. Around the sphere, wrap the eyelids, like two curving bands, and place the iris on the front of the sphere. Note that the mobile upper lid is twice the thickness of the lower lid, which is stationary. The upper lid also overlaps the lower lid at the outer corner.

3 | Darken and sharpen the lines of the lids, draw the iris more precisely, and add the pupil. Add a second line to indicate the top of the lower lid. Compare the upper and lower lids: the upper lid has a steeper slant than the lower lid and juts farther forward.

4 | Lightly block in tone with the broad side of the vine charcoal, using parallel strokes. Darken the eyebrow and indicate the shadow beneath the brow just above the bridge of the nose. Add shadows to the edges of the curved eyelids and place a deep shadow in the eye socket above the upper lid. Note that the upper lid casts a distinct shadow over the iris and white of the eye.

5 | Still using the broad side of the vine charcoal, darken the shadows with clusters of broad parallel strokes. Accentuate the shadows around the eye to make the eye socket seem deeper. Darken the shadowy edges of the eyelids and add a few dark touches to suggest eyelashes. Darken the iris and make the pupil even darker. Just above the lower lid, apply a hint of tone to make the white of the eye look rounder. Block in shadow to complete the eyebrow, keeping the edges soft and out of focus.

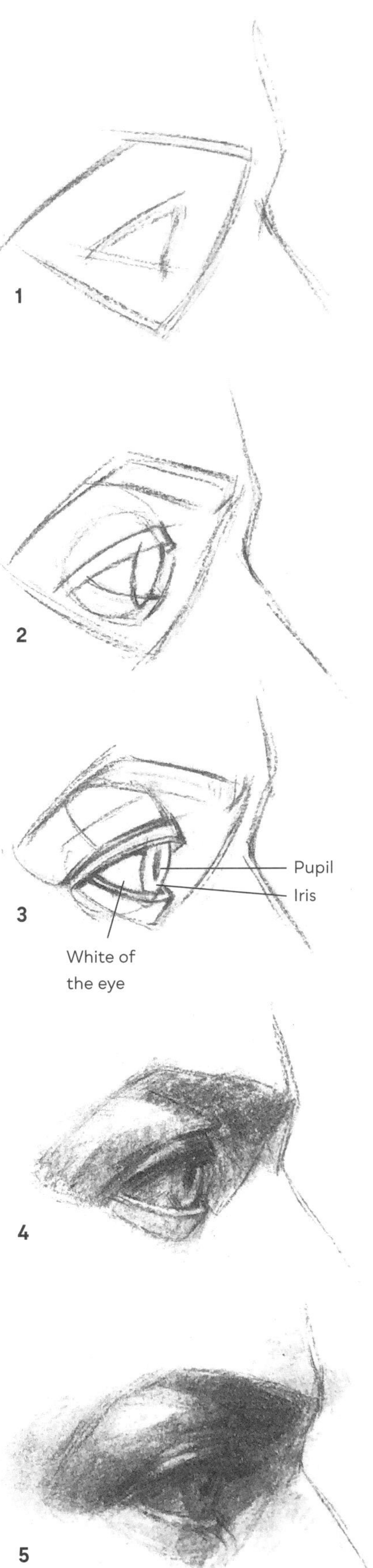

This point of view is especially useful for studying and noting the differences in male and female features.

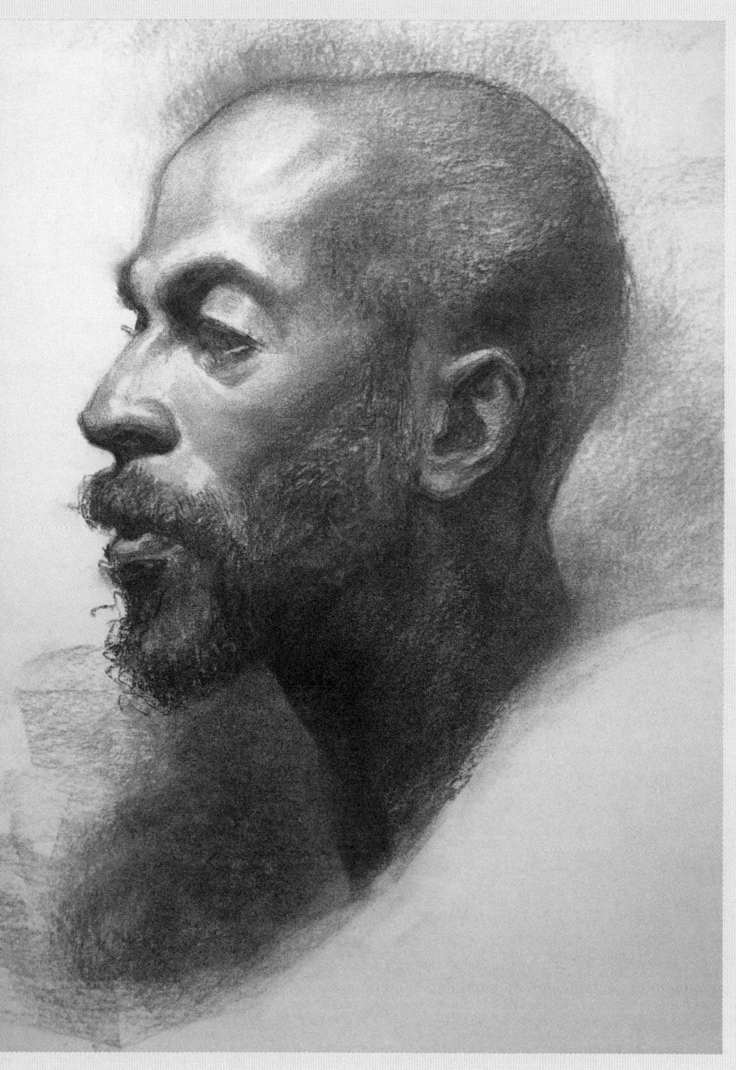

▲ The male brow extends farther than that of a female.

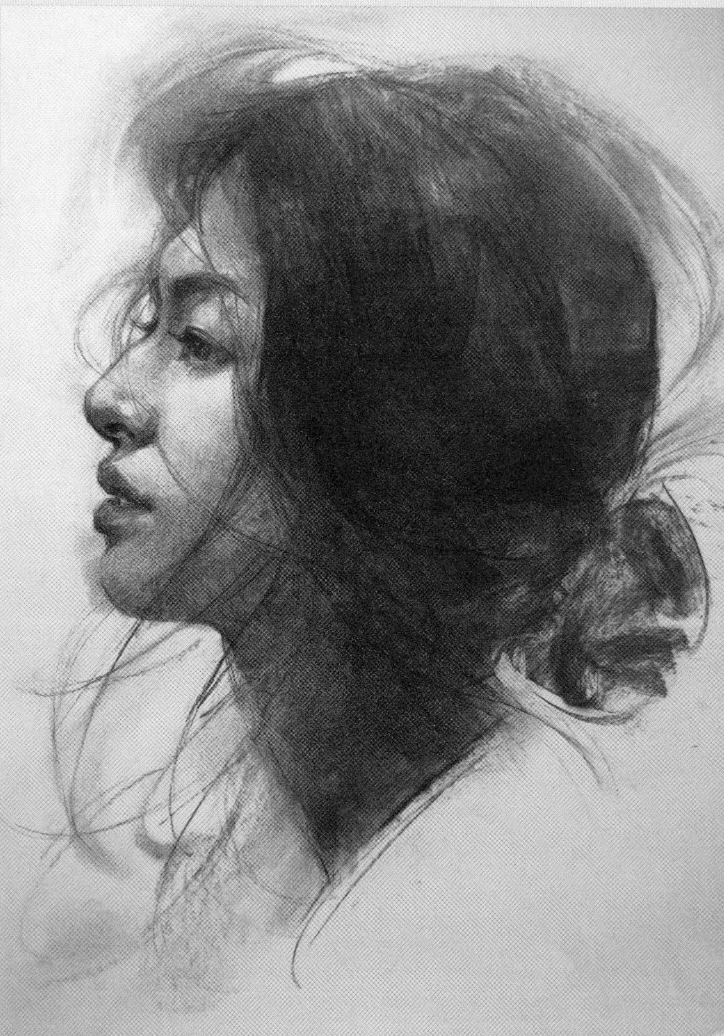

▲ The bridge root of the female nose is typically more rounded than on males, and there is more likely to be a curve between the mouth and nose.

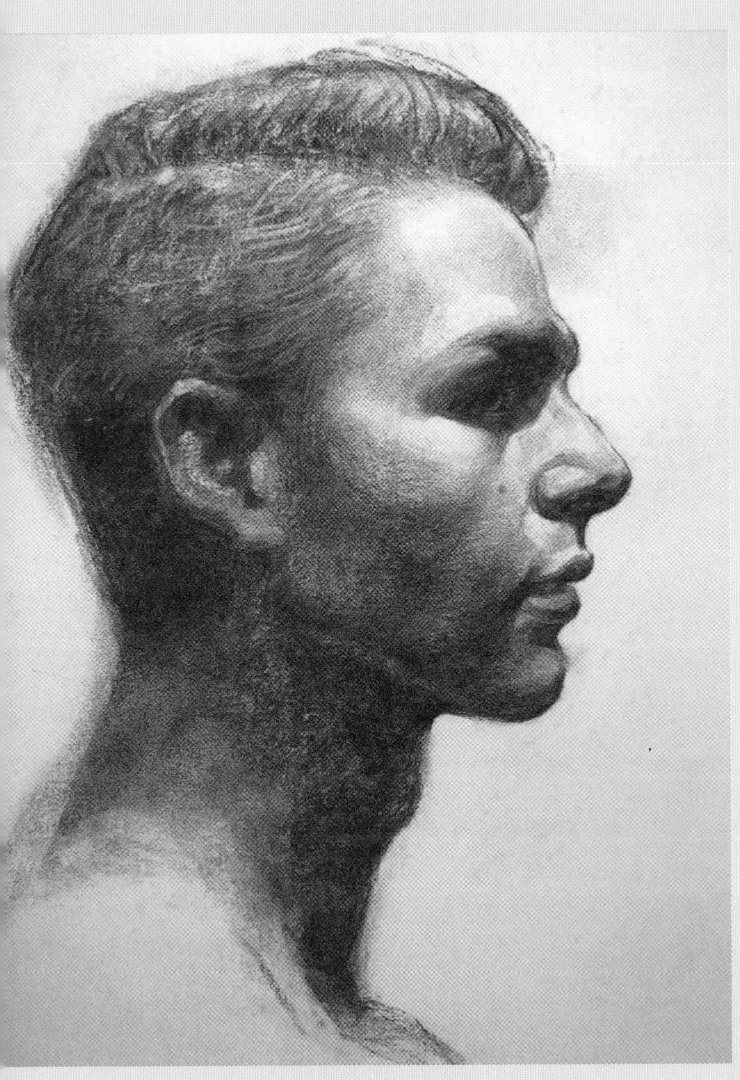

▲ Male noses tend to be longer and straighter on the bottom than the average female nose. Male chins tender to be more pronounced than female chins.

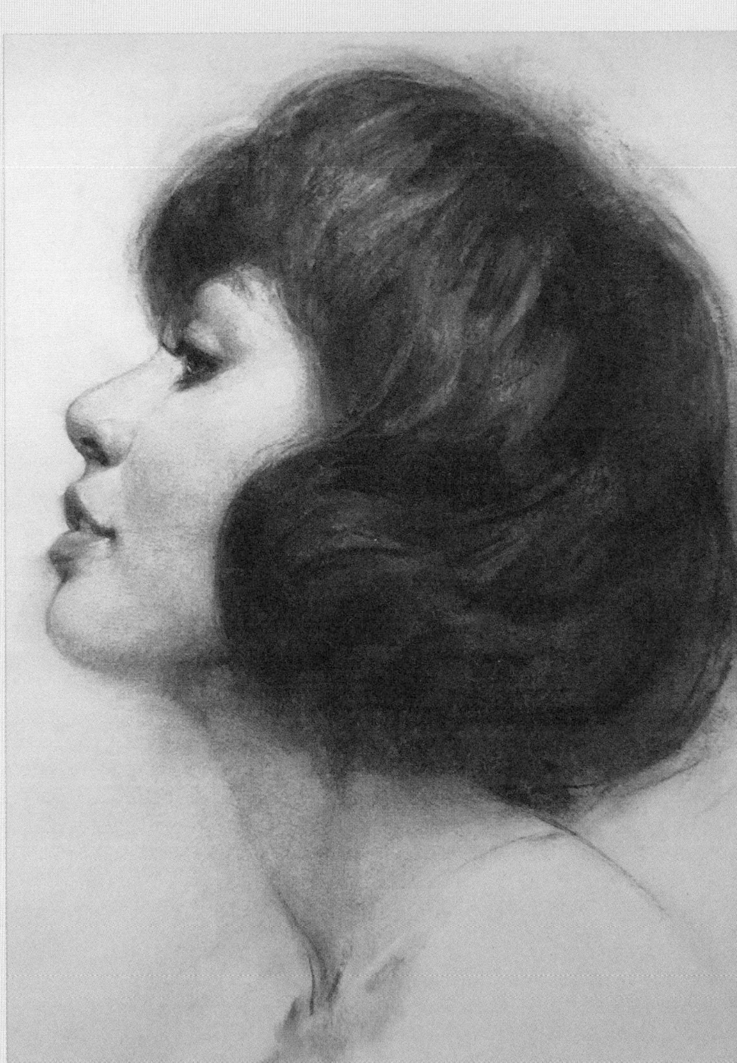

▲ Generally, female lips are thicker than male lips.

Three-Quarter Pose

In a three-quarter pose, the head is turned slightly to the side, about halfway between profile and front view. Though both eyes are visible, only one ear is shown. This pose is ideal for revealing the contours of the face.

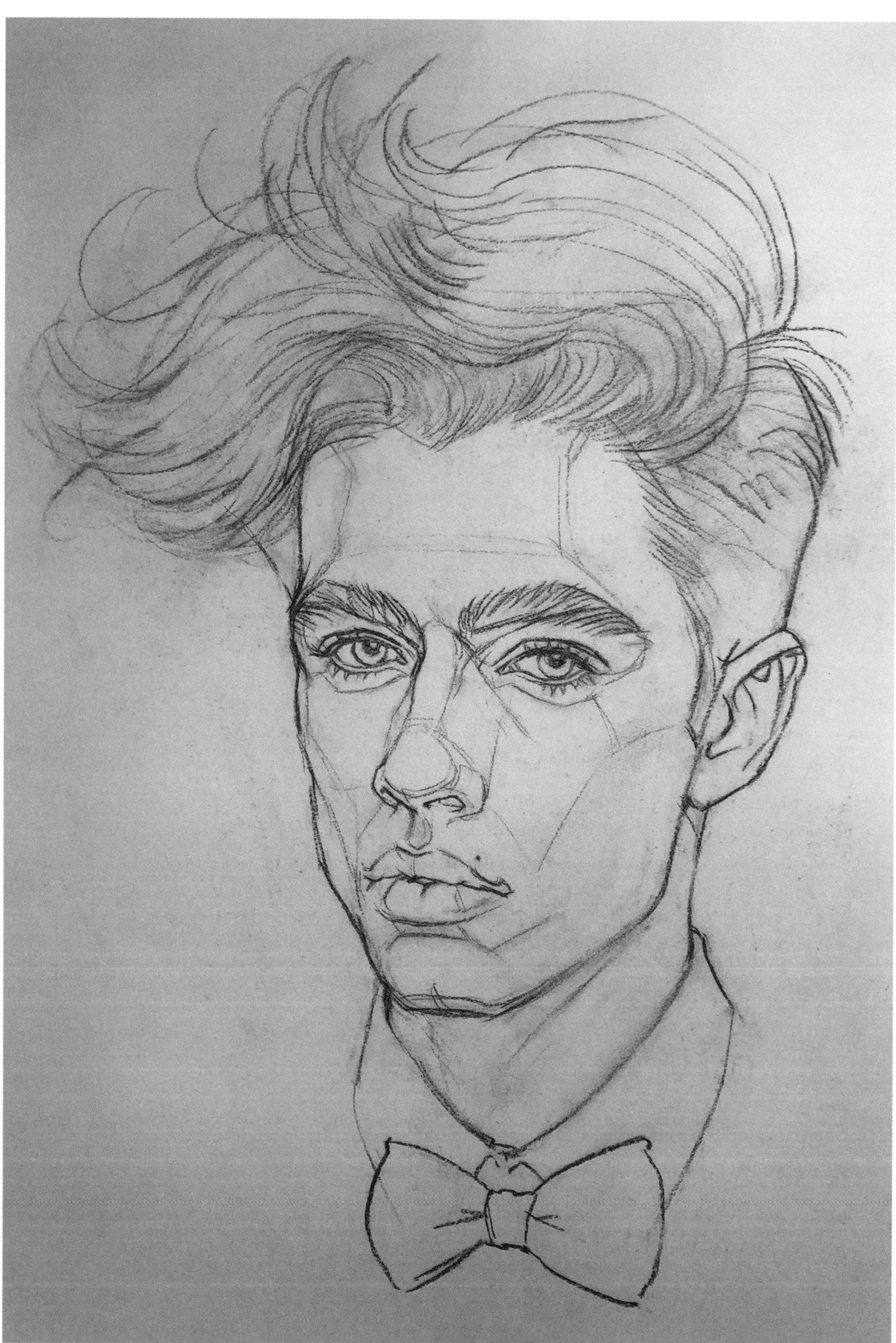

I prefer a slight three-quarter view to the static profile or symmetrical front view because I can center the light on the corner of both the front and the side planes of the head. This creates foreshortened perspective, which also allows for diminished detail and diffusion of the contour lines.

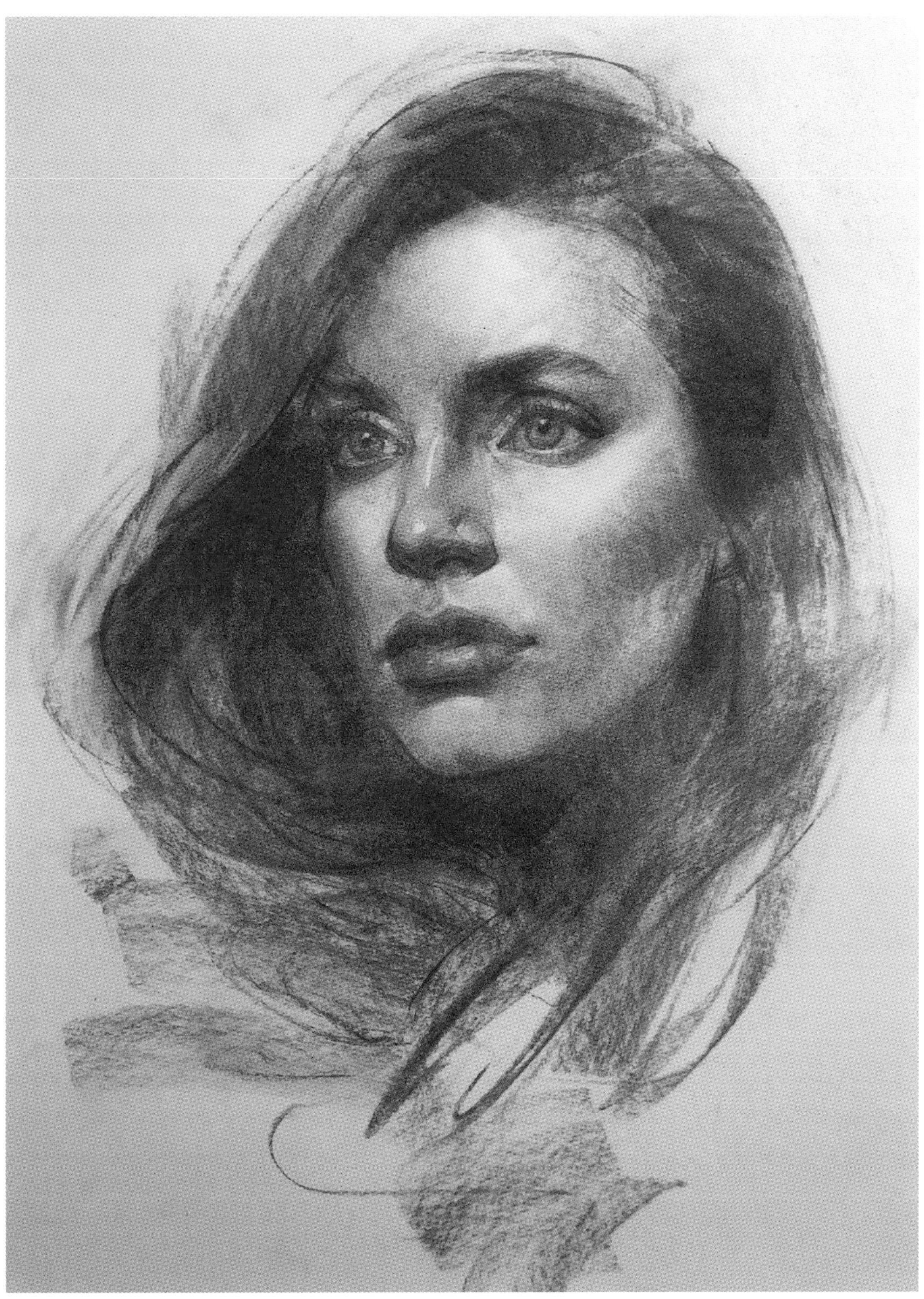

THREE-QUARTER POSE: THE NOSE

At a three-quarter view, the nose no longer looks symmetrical; one side is more visible than the other. In this drawing, the head tilts slightly upward, so we see more of the underside of the nose.

1 | Block in the basic shape of the eye sockets and nose. At this angle, the visible planes are the top, front, bottom, and one side. The bottom plane is triangular and its broad base gently curves on the upper region of the mouth.

2 | Rework the lines to define the shape of the nose. Curved lines indicate the nostrils and the tip of the nose. Pay attention to the width of the top plane, which narrows on the top and widens at the base. Remember, before you begin blending you must start with an accurate line drawing. It's very difficult to correct the shape once you start blending.

3 | Use the broad side of the vine charcoal to begin indicating the shapes of the shadows on the right and beneath the nose with rough, scribbly strokes. Pay attention to the distinction between midtone and shadow on the tip and side of the nose. Notice how the nasal bone comes down almost halfway before the cartilage takes over and the bony part creates a slight shadow by the bridge.

4 | Continue building up the value on the shadow side of the nose and around the tip, working carefully to keep the tones smooth. Define the wings of the nostrils with darker strokes and touches of reflected light, which are important to show roundness. Pull out highlights with your kneaded eraser.

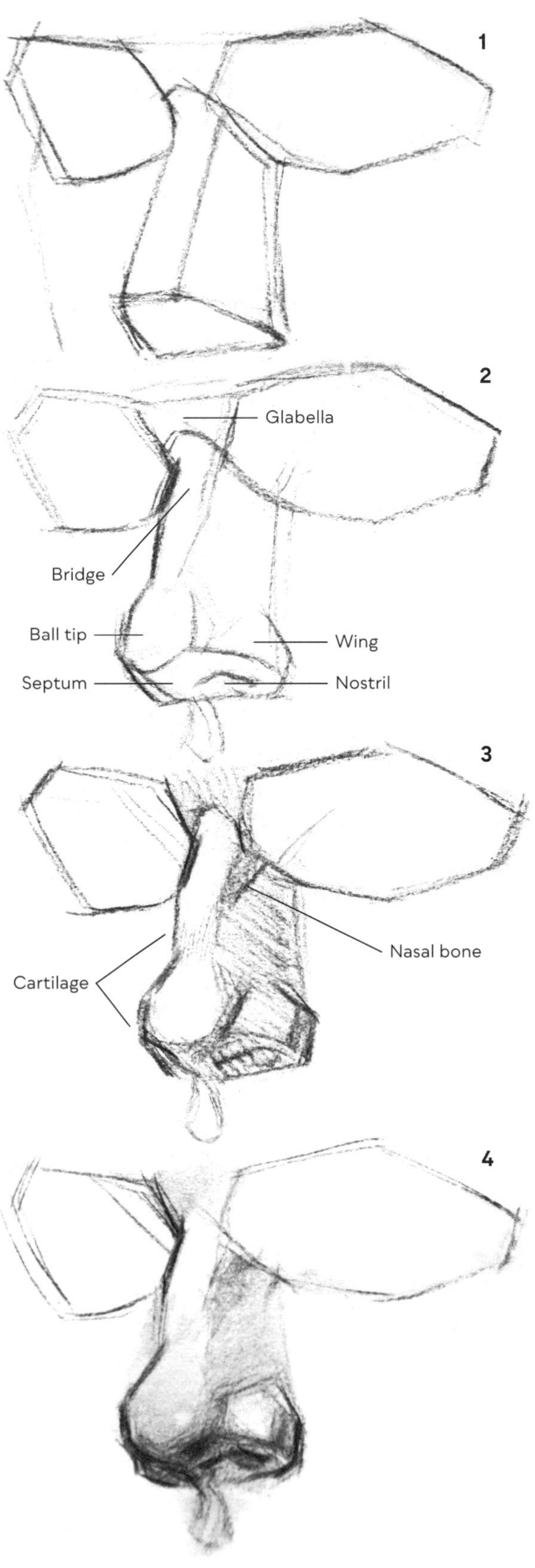

THREE-QUARTER POSE: THE EAR

1 | Only one ear is visible from this viewpoint. Use simple lines to block in the shape, paying attention to the angle, which is not vertical but tips slightly backward.

2 | Curve and smooth the lines to define the shape of the upper ear and lobe. Draw the shapes of the inner ear with short, curved strokes. A dark inner line defines the sinuous shape of the rim, which winds to the deep "bowl" at the center. Notice how the outer rim varies greatly in width.

3 | With the broad side of the vine charcoal, block in the pool of shadow within the ear, making it darkest just inside the rim. Move around the outer edge of the ear and lobe, adding touches of shadow to make the shape look three-dimensional.

4 | Darken the pools of shadow within the ear with heavy strokes. Use small parallel strokes to strengthen the tones around the edge of the ear and then brighten the light areas with an eraser.

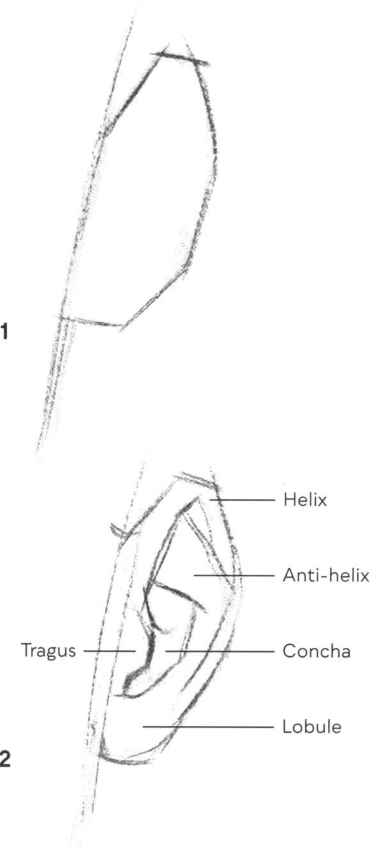

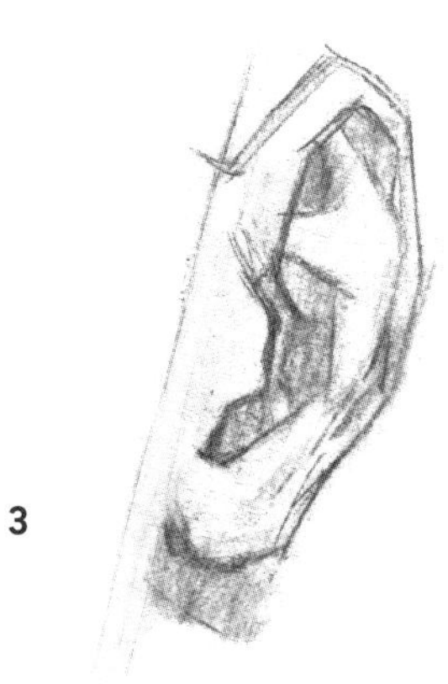

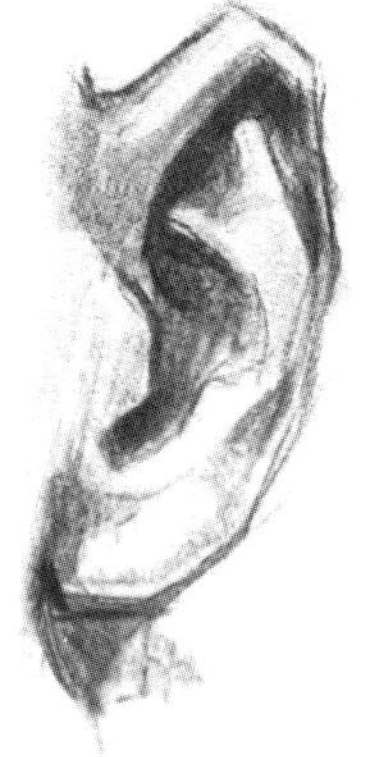

THREE-QUARTER POSE: THE MOUTH

1 | Draw the winged shape of the upper lip
with curving lines to suggest the softness
of the female mouth. Draw the full lower
lip with a single curve and lightly mark the
depression under the lip. Because the head
is turned slightly to the left, the mouth is too,
so we see more of the right side.

2 | Define the shapes of the lips more
accurately. Notice how the center of the upper
lip dips down over the lower. Instead of
drawing dividing lines for the three planes
of the lower lip, slightly square the outer
contour to suggest those planes.

3 | Add tone with the broad side of the vine
charcoal, and begin to indicate the shadows
with rough strokes to darken the upper lip.
Darken the dividing line between the lips,
accentuating the shadows at the corners of
the mouth. Just above this dark line, darken
the shadowy upper lip to emphasize its
roundness. Keep the tone lighter on the
lower lip, which turns upward and receives
more light, but darken the shadow plane at
the right. Apply rough stokes beneath the
lower lip.

4 | Continue to darken the shadowy
upper lip and strengthen the dividing line
between the lips. Add more tone to the
corners of the mouth. Add more tone to the
lower lip, leaving just a patch of light for a
highlight. Strengthen the shadowy underside of the lower lip to make the shape
look rounder. The corners of the mouth are
shaped like doughnuts, so be sure to main-
tain soft edges. Finally, add tone to the chin
and the groove above the upper lip.

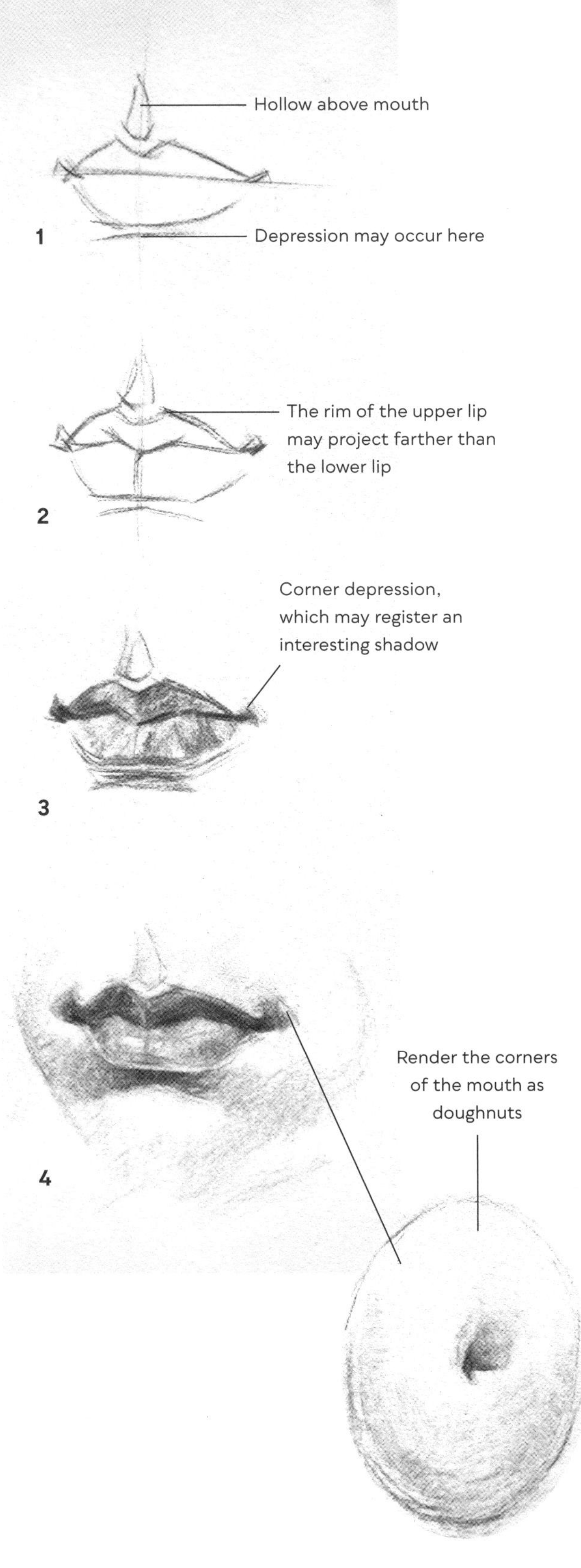

THREE-QUARTER POSE: THE EYES

1 | Start by drawing the shape of the eye socket with angular strokes. The eyes must be carefully placed within the borders of the eye sockets. When you're drawing a portrait, be sure to study the widths of the two different eye sockets, which may vary due to perspective.

2 | Apply quick, causal lines to draw the main contours of the eyelids, iris, and eyebrow. The straight horizontal line that crosses the eye is the guideline that would be drawn across the egg-shaped head to position the eyes.

3 | Go over your lines with darker, more precise expressive strokes, defining the curves of the eyelids, the disk shape of the iris, and the pupil. The top lid begins as a long, flattened curve that turns steeply downward at the inner corner, while the lower lid starts at the inner corner as a long, flattened curve and turns sharply upward at the outer corner. The lower eyelid is thinner and more obvious because it is moist and catches the light.

4 | Begin applying tone with clusters of parallel strokes with the broad side of the vine charcoal. Curve these strokes around the contours of the eye sockets to show their form. Sketch dark and light values in the eyeball; the range of values varies with the color of the eye. Carefully draw the shadowy edges of the lids, paying attention to the shadows cast across the eye by the upper lid. The lower the upper lid, the deeper the shadow over the iris. Darken the pupil and eyebrow.

5 | To finish, blacken the pupil, darken the iris, and strengthen the shadowy edges of the eyelids. Add just a touch of shadow on the whites of the eye. Apply more groups of parallel strokes that curve around the eye socket to darken the tones and make the shape rounder. Use long, graceful lines to suggest eyebrow hairs and short, curving lines to suggest eyelashes. Finally, pull out highlights with a kneaded eraser.

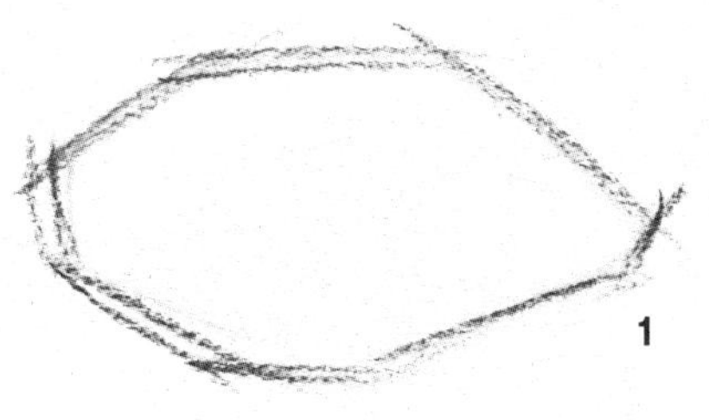

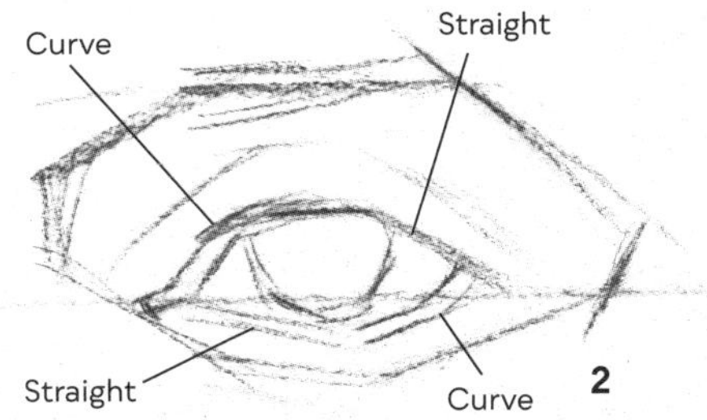

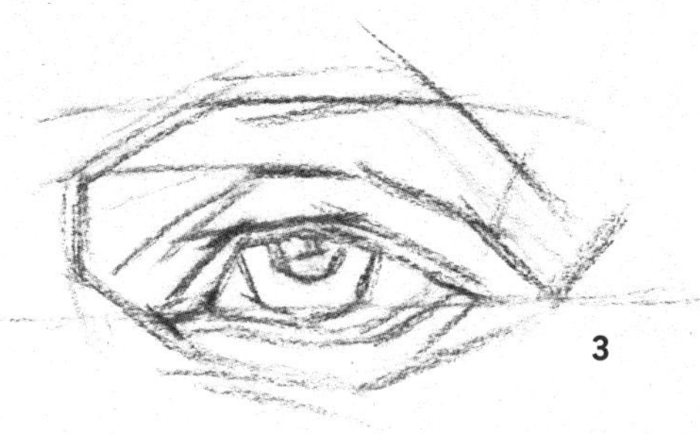

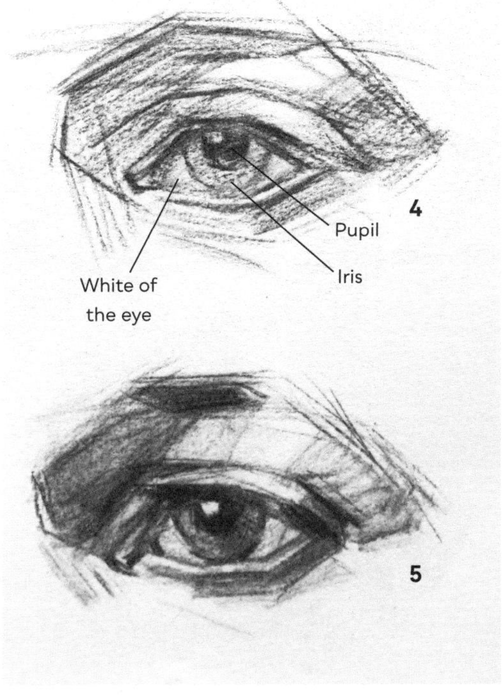

FORESHORTENING IN THREE-QUARTER VIEW

When the head is viewed at this angle, the perspective of the face and features is skewed. Foreshortening causes the closest parts of an object to appear larger than parts that are farther away. When you draw from this viewpoint, be sure to carefully study proportion variation and measure the distance between features.

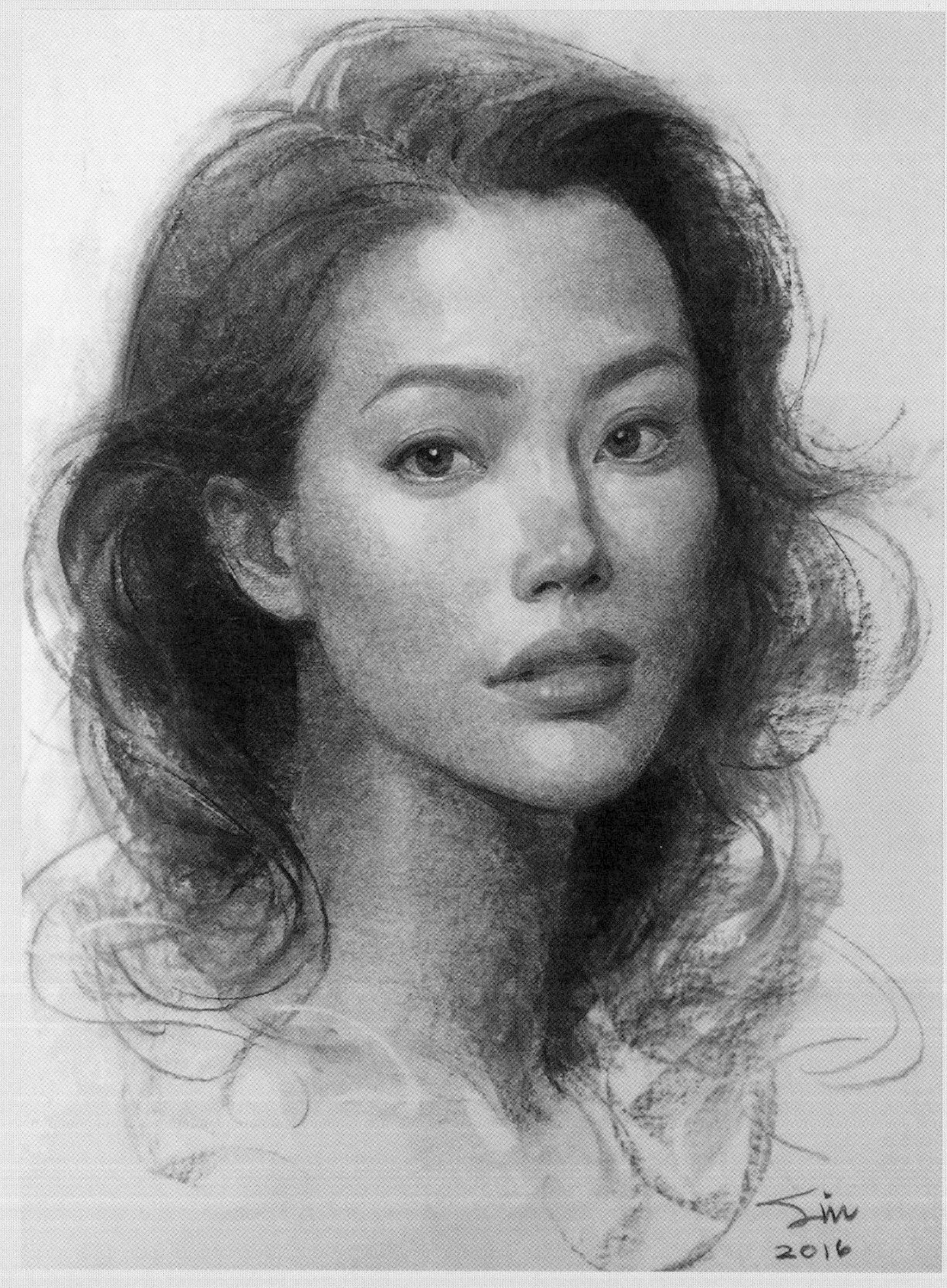

▲ Three-quarter view places an emphasis on the closest eye as the focal point. The eyes, along with the eyebrows, reveal the mood of your subject. The distance between the two eyes is generally the width of one eye, but it may be smaller depending on the angle of the head or the subject.

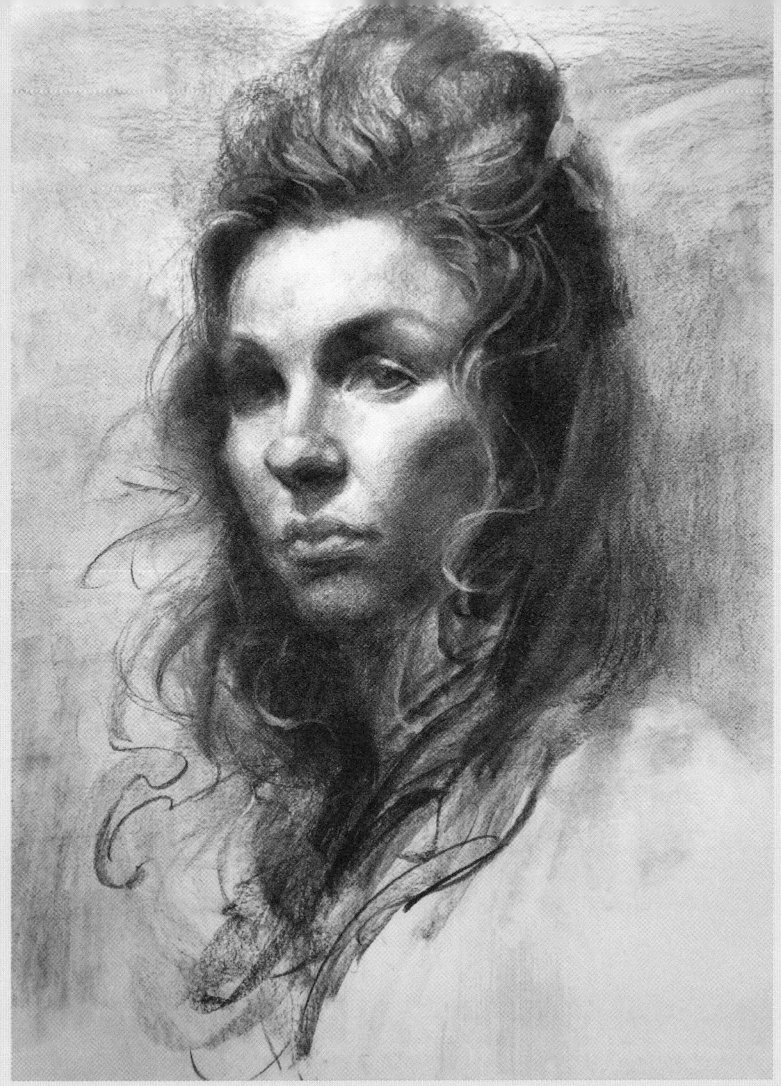

The near side of the face is wider than the far side, due to the foreshortened perspective. The cheekbone is more defined on the far side of the face, with a harder contour line.

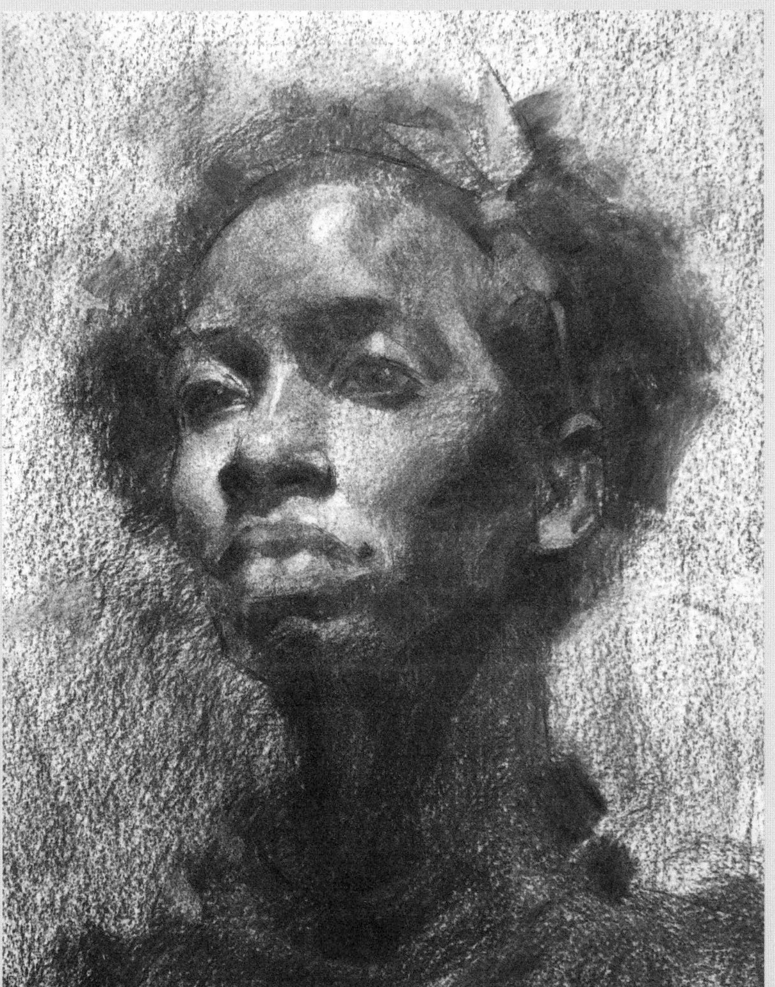

As the subject lifts his or her chin, the tip of the nose is closer to the eyes.

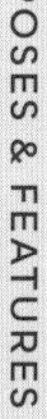

DEVELOPING A PORTRAIT FROM START TO FINISH

1 | Use vine charcoal to map the position of the head by marking the top, bottom, and side boundaries with straight lines. Avoid drawing curved lines to fit the contour; it's easy to make mistakes that result in incorrect proportion or perspective. Straight lines allow you to observe the subject as a whole and examine the relationships between key blocks so you can define them accurately on paper. Draw a ball shape for the skull and U-shape for the jaw. Establish the cross where the middle line crosses the brow line. Notice how the brow line slightly curves due to the tilted gesture of the head.

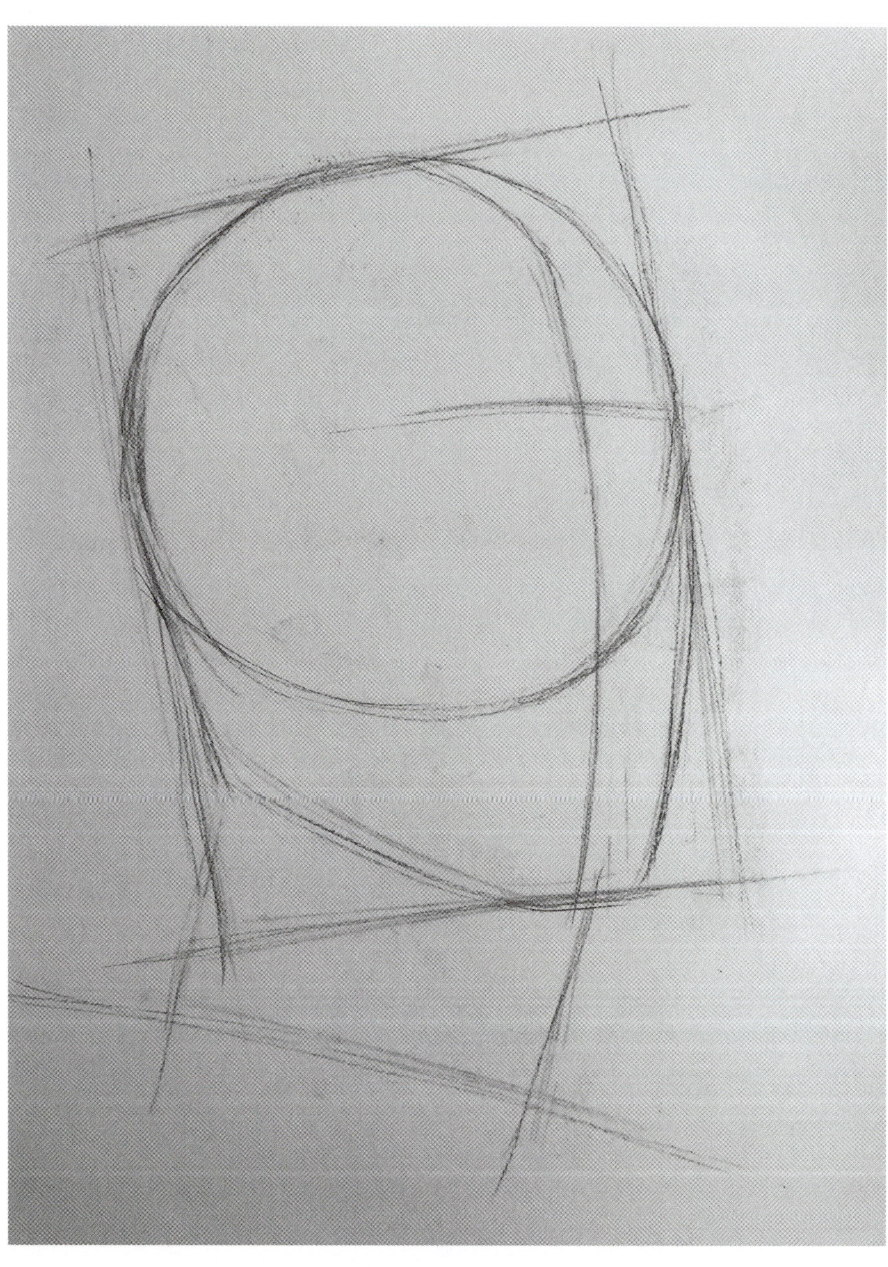

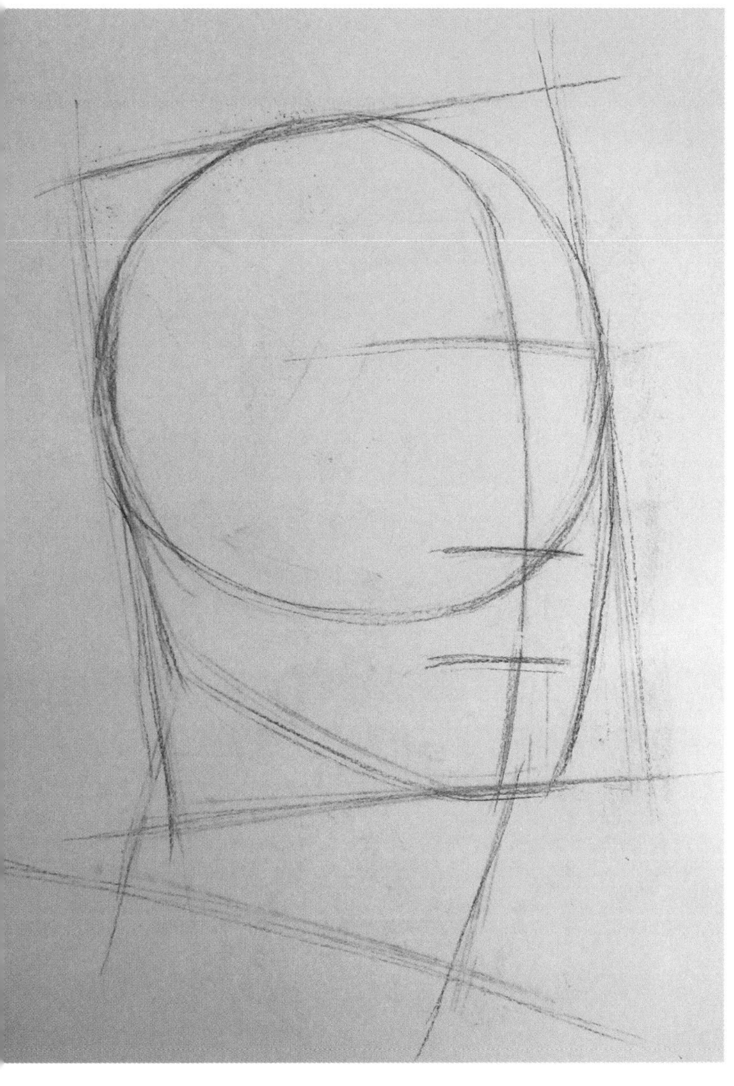 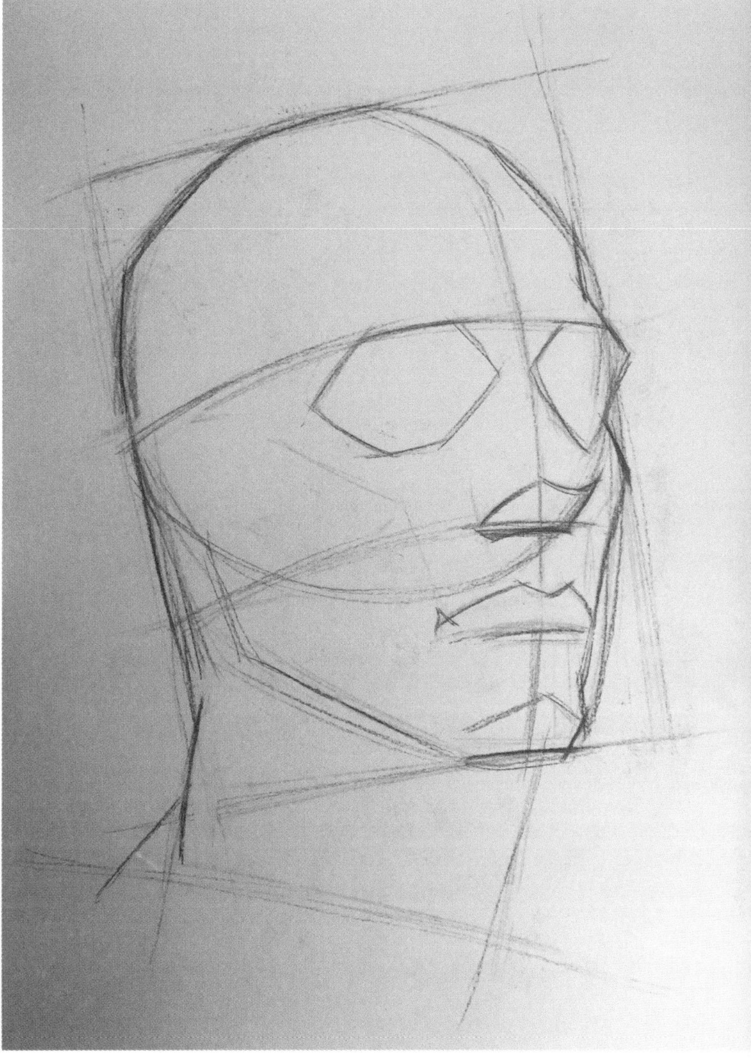

2 | Identify and divide the head into thirds: one-third from the hairline to the eyebrows, one-third from the eyebrows to the nose, and one-third from the nose to the chin. The lower lip is halfway between the nose and the chin.

3 | Continue to use straight lines to define the large shadow areas, such as the eye sockets, mouth, and base of the nose. Define the approximate shapes of the head's outline and mark the brow. Notice the shape of the chin's bottom plane, which is foreshortened due to the angle of the head.

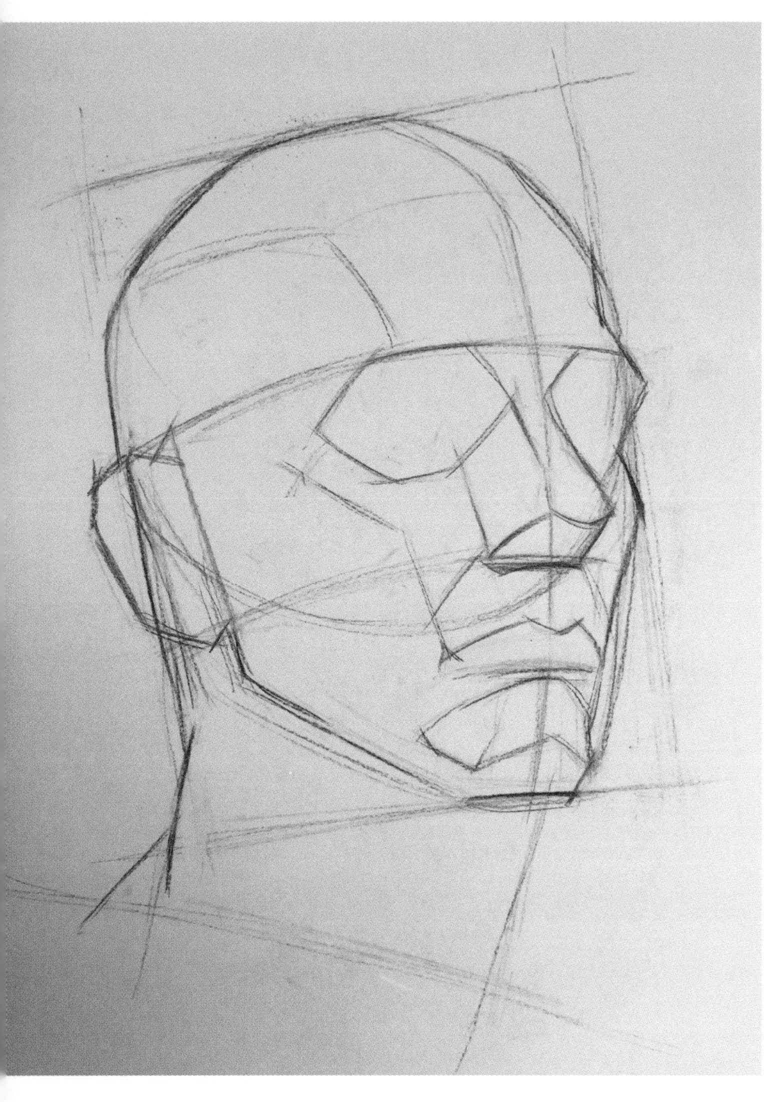

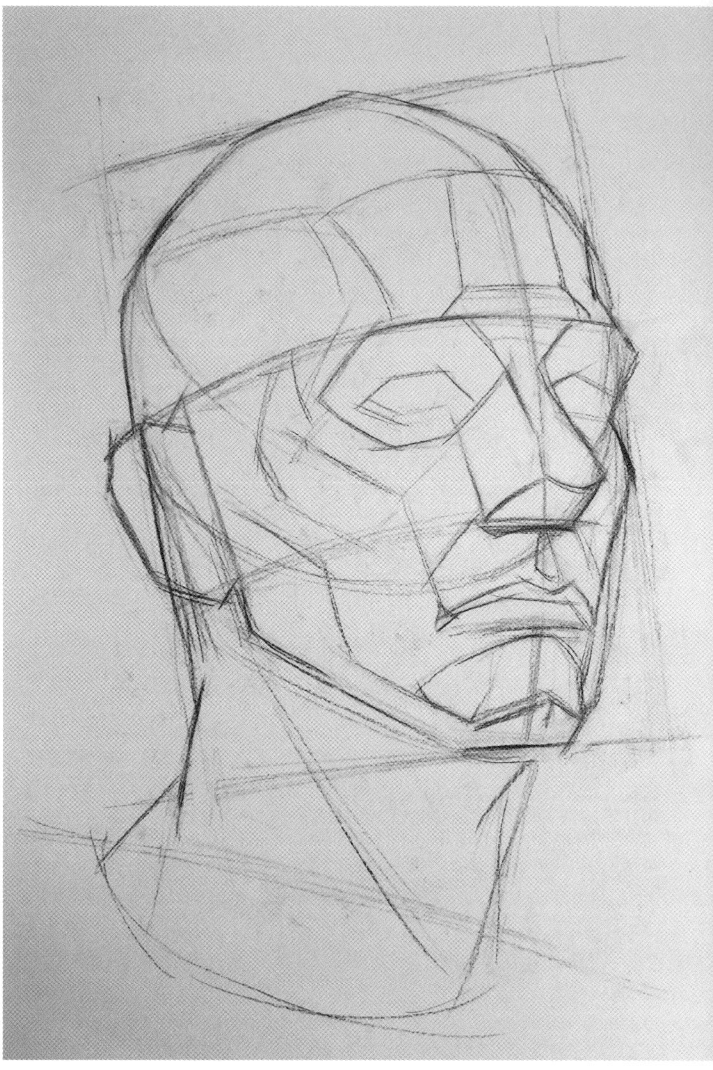

4 | Draw the shape of the ear, which aligns with the brow line and the bottom of the nose. Continue to define the planes of the forehead, cheekbones, nose, and chin with straight lines.

5 | At this stage, focus on studying and exploring the proportions and relationships of the shapes to one another as you further refine the face. Avoid adding details, such as the pupils and nostrils, for now.

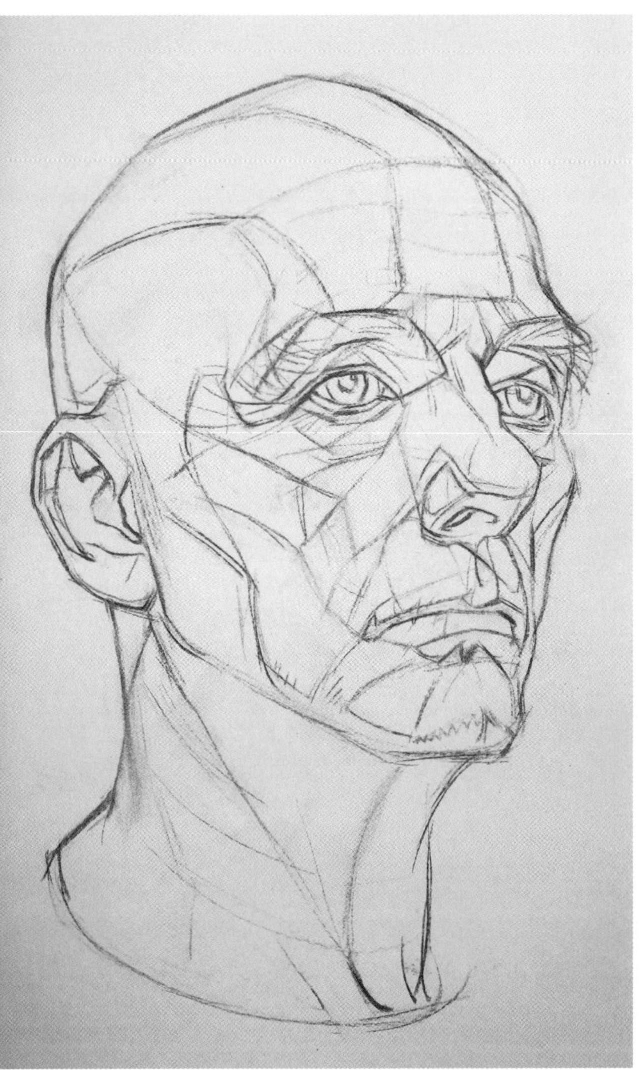

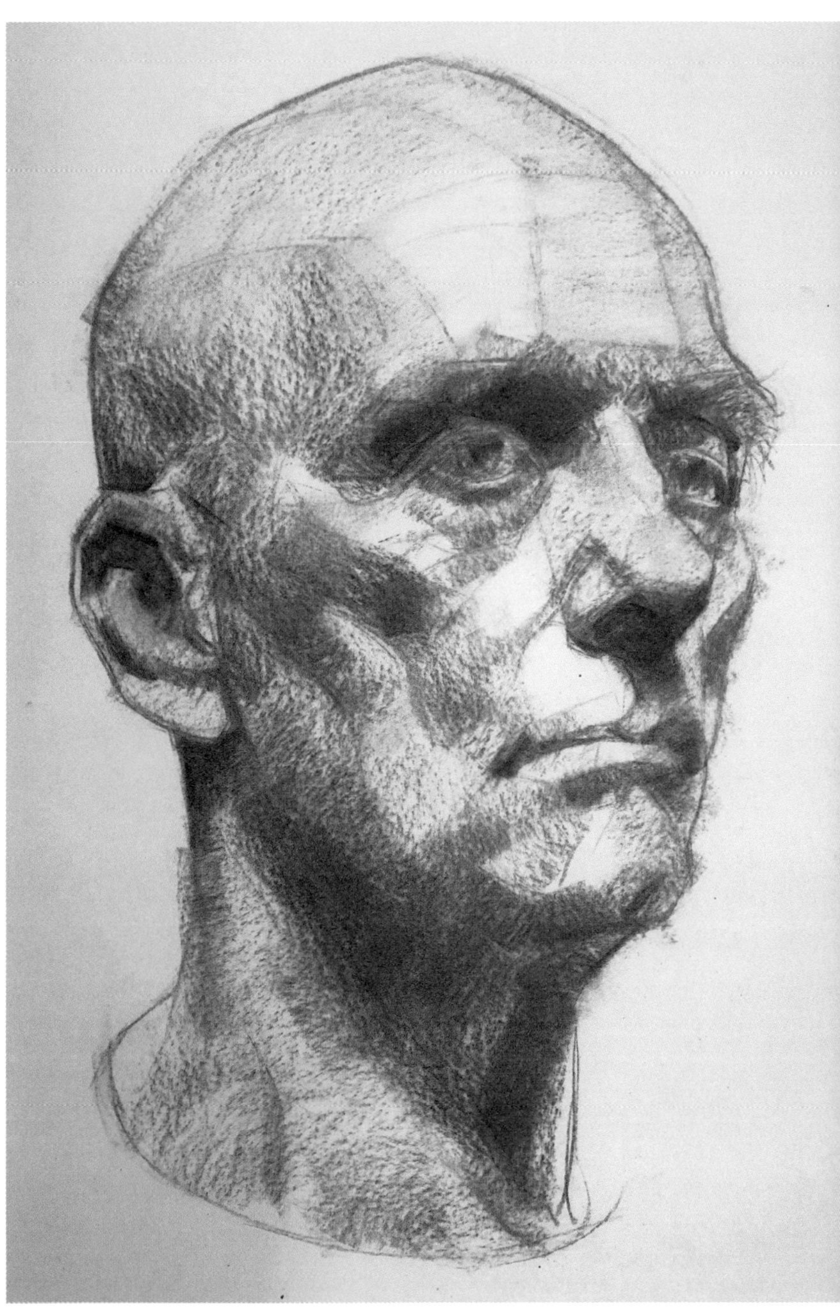

6 | Continue to use lines to define areas of shadow and where planes meet, such as the front, sides, and slope of the forehead, and the front, wings, and base of the nose. Mark the approximate shapes and positions of the brow arch, cheekbones, temporal bones, chin, and jaw.

7 | Use the broad side of the vine charcoal to begin blocking in values to build the structure of the head. Remember that all objects have light, middle, and dark values when exposed to light. That applies to each of the individual facial features. Hatch the entire shadow area of the nose and continue into the dark shadow of the cheekbone and other areas. If you like, you can reduce the textures by blending the surface with your fingertip or a stump.

8 | Next, begin to add and develop the details, which is a process of repetition. In each area where you work on details, reexamine the shapes of the different parts, paying attention to the strokes so that there is variation in hard and soft edges.

Wherever you add detail, shade the entire area first. Then pull out highlights with an eraser and use a charcoal pencil to emphasize the shadows. Wrinkles can be challenging to draw, but they also add interest by enriching the drawing with texture and details. Wrinkles should not stand out and must correspond to the shape of the facial features. Focus on conveying an impression of wrinkles, rather than drawing every single wrinkle visible. (See also "Drawing Elderly People," page 124.)

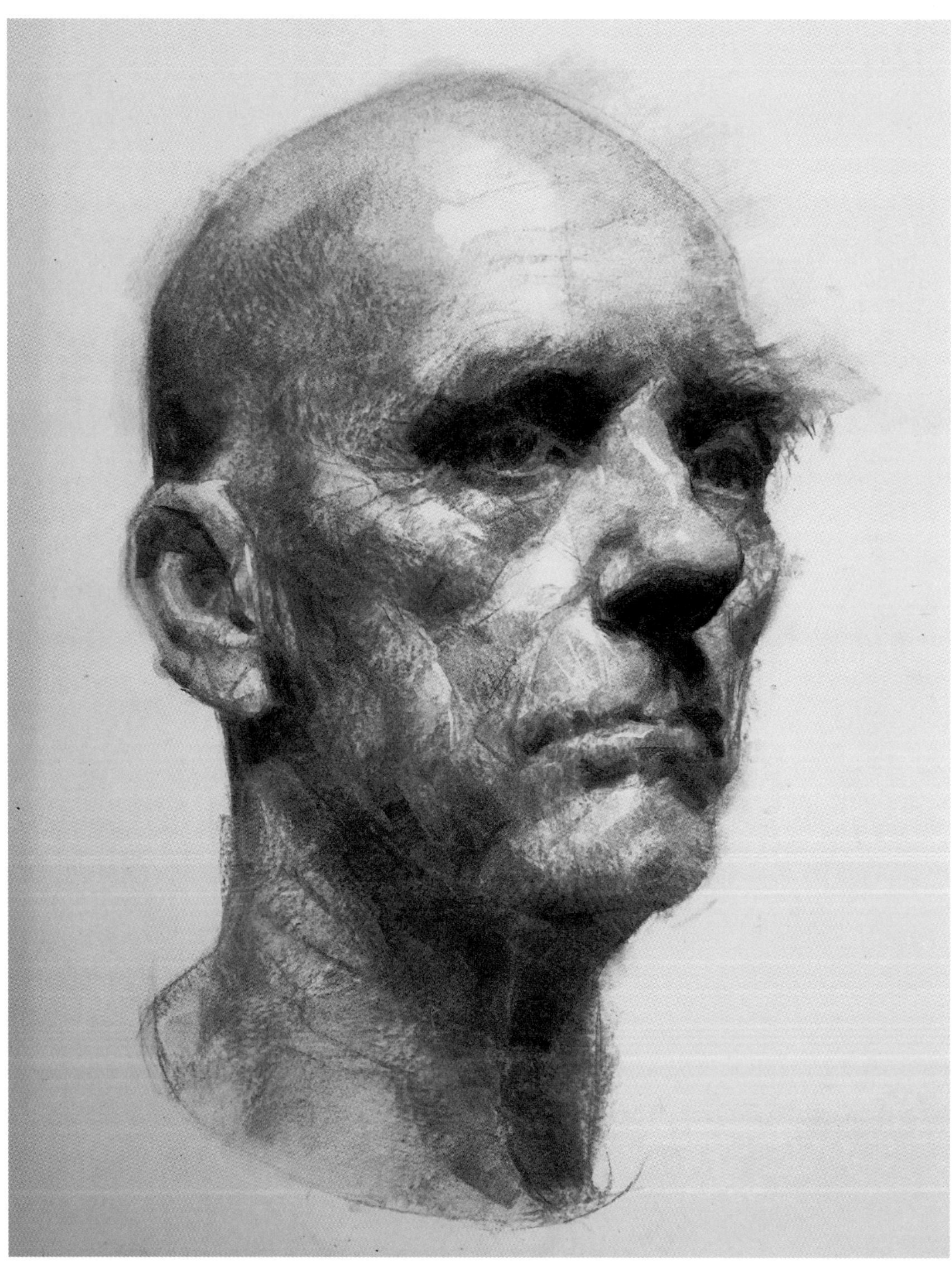

9 | Finish by reexamining the light, midtone, and dark values, as well as the edges of the face. Each of the three major values should be further rendered into three more values, plus the highlight, for a wide value range that captures the forms. The edges of the face shouldn't form one continuous line, but contain rhythm, spatial relationships, and variation.

Reinforce the boundary between light and dark on the chin to solidify this feature and softly represent the structure and texture. Last, reinforce the dark areas even more. When you're happy with the likeness, immediately cover the drawing with spray fixative to prevent smearing the fragile vine charcoal.

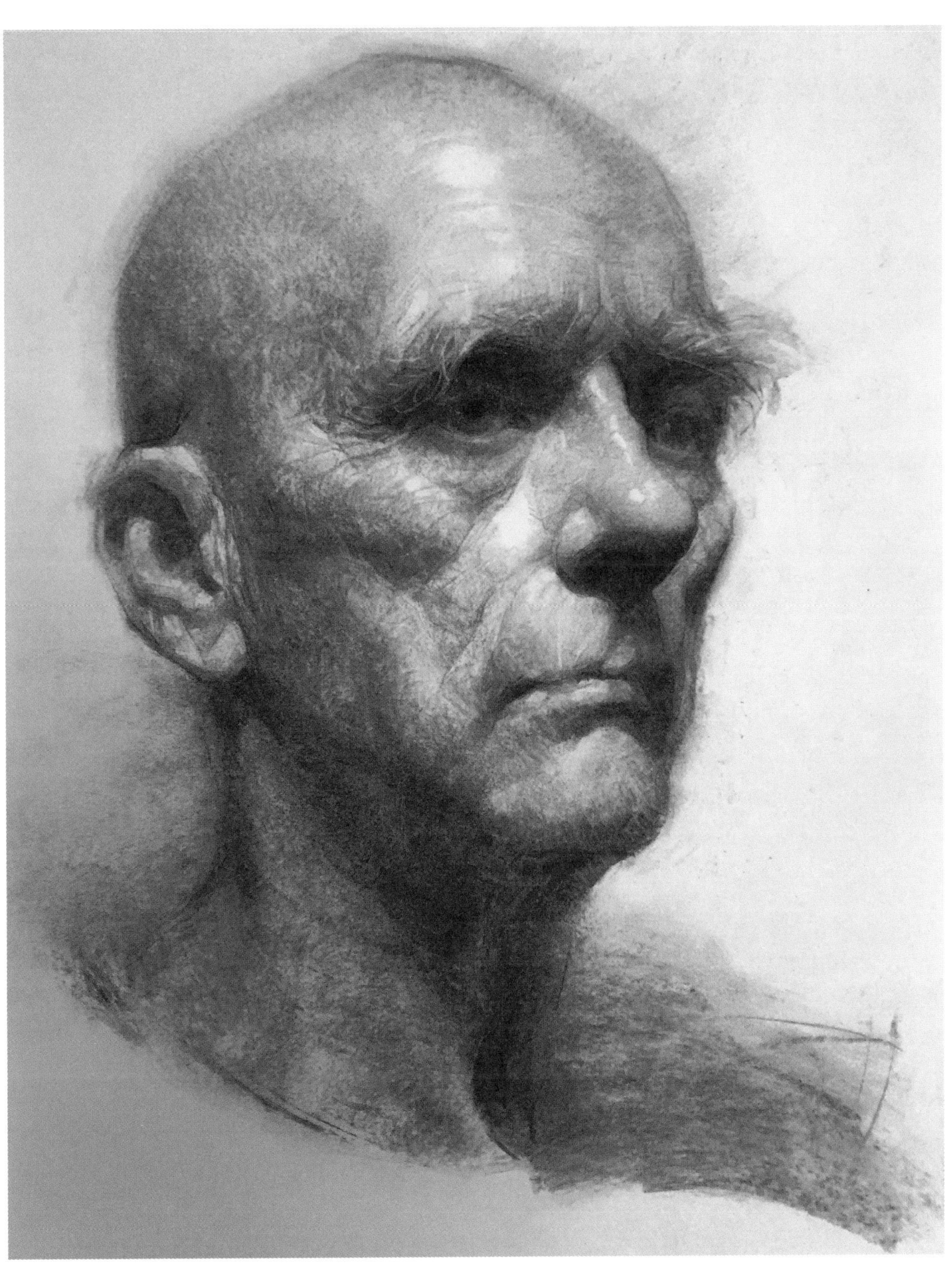

DRAWING HAIR & FACIAL HAIR

Hair has fullness and depth and must be built up in layers to achieve this fullness and look realistic. Like every other aspect of portraiture, look for shapes or patterns in the hair growth, and render hair as a three-dimensional mass of light and shadow. Rather than trying to draw each individual strand of hair, focus on creating areas of light and dark, adding a few defined strands for flyaways.

Defining the Hair

1 | To draw hair, start by defining the outer contour of the general shape. Then break it up into the shapes you can see within the hair, using rough gestural marks to define the shapes and identify the direction of hair growth.

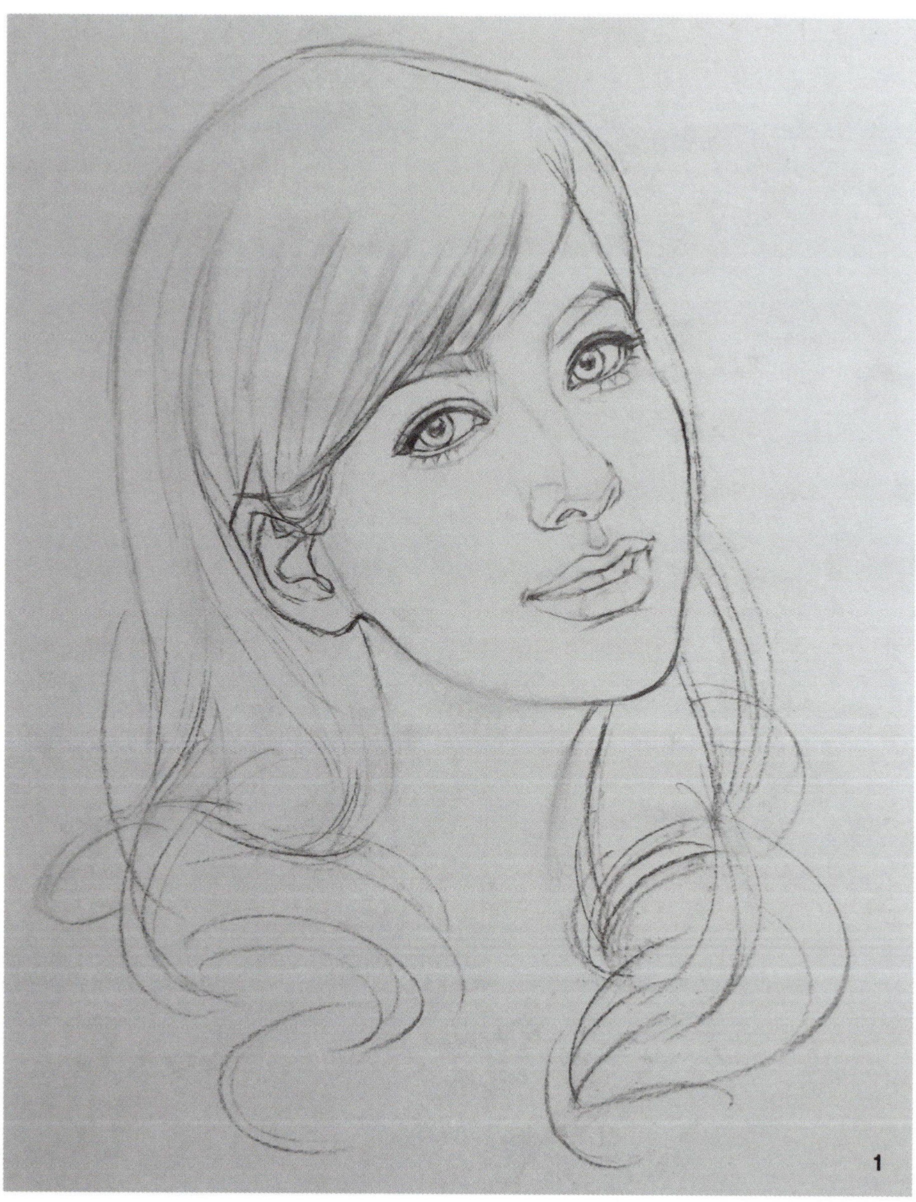

2 | Once you've identified the shapes, you can render the hair just like any other part of the head. Look for the areas of shadow first and develop the dark tones before working your way to the midtones and highlights. Keep the outer contours of the hair soft and blended, and use defined strokes to suggest the stray strands and flyaway hairs.

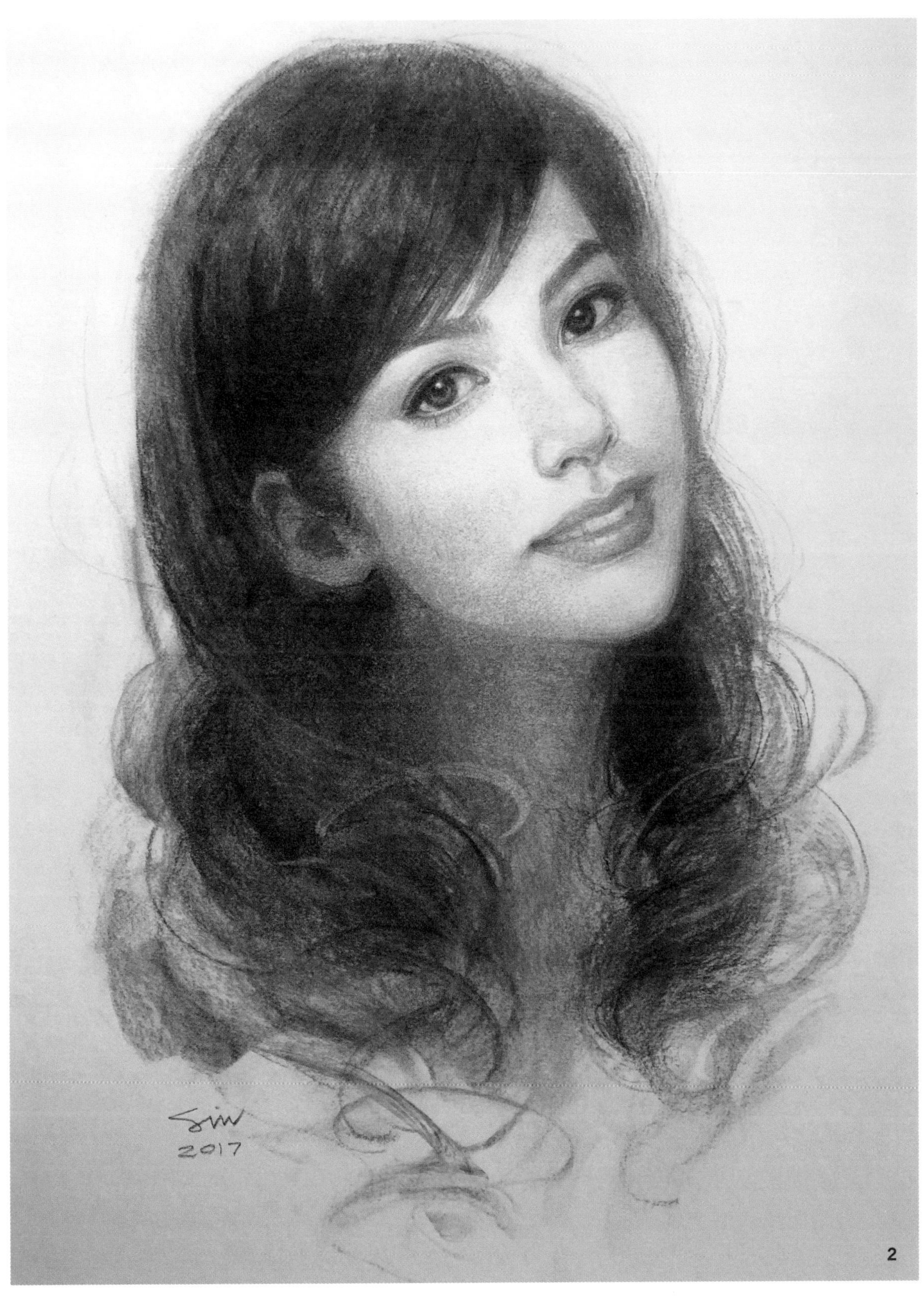

2

Facial Hair

If you simply draw a mustache or beard on the face, that is how it will look: drawn on. The mustache or beard is a mass of planes of different values, just like any other facial feature. Study the shape, fullness, coloration, and growth pattern before drawing so that you can accurately render a true likeness.

Every beard or mustache is different, but there are several key things to look for.

1 | Relationship to the nose and mouth. The nose casts a shadow on the mustache, and the mustache casts a shadow on the mouth.

2 | Upper lip. If the mustache is very full, it may cover the upper lip, either partially or completely.

3 | Planes of the head. Follow the light and shadow on the head if the planes are not readily visible in the facial hair. For example, if the cheek falls into shadow, so will the beard. If the front plane of the head is in light and the side plane is in shadow, the beard will follow.

4 | Color. Pay attention to how the color of the hair looks next to the skin. Is it light against dark, or dark against light?

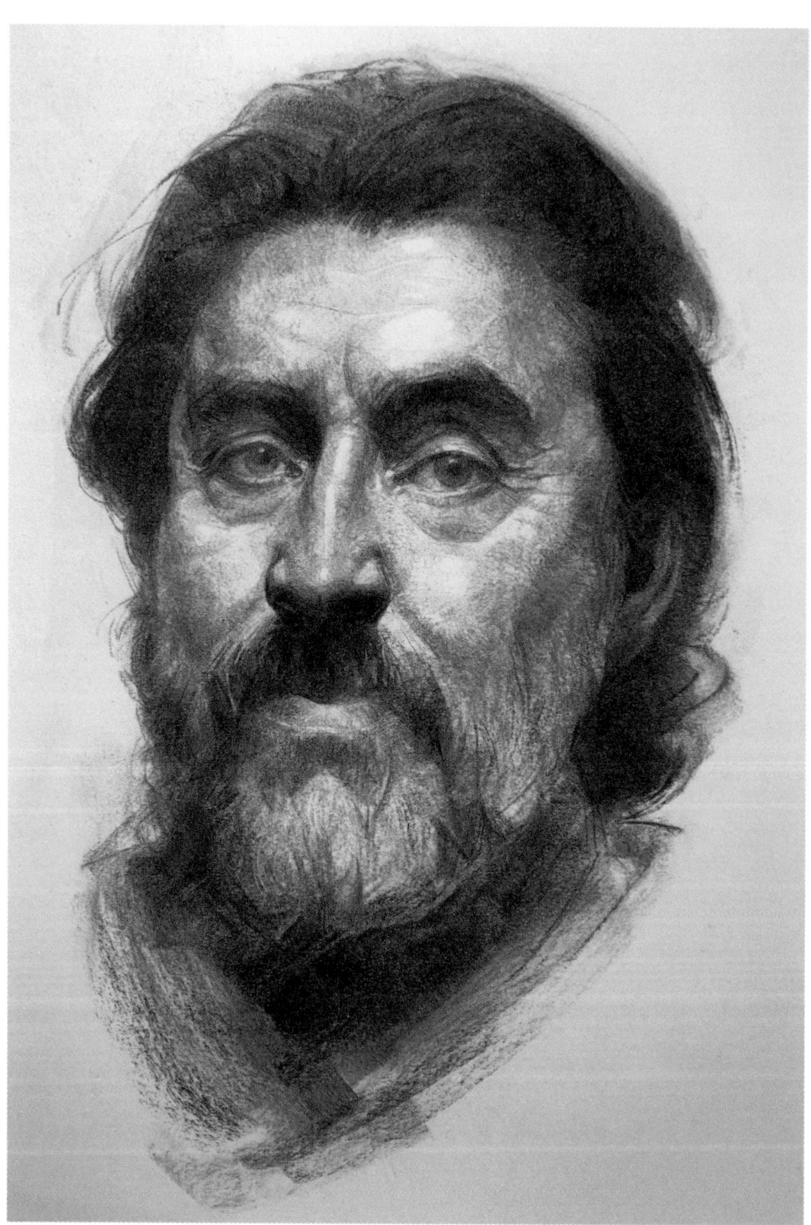

◄ Think of the mustache as a large upper lip that wraps around the doughnut shape of the mouth, producing larger shadows.

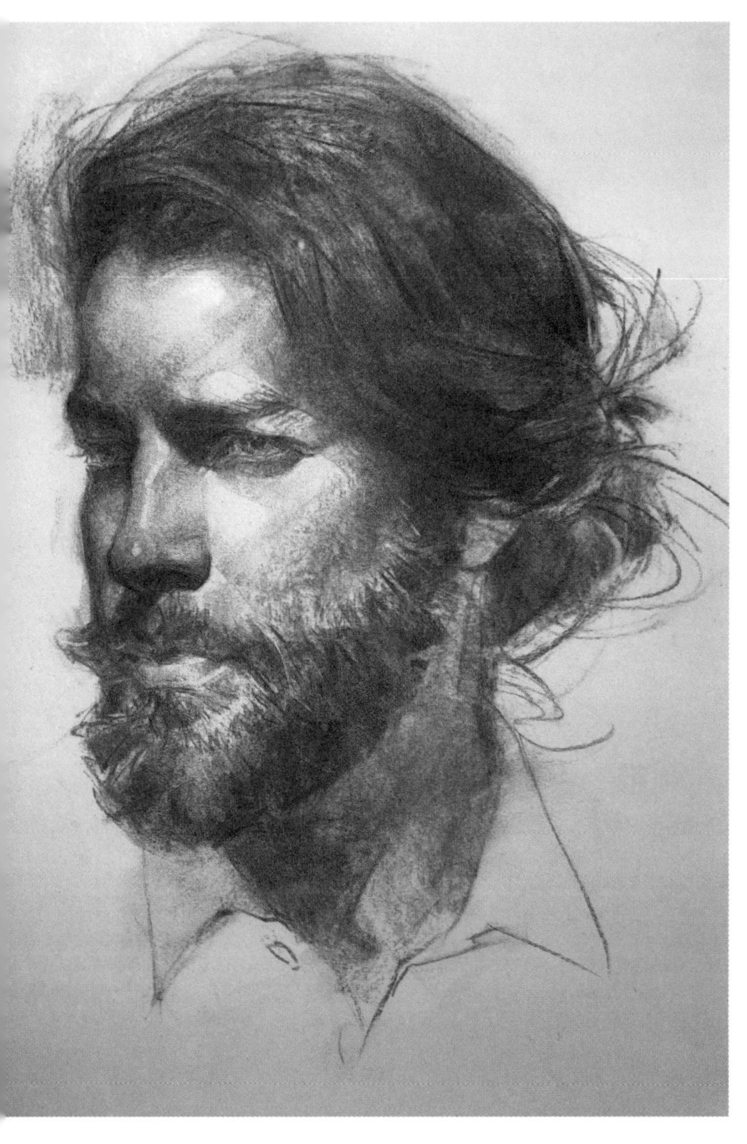

▲ Light hairs can be picked out of the beard or mustache with a kneaded eraser.

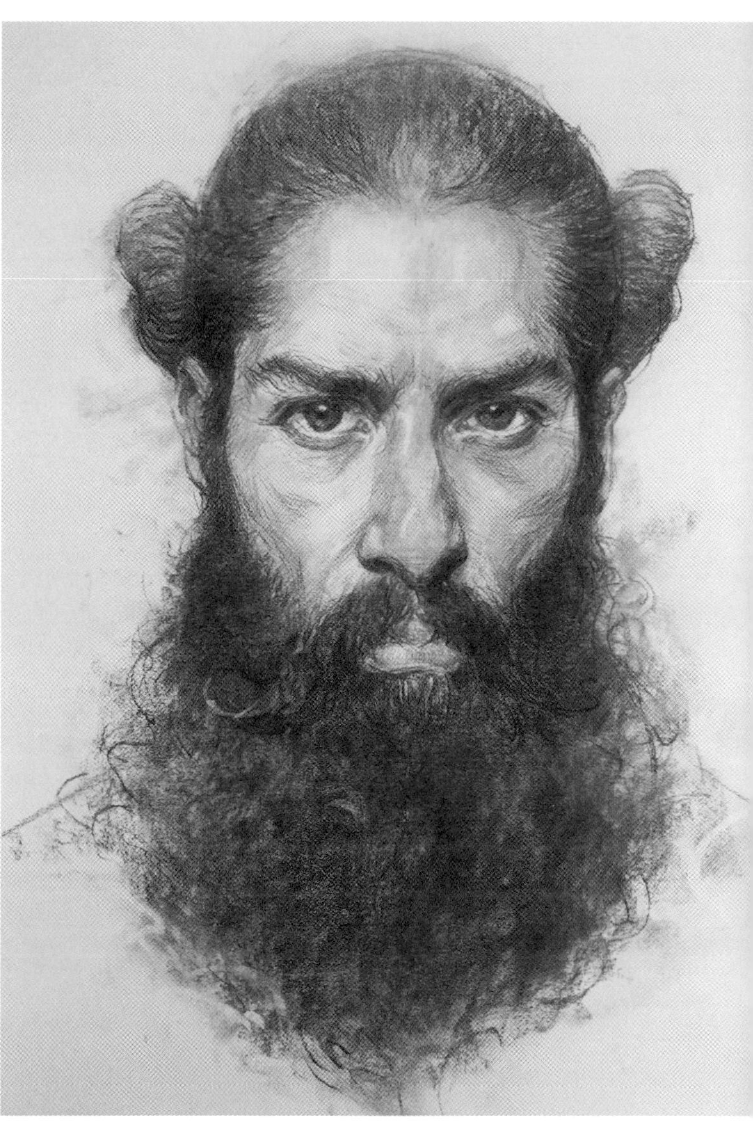

▲ Pay attention to beard shape, and train your eye to see that hair has no definable edge, like smoke. Rather than drawing individual hairs, treat the beard as a mass of light and shadow, keeping the edges soft and blurred.

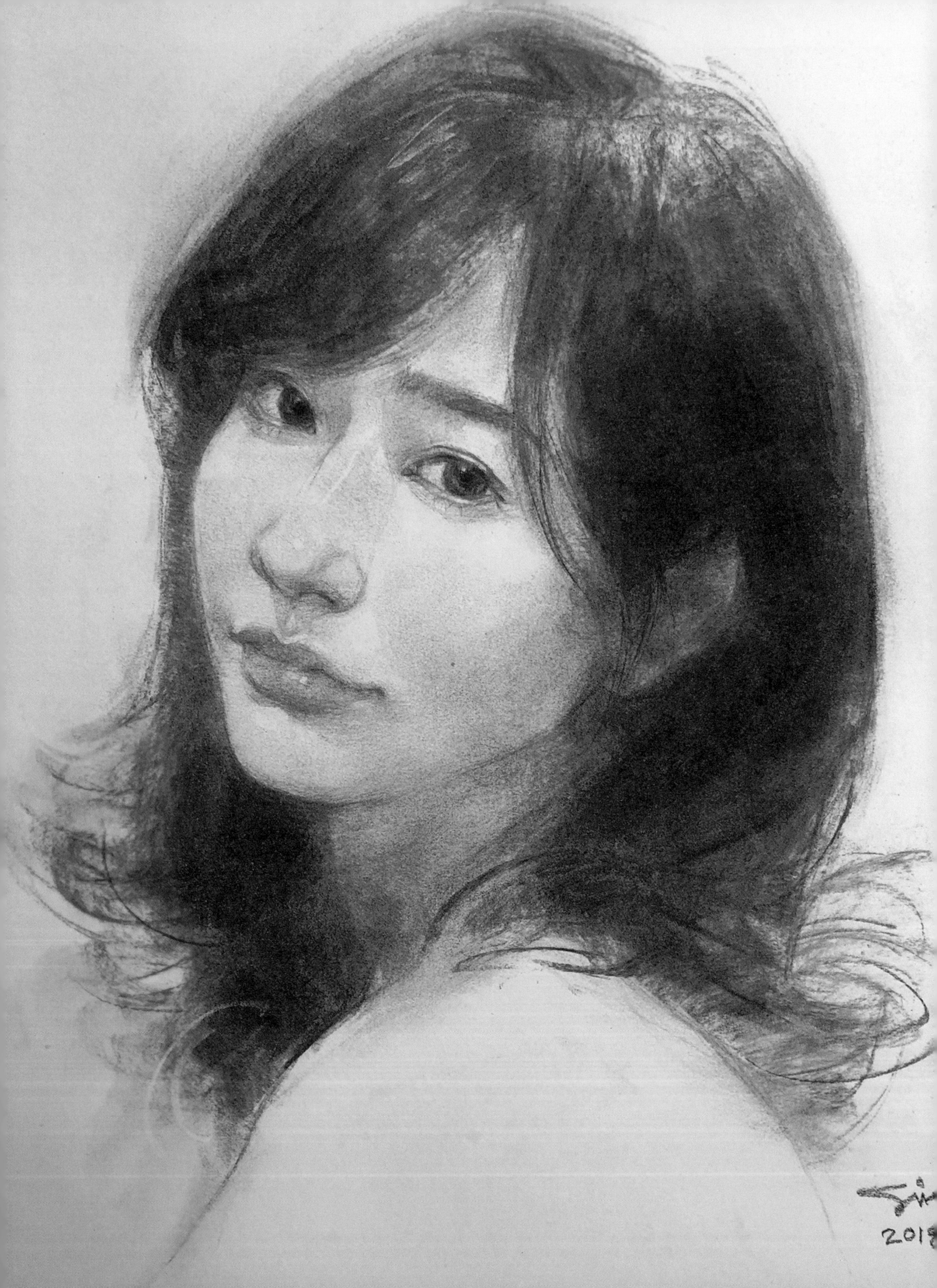
2018

4

ENHANCING DEPTH & DIMENSION

EXPLORING THE USE OF LIGHT

It's best to use a single light source to light the head for portraiture. The position of the light source should ideally be above and slightly to the front left or right of your model. This lighting setup, called "three-quarter lighting," produces light and shadow not only from top to bottom, but also from side to side on the model's head, a crucial factor in creating the illusion of three-dimensionality.

If all the planes are equally lit, the head appears flat.

Note that all of the lighting configurations can be used to enhance any pose.

Three-Quarter Lighting

In three-quarter lighting, most of the face is brightly lit, but there are narrow shadows on one side of all the forms. This is a flattering lighting setup for most sitters.

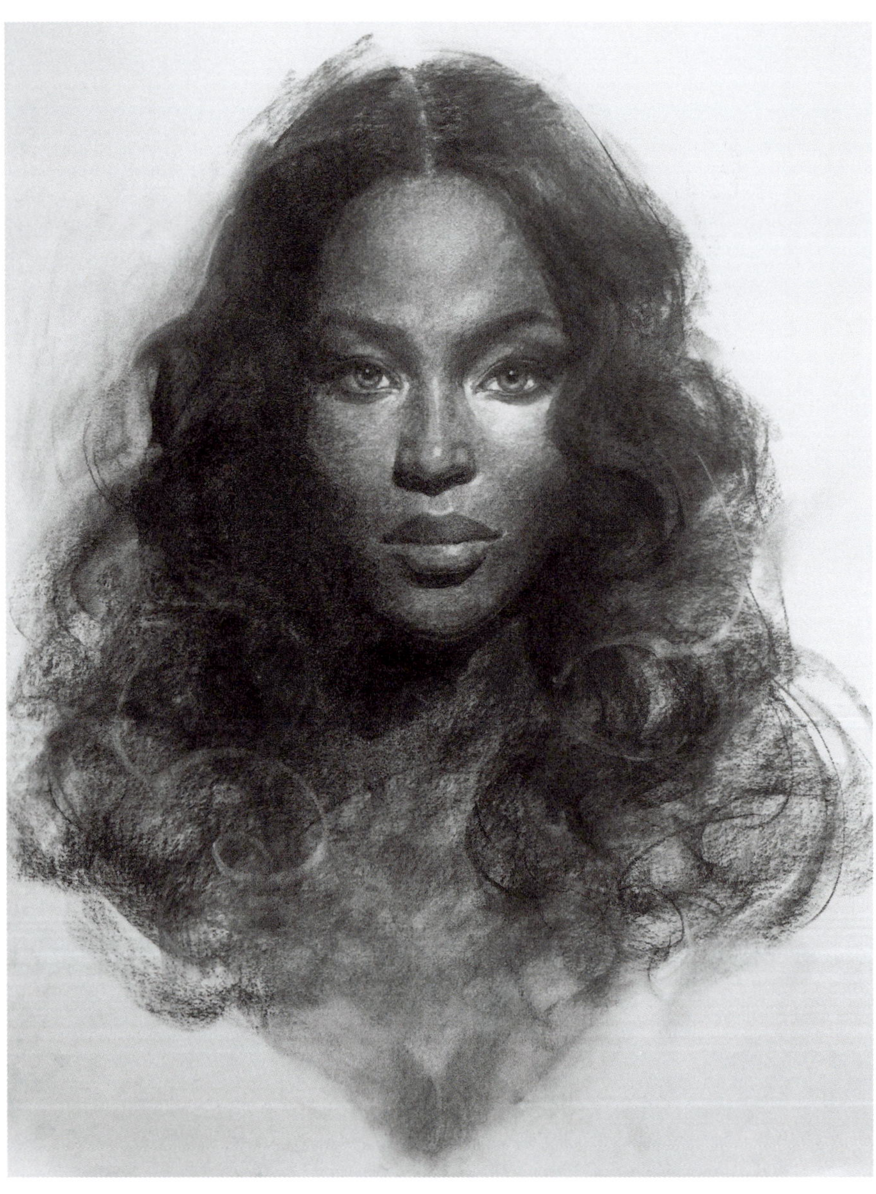

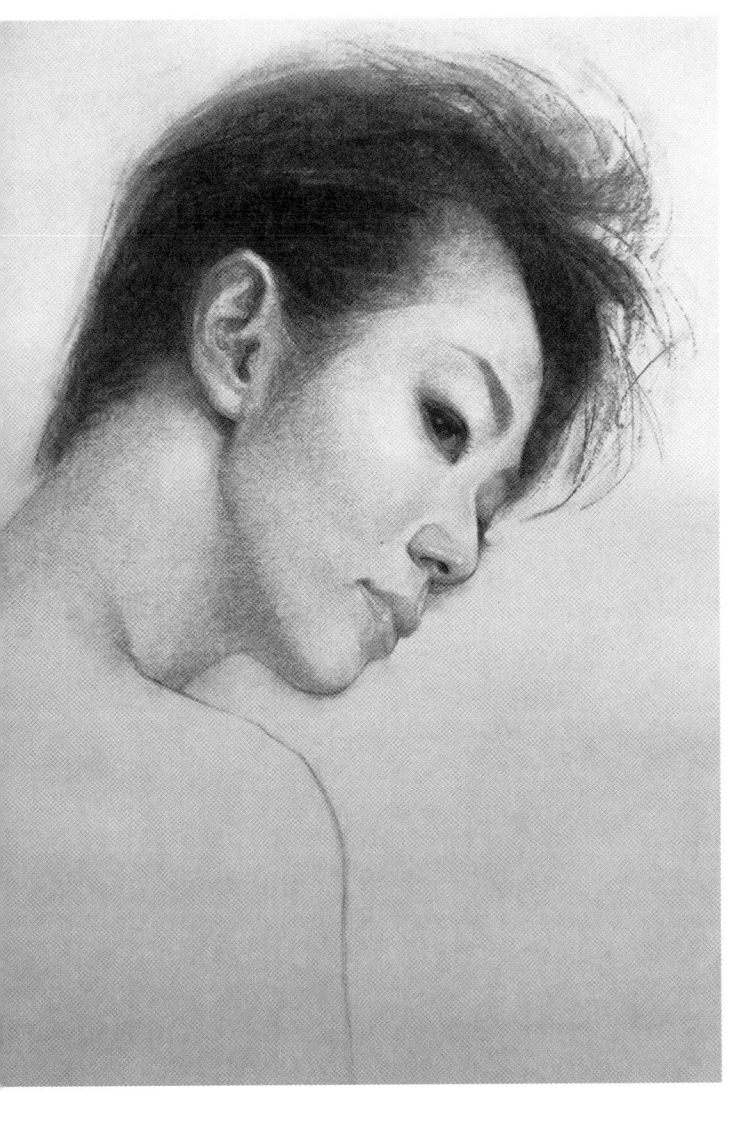

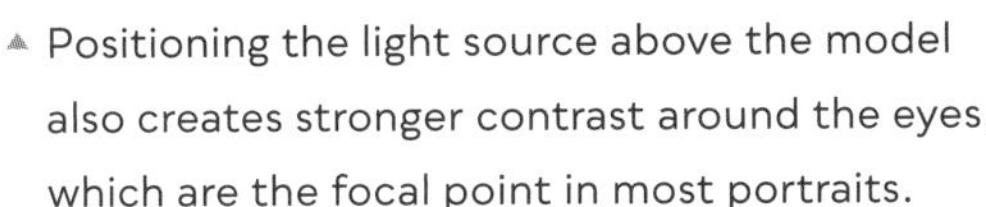

Positioning the light source above the model also creates stronger contrast around the eyes, which are the focal point in most portraits.

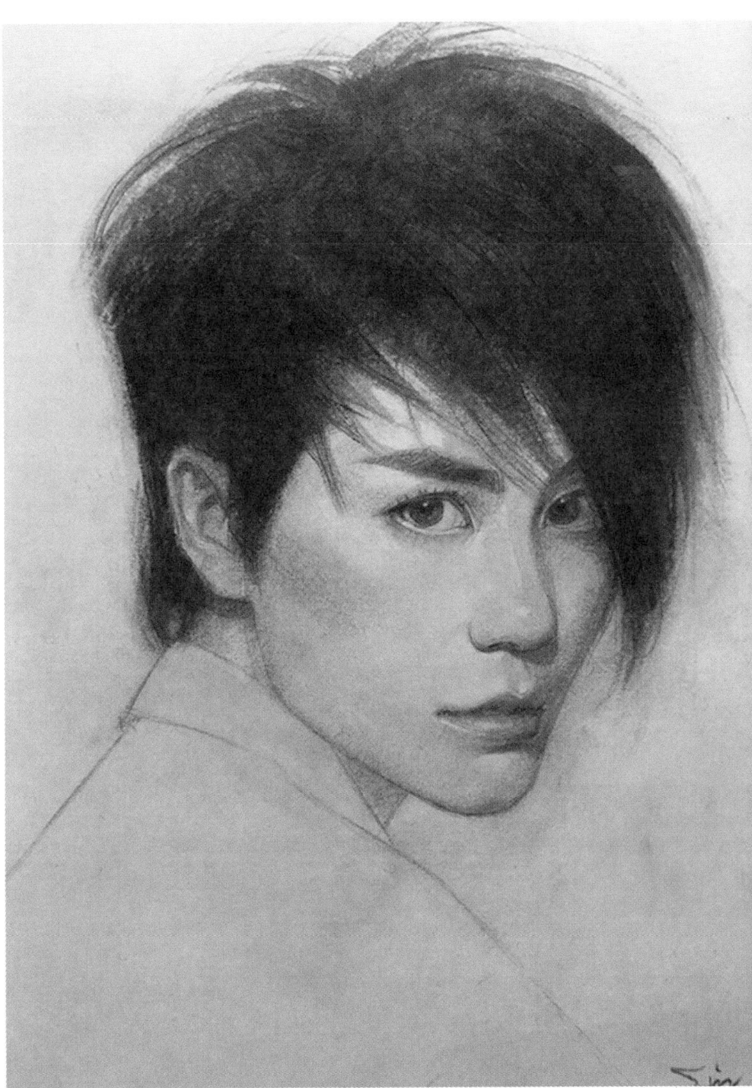

Reflections of the light source, called "catch lights," give the eyes a lifelike quality. Avoid overstating the catch lights for a pensive or mysterious mood in the portrait.

Rim Lighting

In this setup, the light source is behind the model and most of the face is in shadow. The light creeps around the edges, or the rim, of the face. Although the front of the face is in darkness, there is a distinct contrast between the shadows and midtones that defines the features. The shadows are rarely pitch-black, and instead are filled with subtle light.

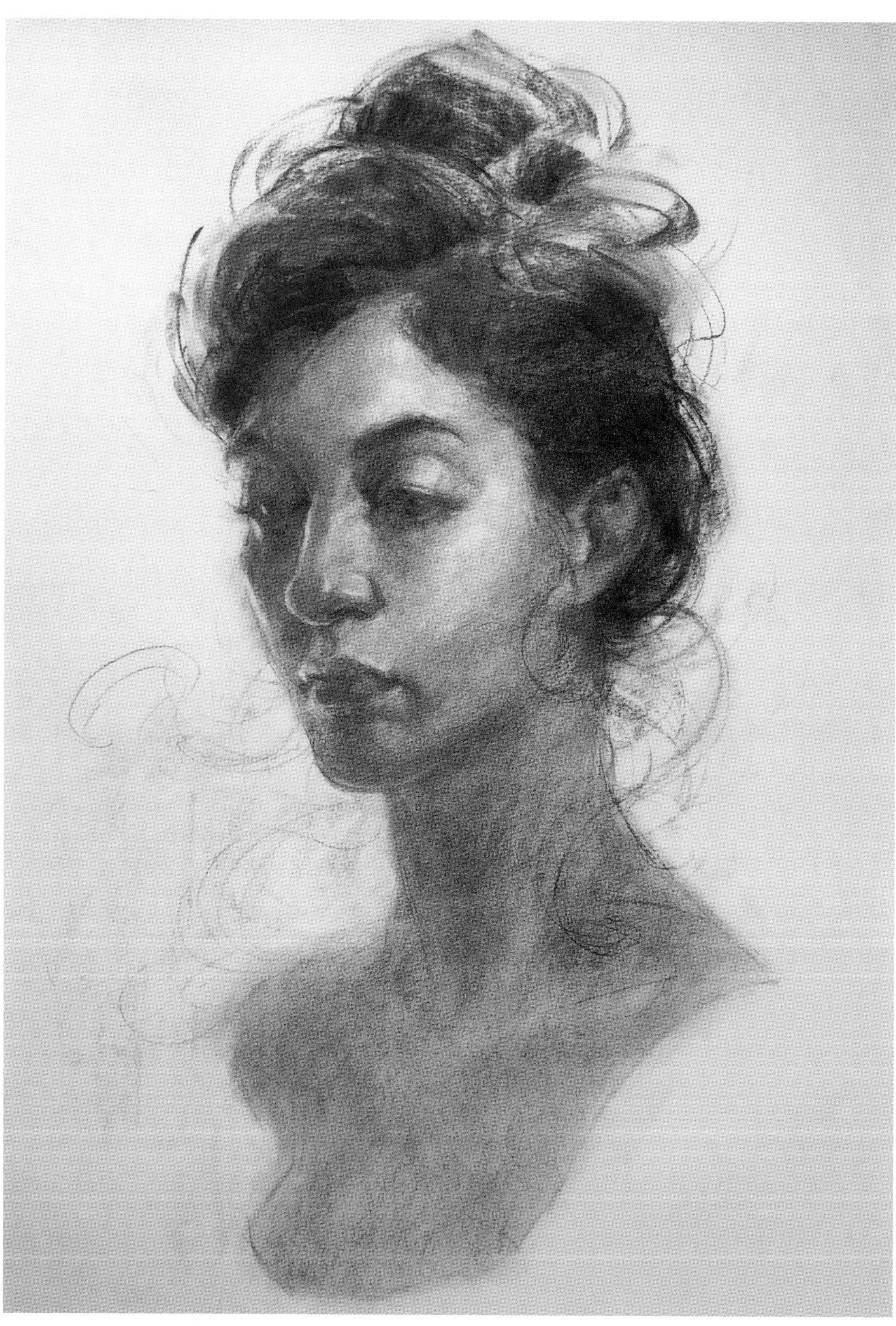

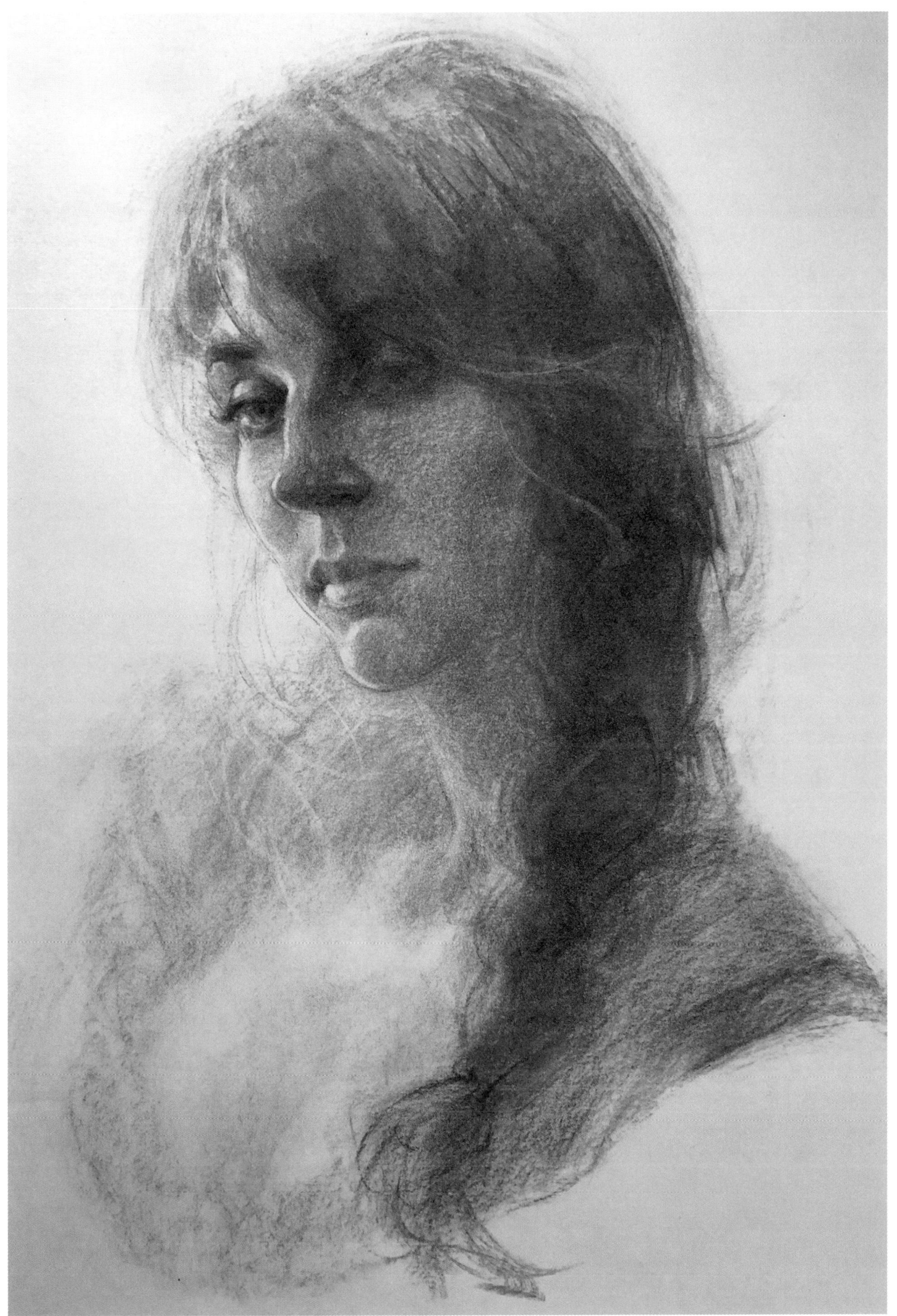

Top Lighting

Top lighting comes from above the subject, highlighting the top-facing planes and casting extreme shadows.

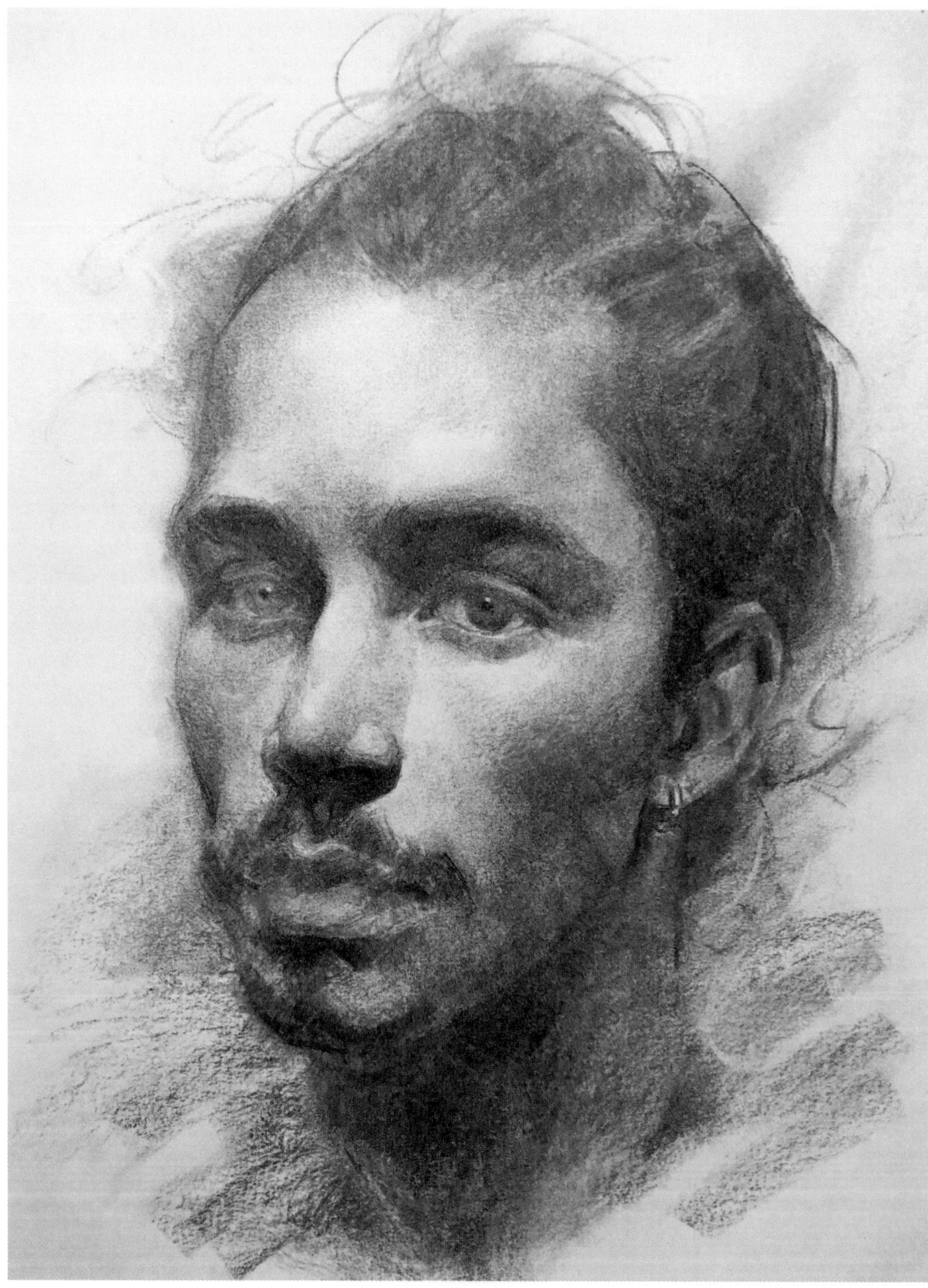

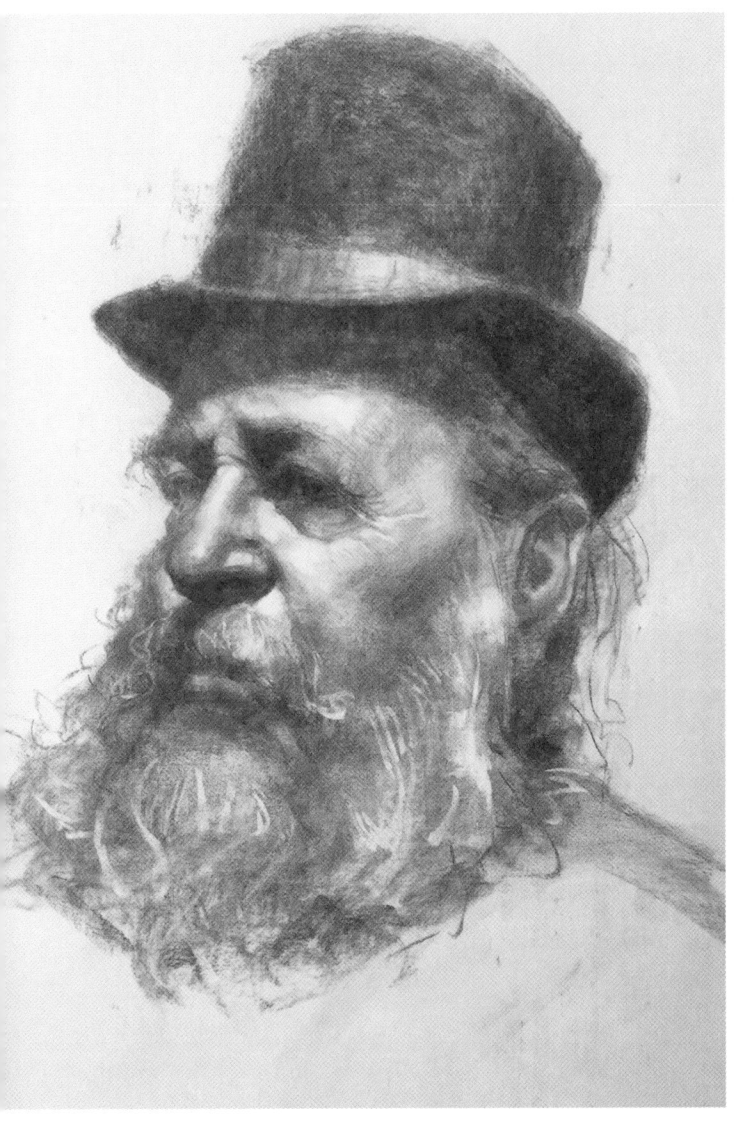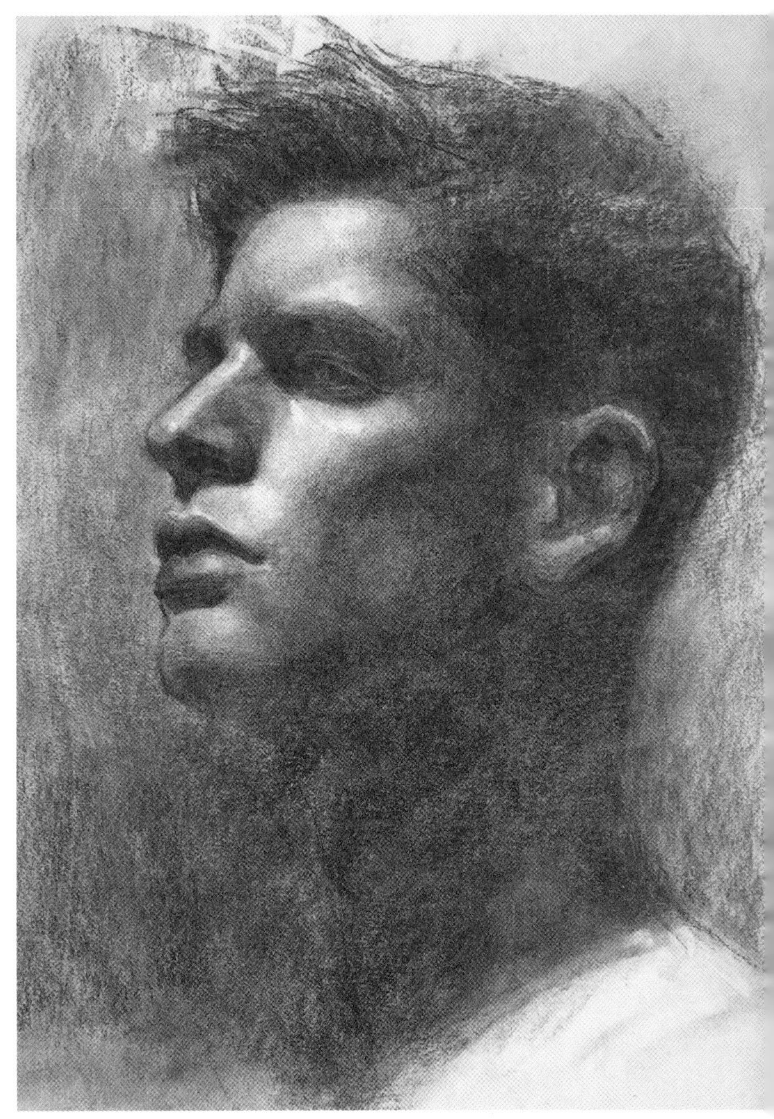

Side Lighting

In this setup, the light comes from the sitter's left or right side, placing more of the face in shadow. One side of the face is dark, with a small, bright triangle on the cheek that curves forward to catch the light. The nose casts a dark shadow on the left or right side. The eye sockets are also in deeper shadow.

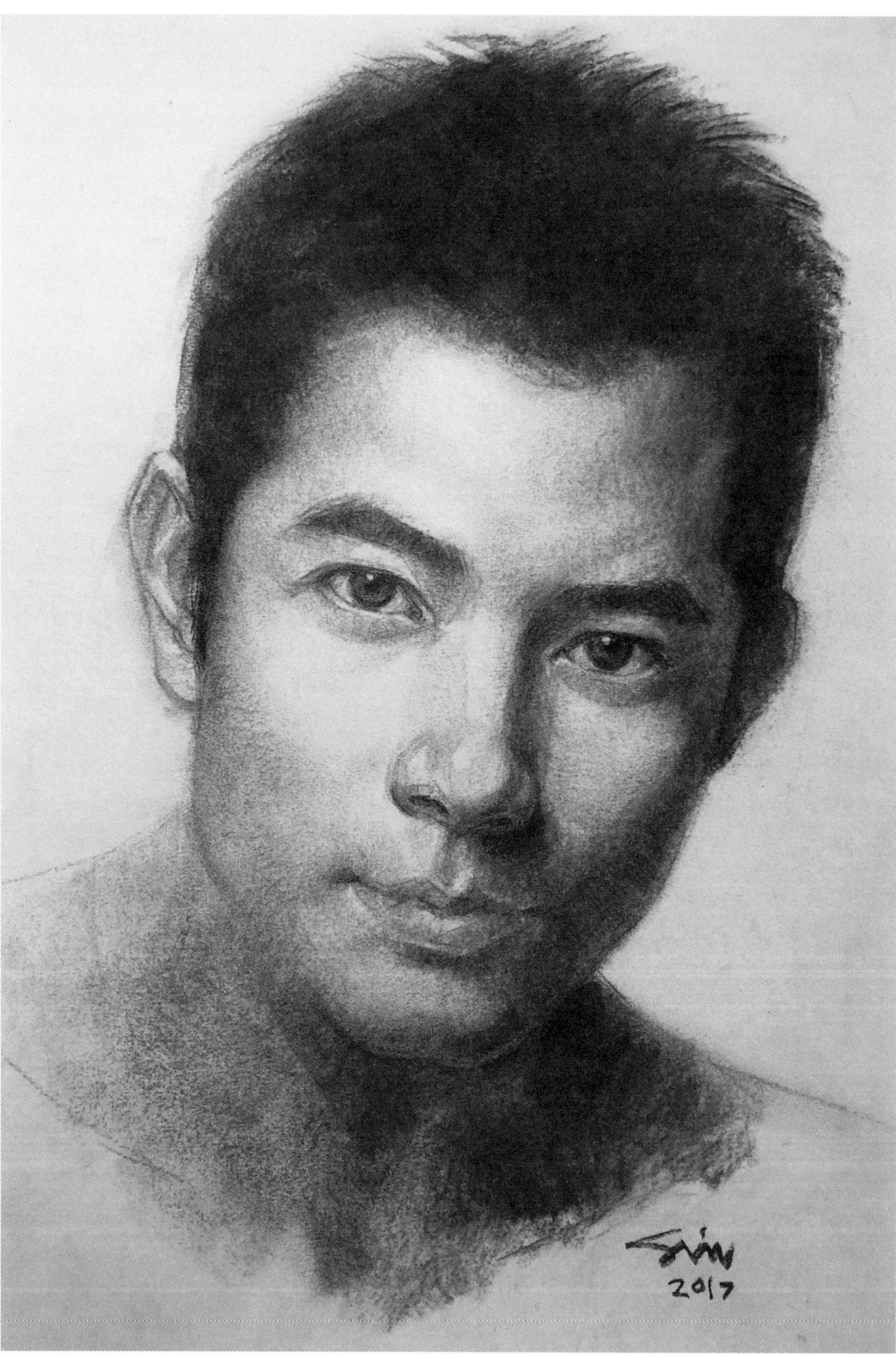

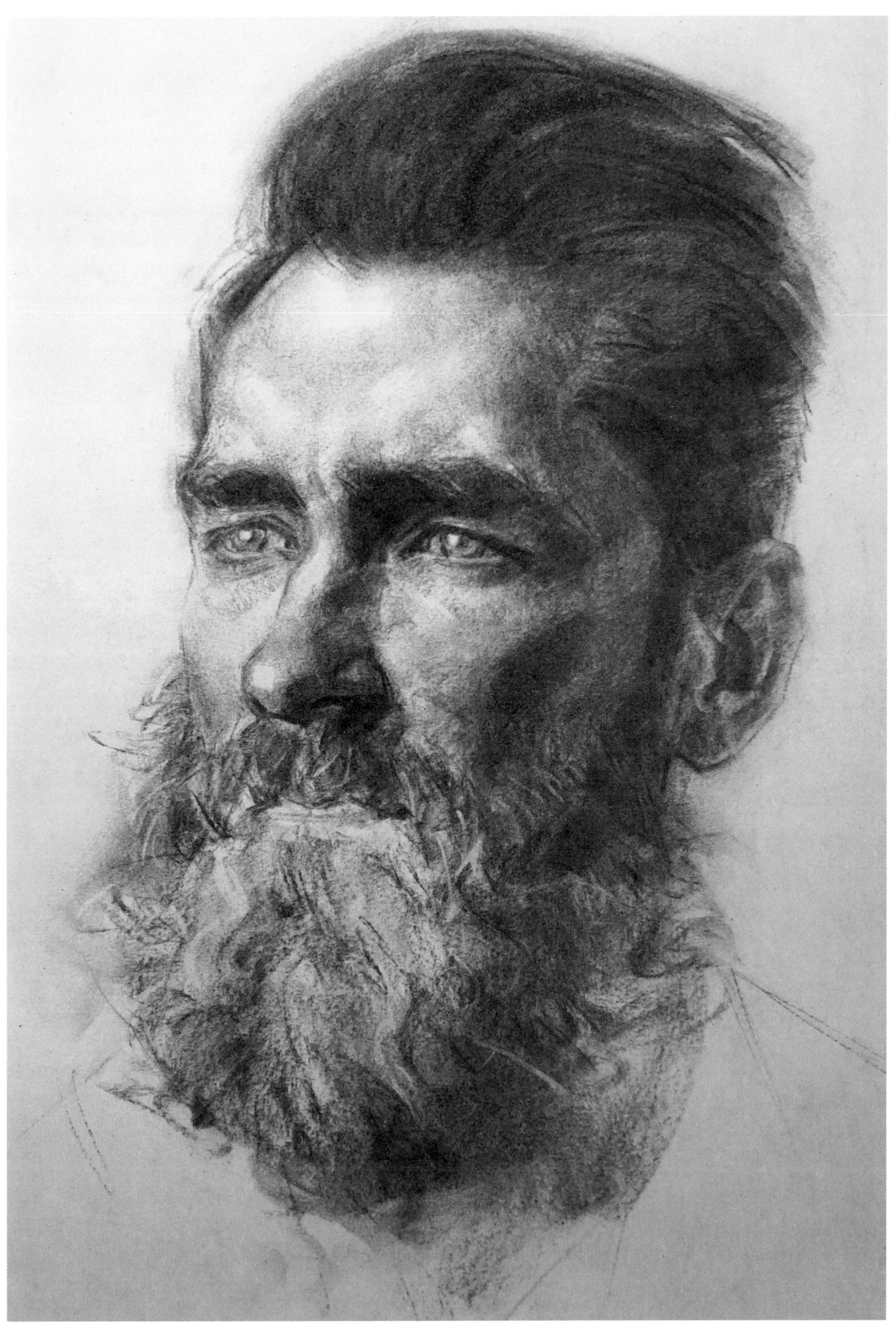

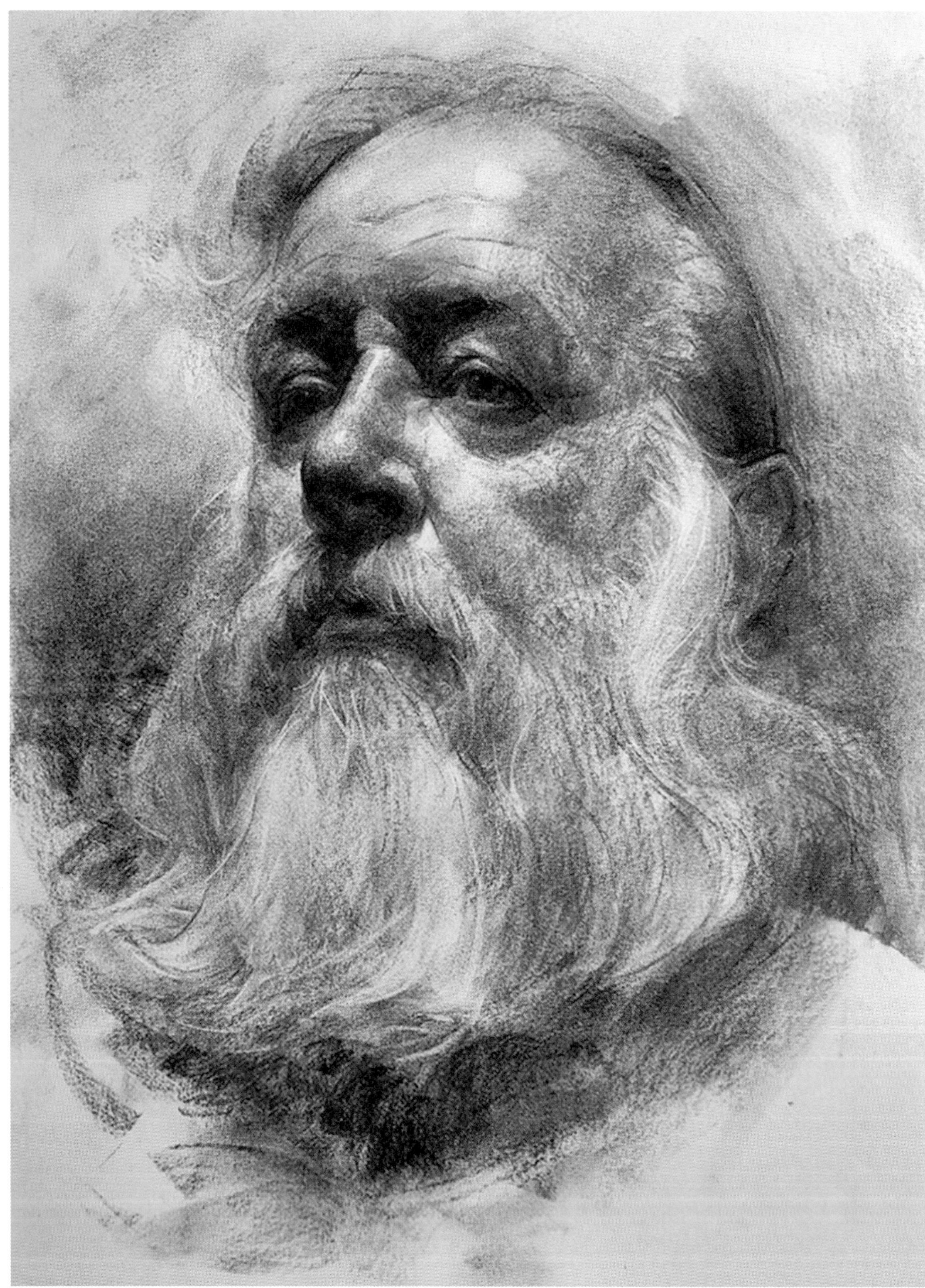

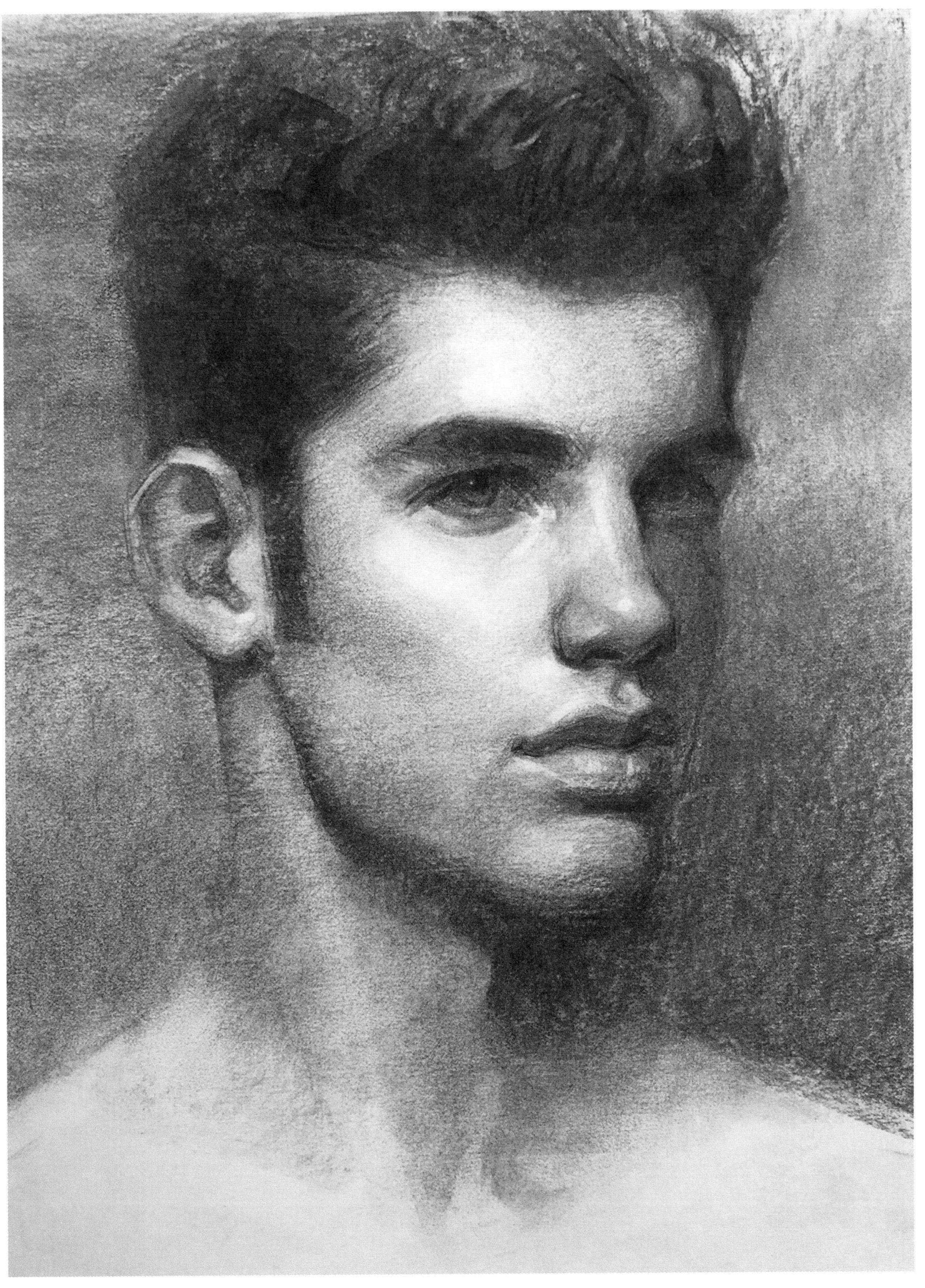

Frontal Lighting

In this setup, the light hits the sitter directly
in the middle of the face, creating big
patches of light in the centers of all the
forms, with shadows around the edges.

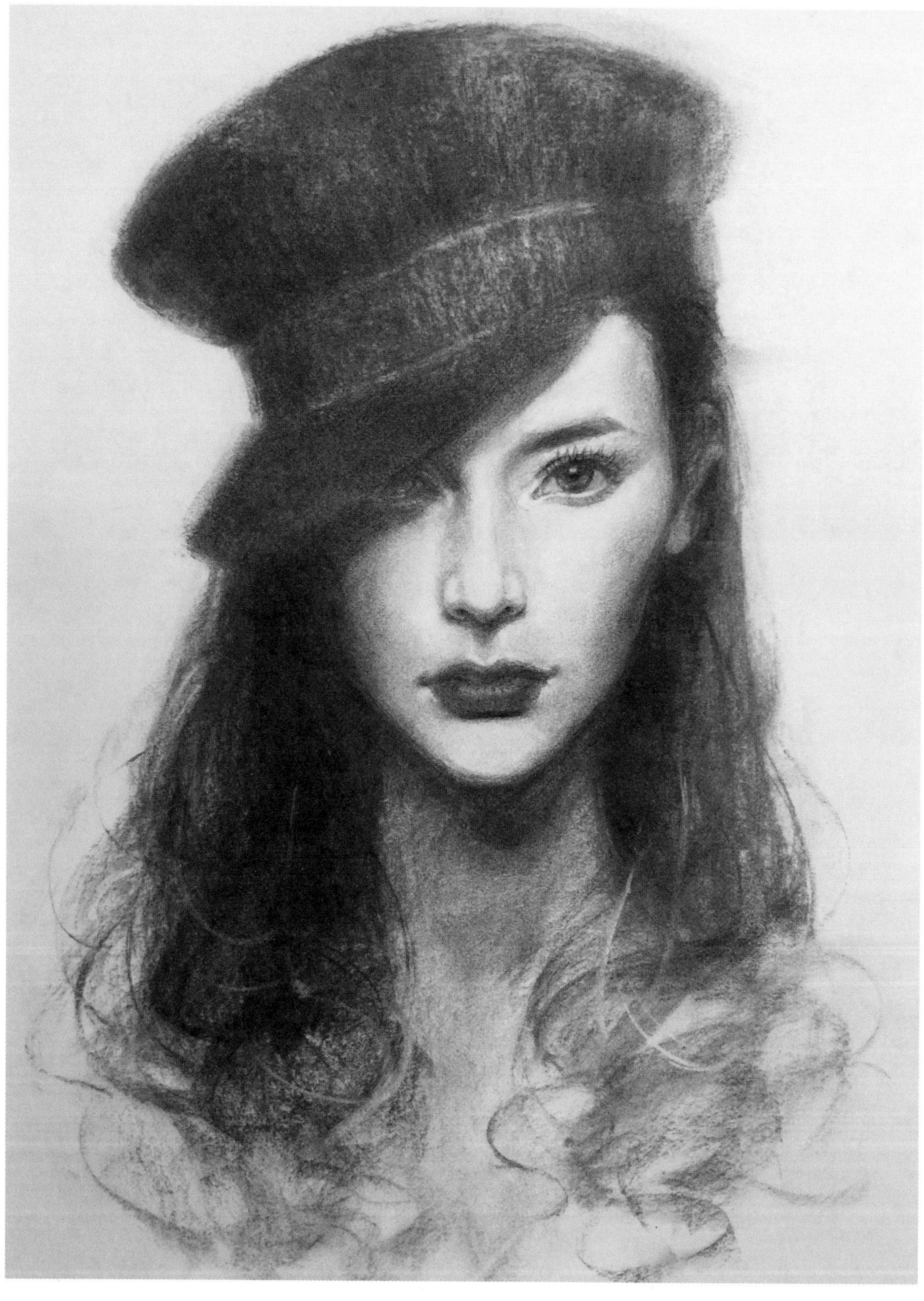

▲ The chin and jaw cast a strong shadow down the center of the neck.

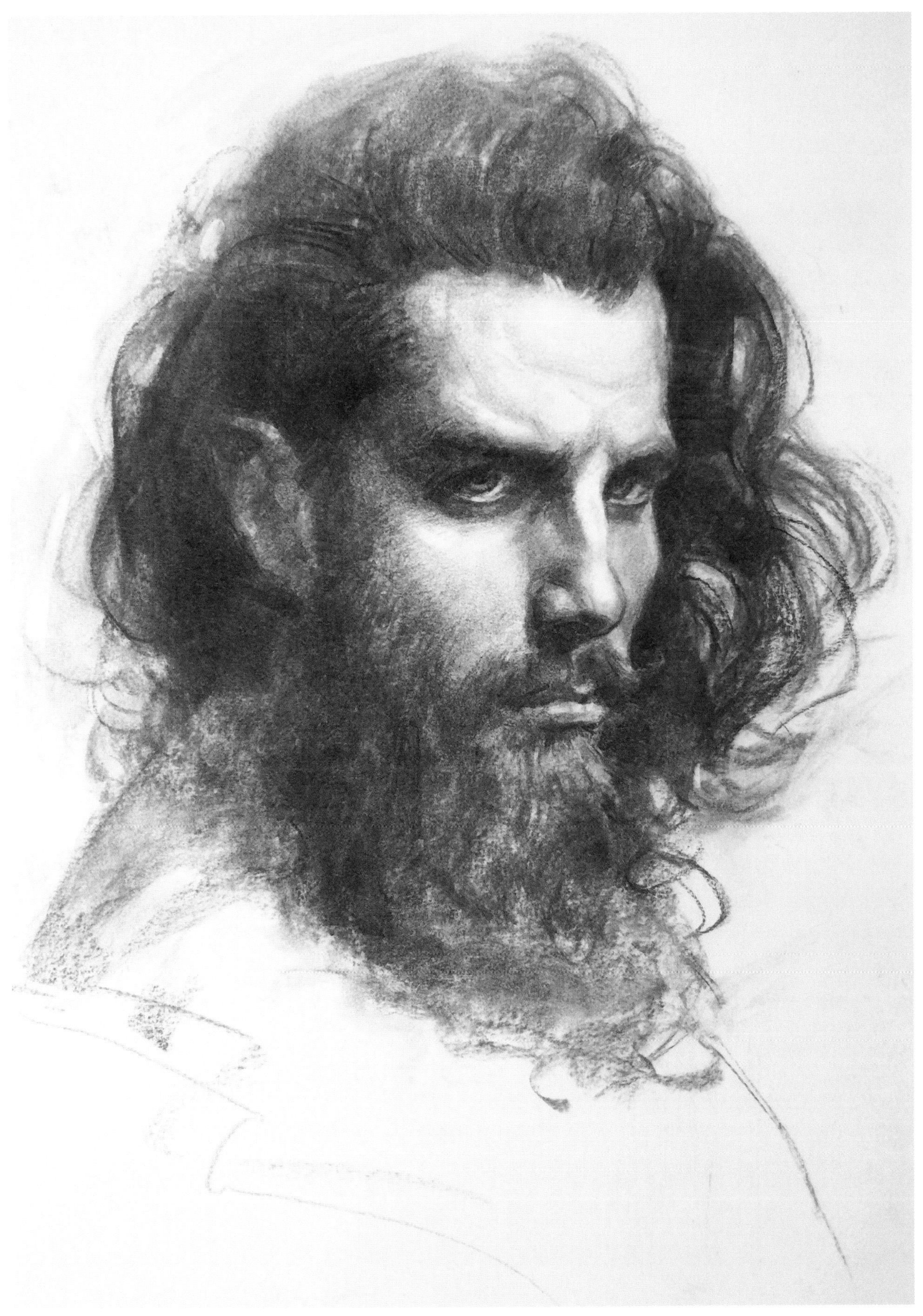

▲ The forehead, nose, cheeks, and chin are bright in the middle and shadowy at the sides.

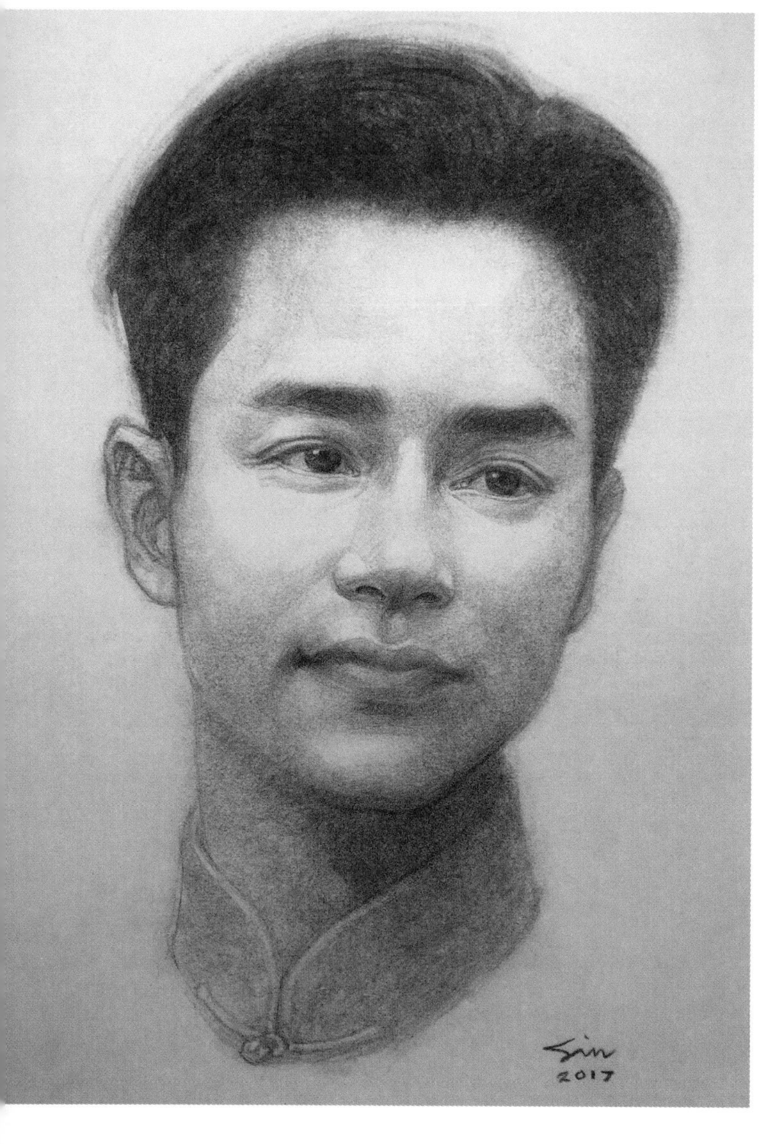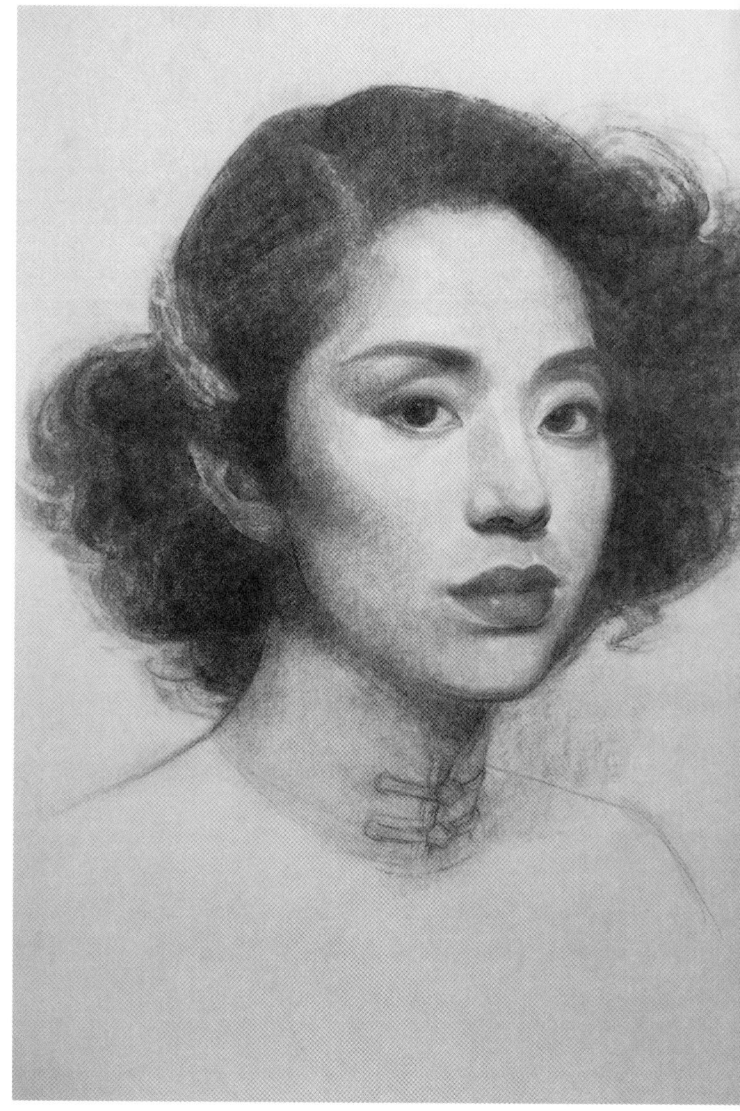

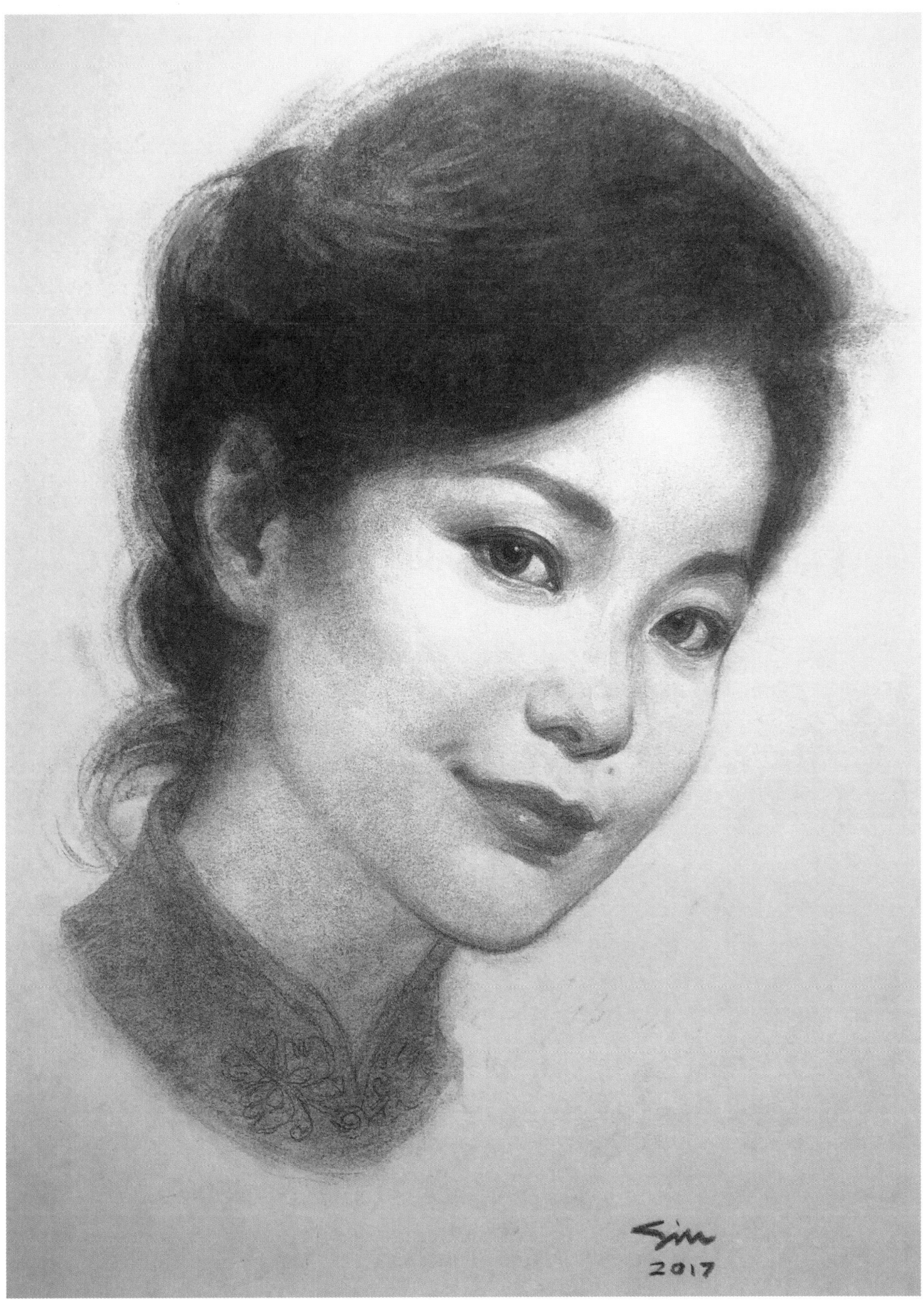

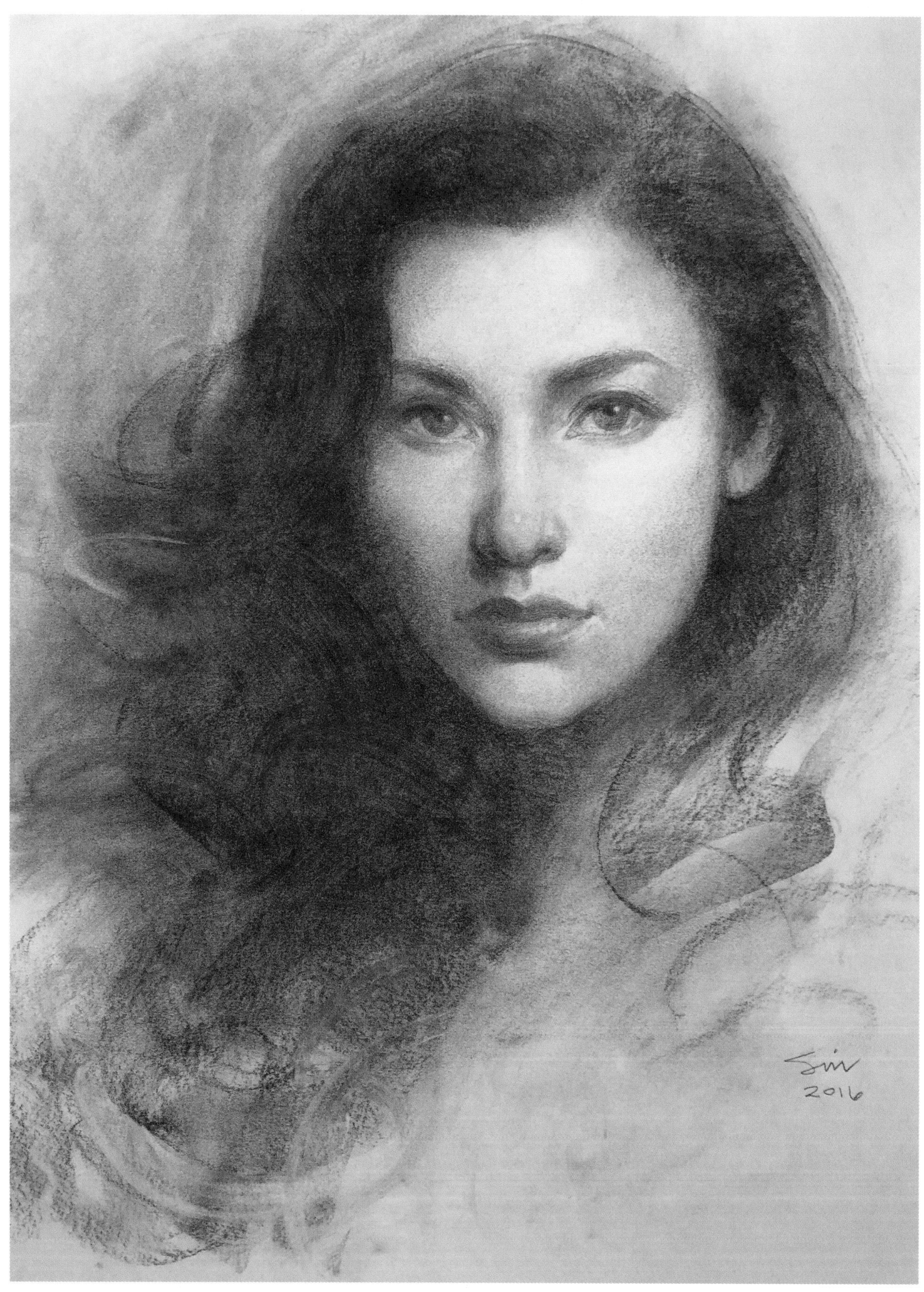

94

▲ Frontal lighting evenly illuminates the subject, but it also results in fewer shadows,
which are what give the subject shape and form, thus flattening the subject.

Bottom Lighting

Bottom lighting is commonly used in theater
for an eerie effect that distorts the features,
making the subject appear frightful.

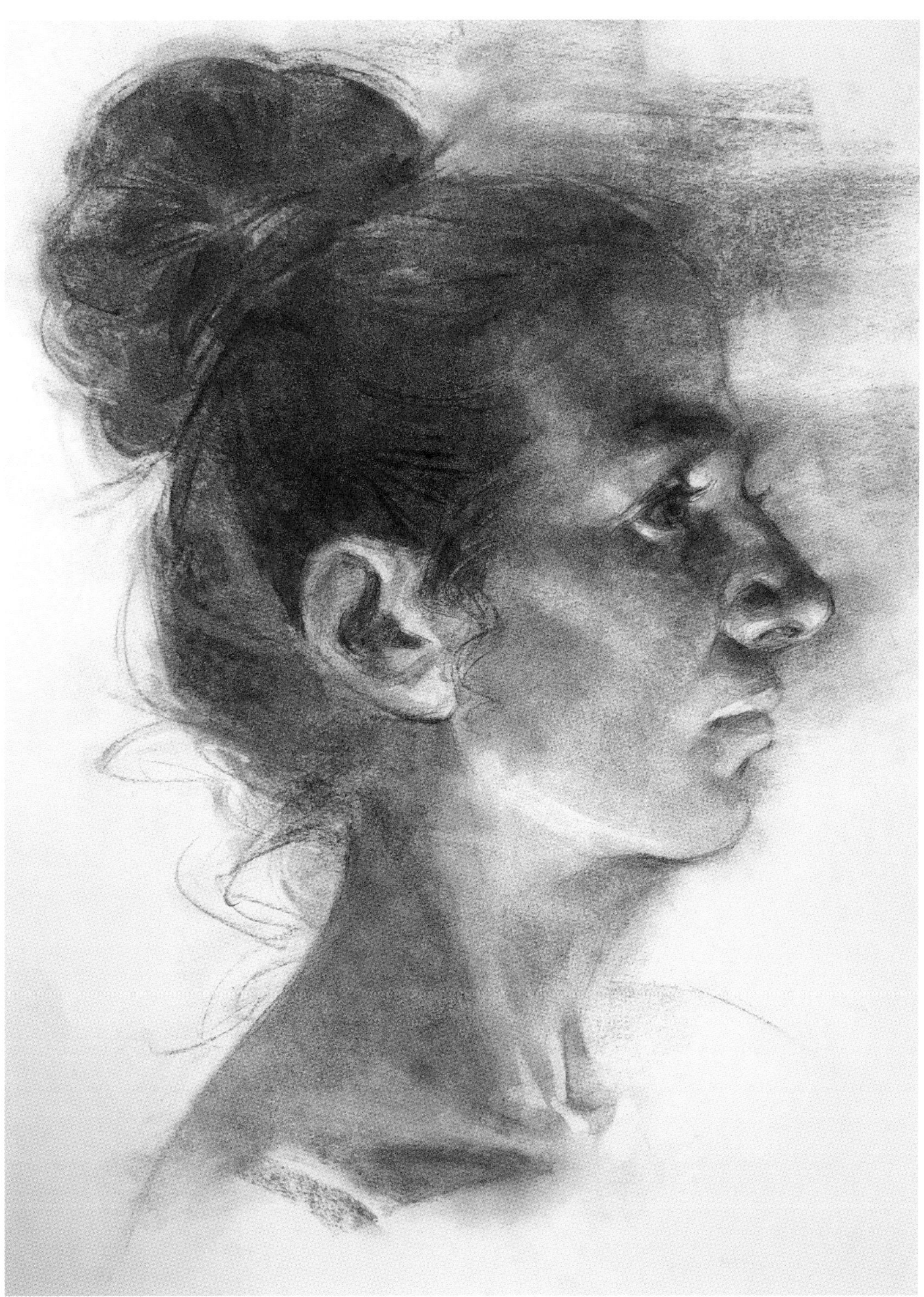

USING EDGES TO CONVEY FORM

One of the techniques that will improve your drawings immensely when you master it is the proper use of hard and soft edges. In a line drawing, the lines not only delineate and define spaces and shapes, they also play a vital role in the composition. Lines can thrust elements forward visually, or can make them recede into the distance. In other words, lines can create a sense of depth.

When an artist skillfully mixes soft and hard lines, or edges, in the right places, it sets up a path for the viewer's eyes, creating the illusion of three dimensions on a two-dimensional (flat) surface. When edges are soft, an area or element can seem to recede.

You can further blend a subject into the background by making its lines extremely soft.

Some subjects—for example, clouds, waves, hair, and fabric—inherently call for soft edges. A soft-edged drawing creates a fuzzy, dreamy effect, whereas a drawing with too many hard edges will look unnatural, creating visual tension because too many areas are competing, which will confuse viewers because there's nowhere for their eyes to rest.

I don't mean that you should never use hard edges, but that you should use them sparingly for effective emphasis, keeping lines hard at your focal point and wherever they're directed toward the viewer.

▸ In my portrait drawings, I generally use a proportion of roughly 85 percent soft lines and 15 percent hard lines. If you understand and master the power of controlling edges in your drawings, you'll be amazed at how much your portraits will improve.

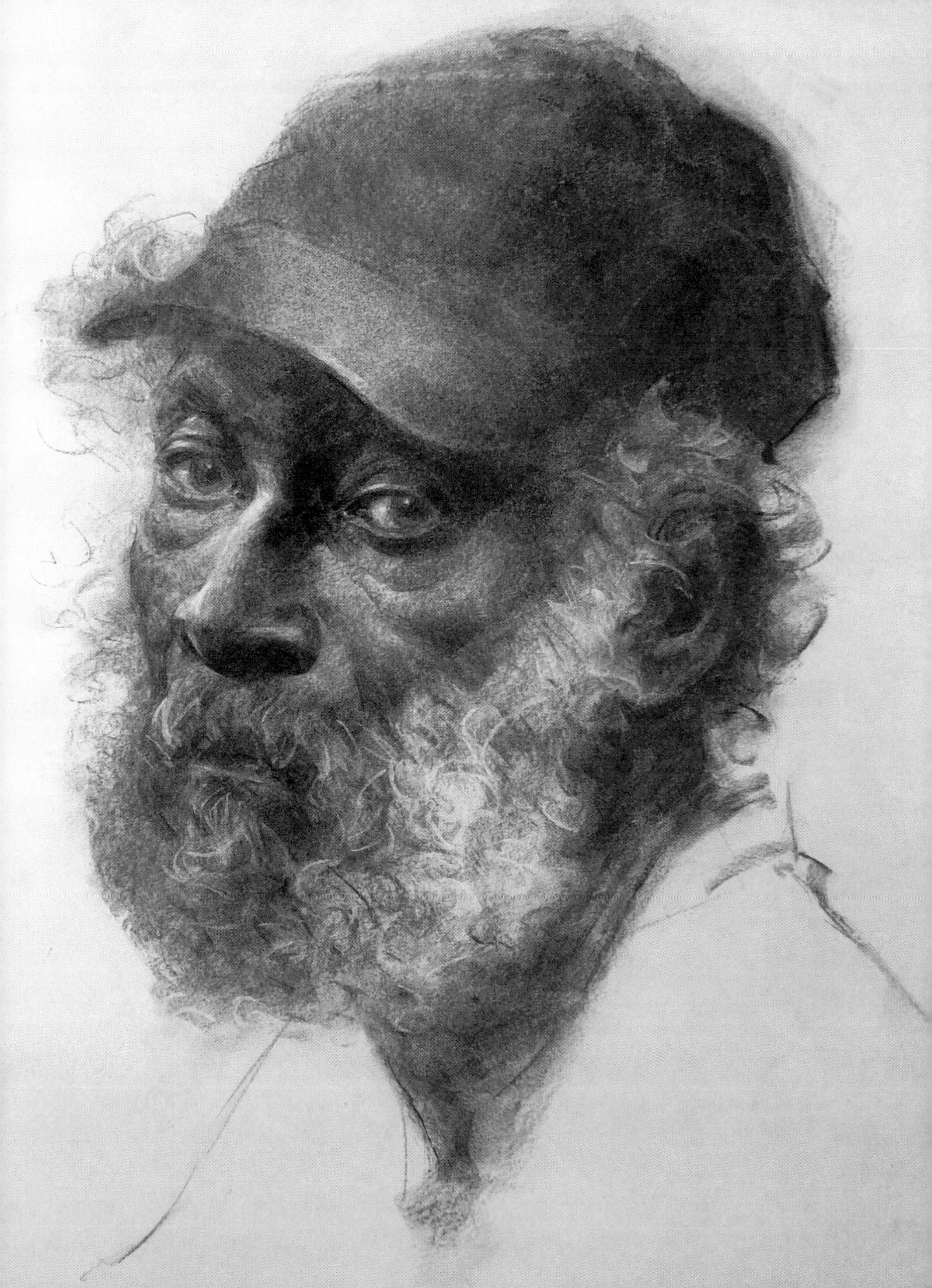

ATMOSPHERIC PERSPECTIVE

All realistic art is dependent on creating an illusion of three dimensions on a two-dimensional surface. Another important technique for creating depth is atmospheric, or aerial, perspective, which is the effect of the atmosphere, or distance, on objects. Within atmospheric perspective, there are seven methods/elements that when used together can maximize the illusion of depth and dimension.

1 | **Linear perspective.** By using one-, two-, or three-point perspective–techniques for using lines that converge at a vanishing point to convey how the elements in a composition appear in space relative to a horizon line–an artist can establish the illusion of depth.

2 | **Overlapping.** When one object is positioned in front of another–for example, when part of an object behind another is partially blocked from view–it gives the illusion of depth.

3 | **Manipulating size.** Objects that are visually closer within a composition appear larger than those that are farther off in the distance.

4 | **Manipulating value and/or value contrast.** Objects that are visually closer appear darker in value, while those that are farther away appear lighter in value. The most important is value contrast: areas with a lot of contrast will come forward; areas with little contrast will recede.

5 | **Manipulating detail.** Objects that are closer appear more detailed than objects that are farther away. In my portraits, I'll often push an area closer to the value of the background to make it recede.

6 | **Surface placement.** Generally, objects that are positioned lower on the picture plane will appear closer than objects that are positioned higher on the picture plane.

7 | **Controlling line weight and thickness.** Lines in the foreground are the darkest, the middle ground lighter, and the background the lightest.

You also can make the lines in the foreground the thickest, the lines in the middle ground thinner, and the lines in the background thinnest.

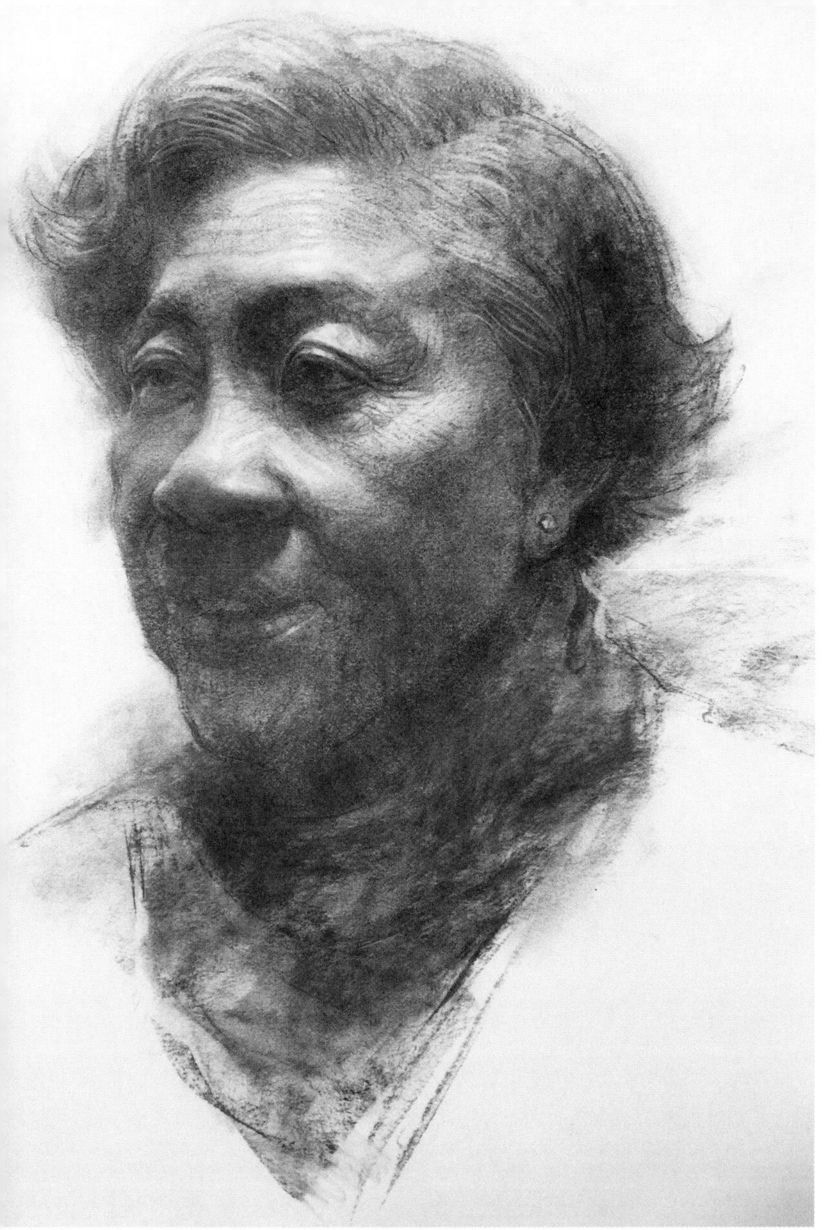

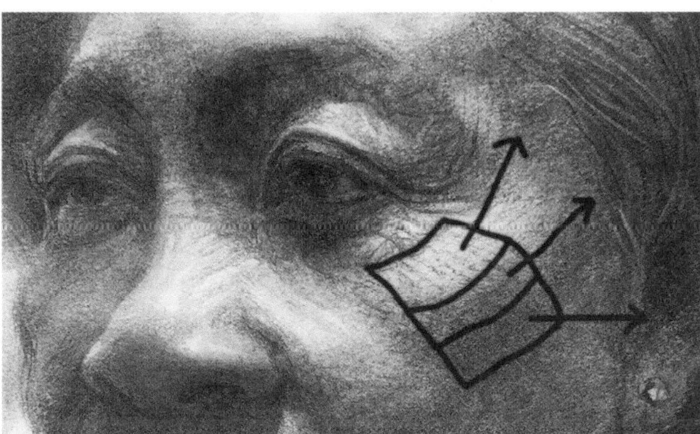

▲ A change of plane on a three-dimensional object indicates
the turning of form. The portrait subject sits facing to the left,
toward the light source, so the halftone to the right of the
highlight faces the viewer, and the shadow plane on the side
of the cheek faces the right. These three transitions, which
individually look like flat values, together as a subtle gradation
express the three-dimensional form of the left cheek.

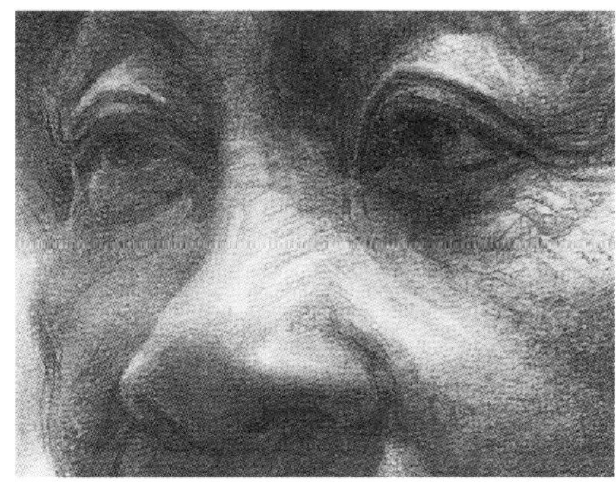

▲ I also applied the concept of atmospheric
perspective by decreasing the contrast within
the subject's right eye and increasing it within
her left eye so it would advance toward the
viewer and become a focal point. I did the same
with the nostrils. A common mistake is to make
nostrils too dark and defined, but they should be
inside the nose, in the shadows.

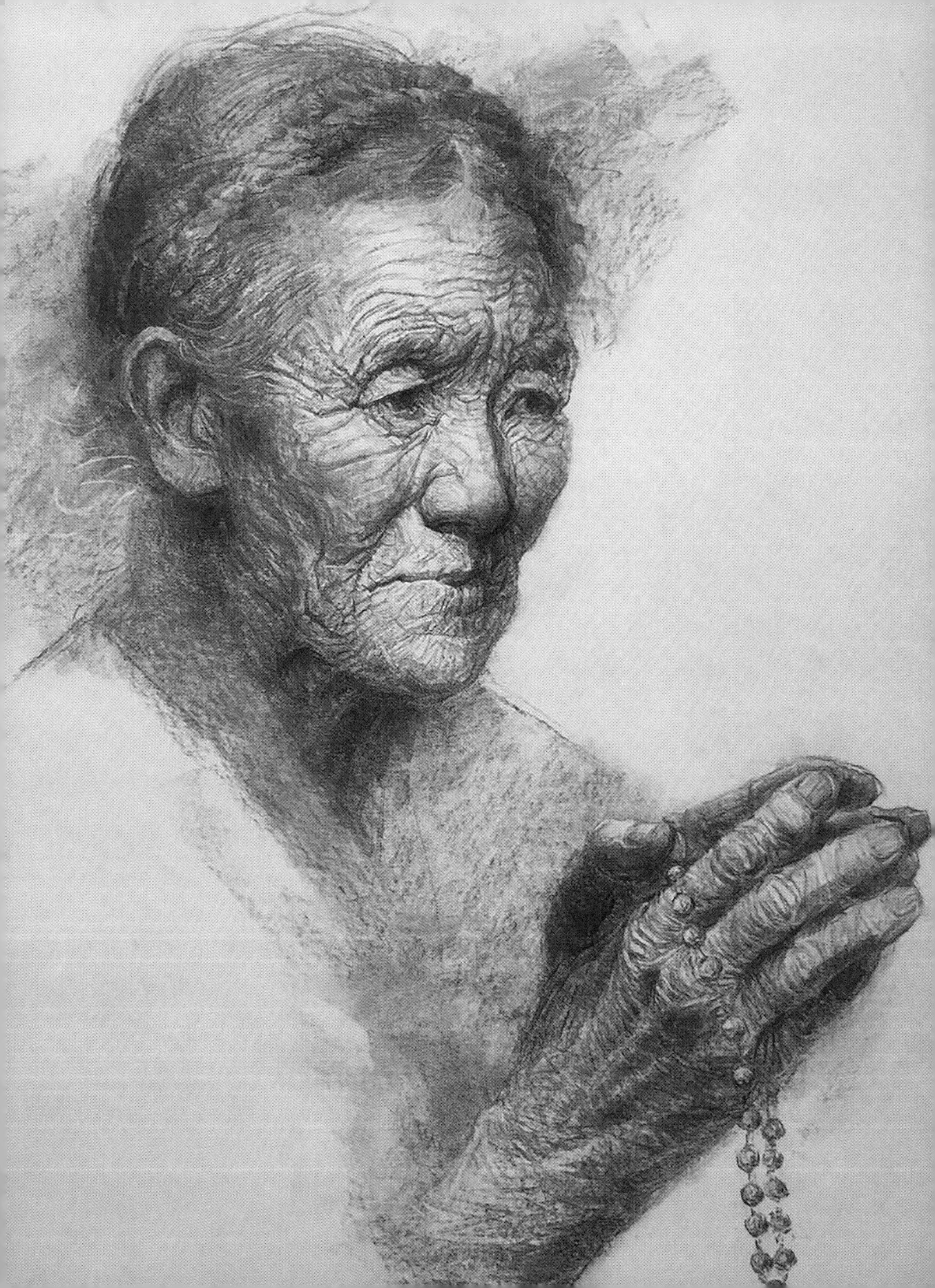

5

BRINGING LIFE INTO PORTRAITS

BEYOND BASIC POSES: CONTRAPPOSTO OF THE HEAD & NECK

The position of the head and the neck establishes the attitude of the portrait and hints at the emotion of the sitter. Besides the angle of the head, look for stretch and compression in the neck that reinforces the gesture. The word *contrapposto* describes the twisting action of the torso. When a figure twists the torso, it often stretches and compresses, as does the neck. Train your mind to recognize contrapposto and its effect on the neck.

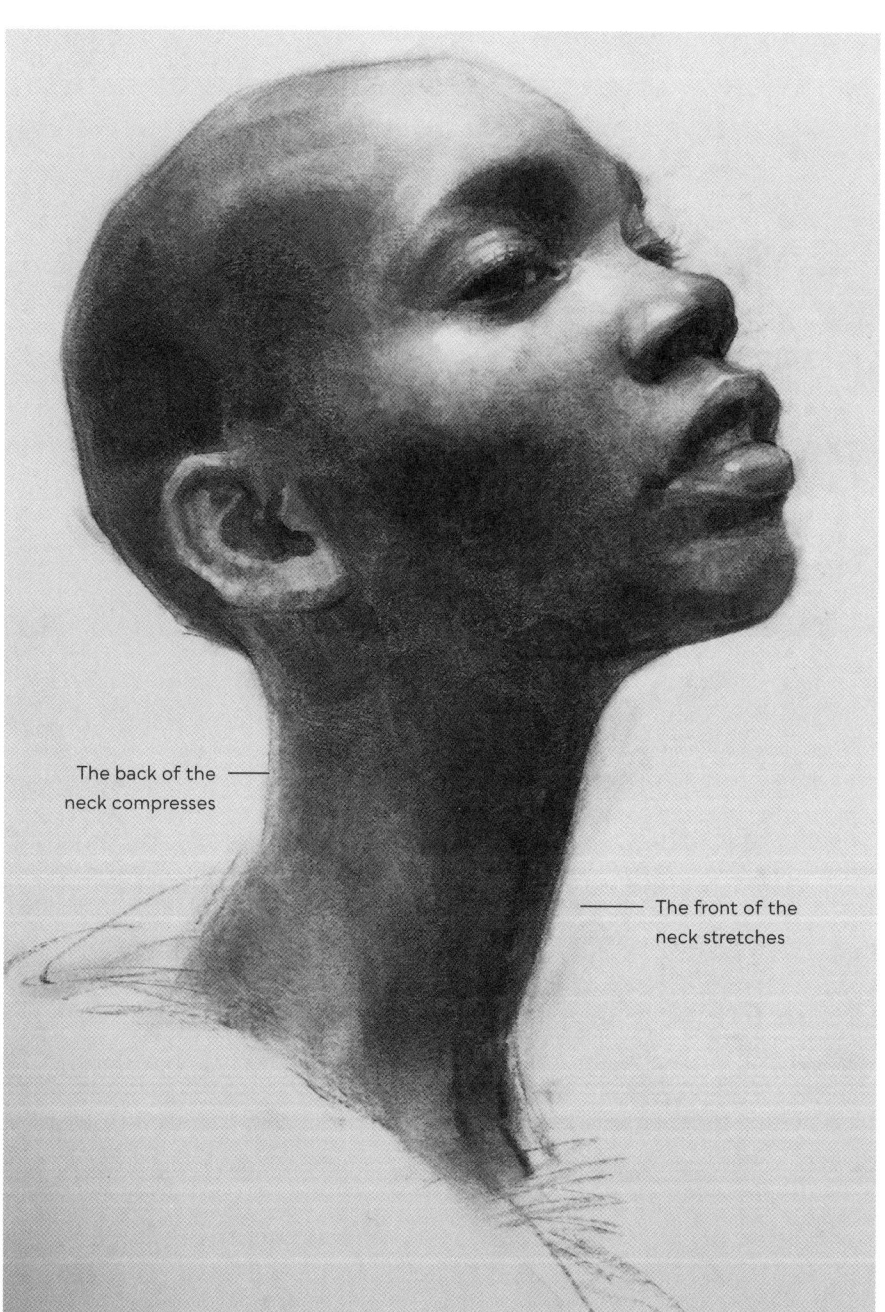

As she thrusts her head forward and upward, the stretch of this model's neck expresses a haughty gracefulness.

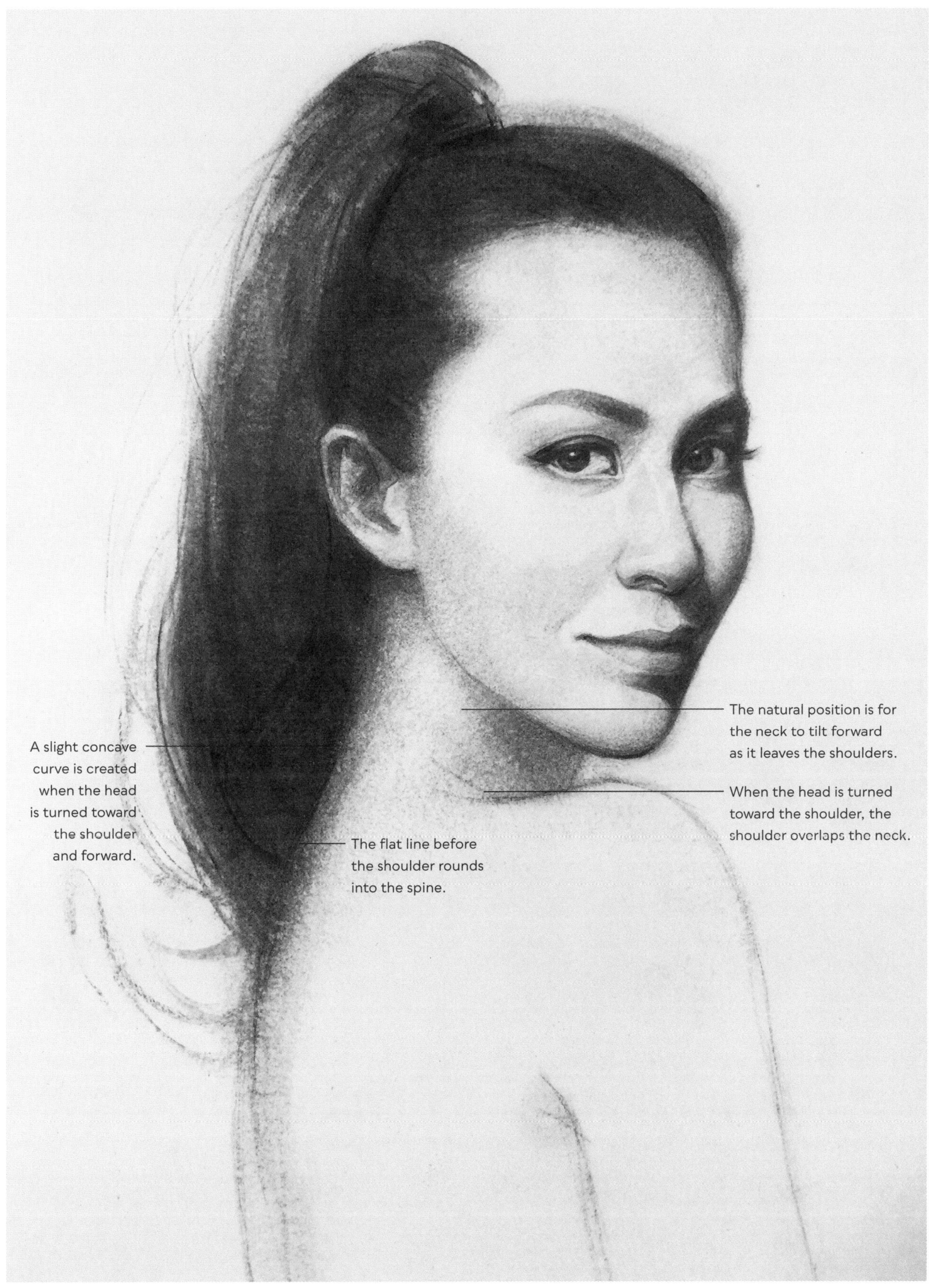

▲ This is one of my favorite poses: the model, with a soft, dreamy look in the eyes, looks back at the viewer over her shoulder.

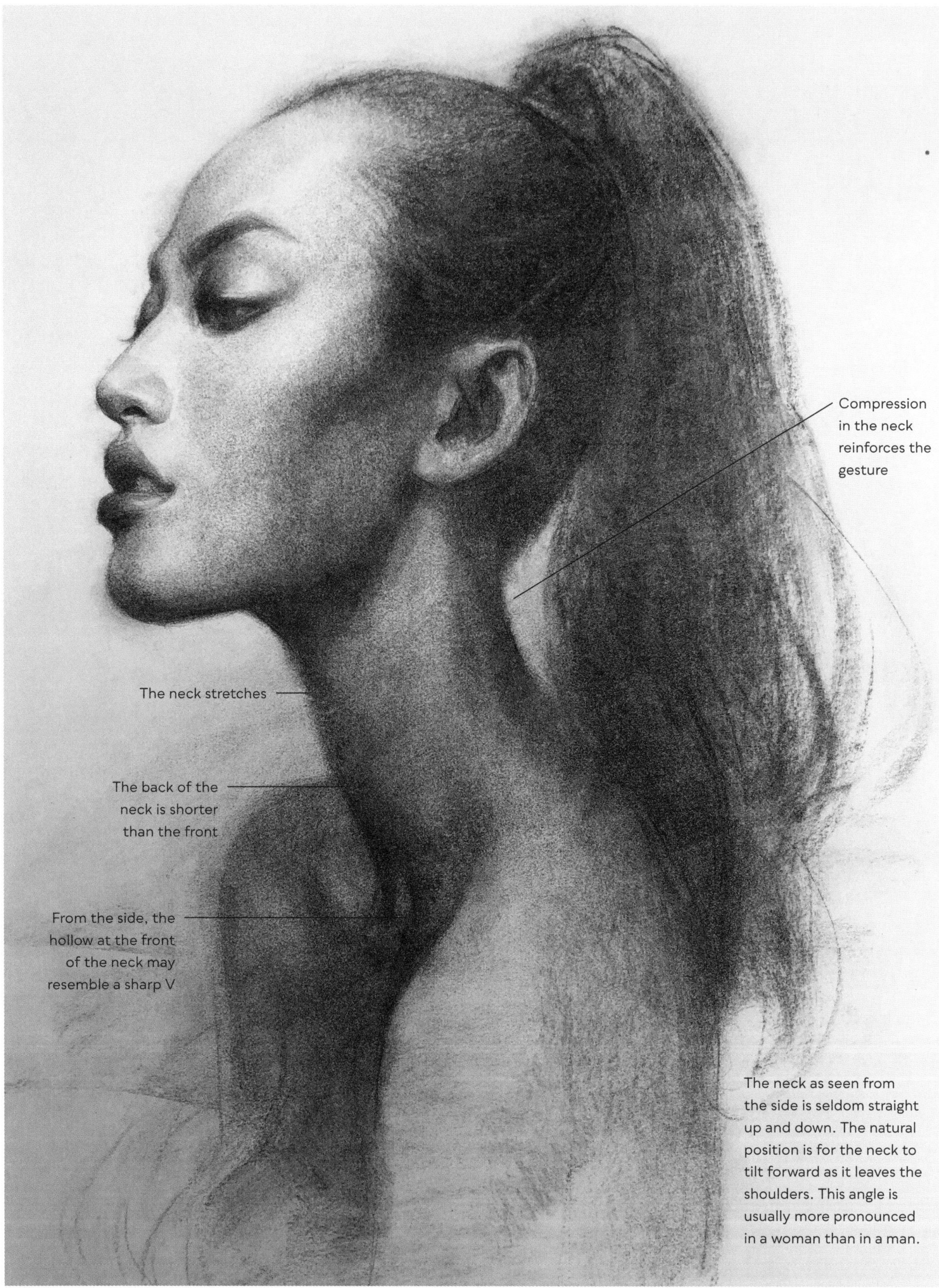

▲ As this model thrusts her head forward slightly and lifts her chin, the back of her neck compresses, while her downward gaze communicates an arrogant attitude. A long neck will look even longer in the front if the chin is lifted slightly. When the head is lifted and the shoulders are pressed forward, the line of the neck descends to a hollow between the collarbones.

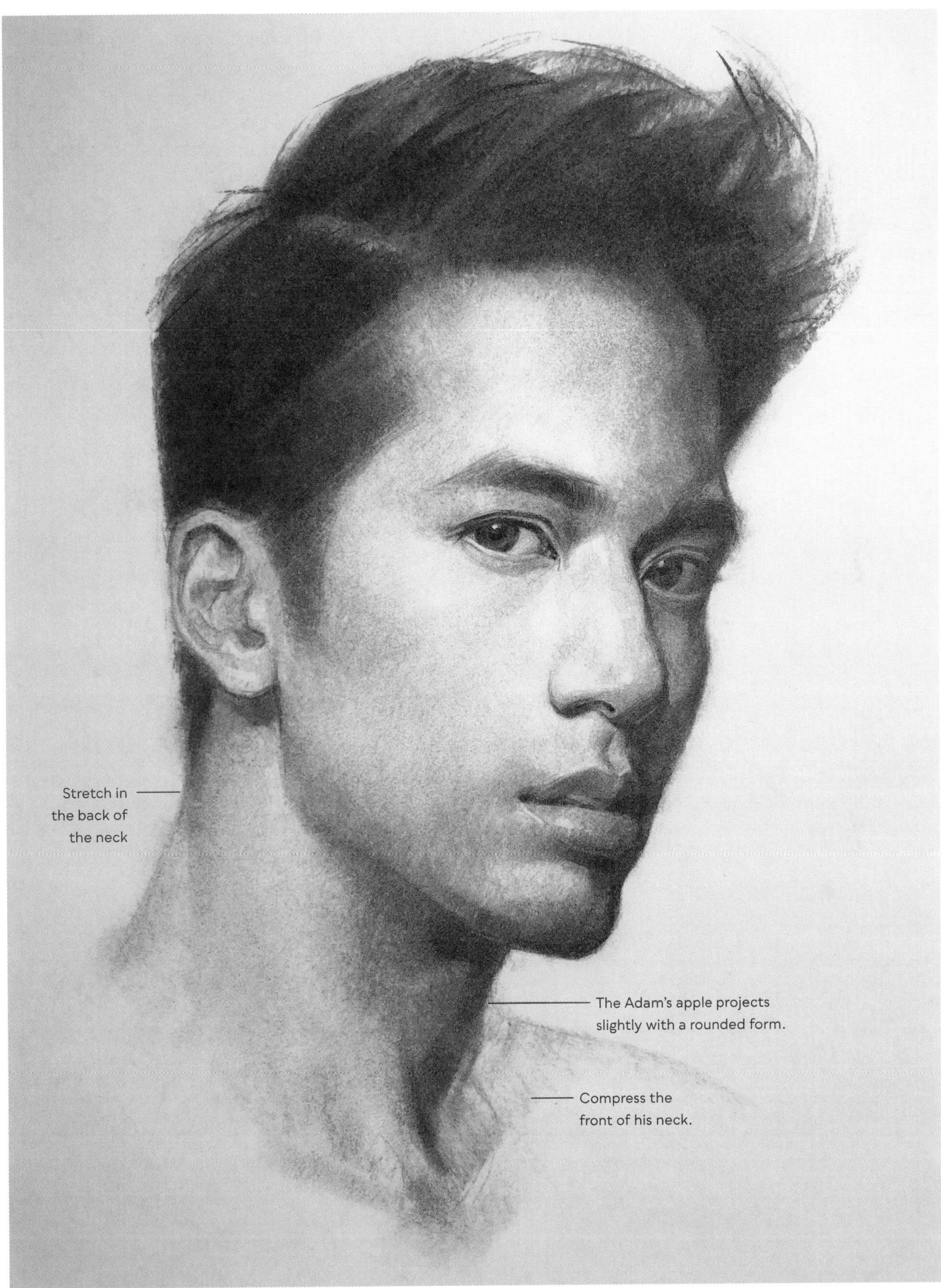

▲ In front and modified front poses, the lines at the top of the neck appear to extend down and cross over the ones in the center and at the bottom of the neck. The slashing angle of the sternomastoid, the largest muscle in the neck, communicates strength and power.

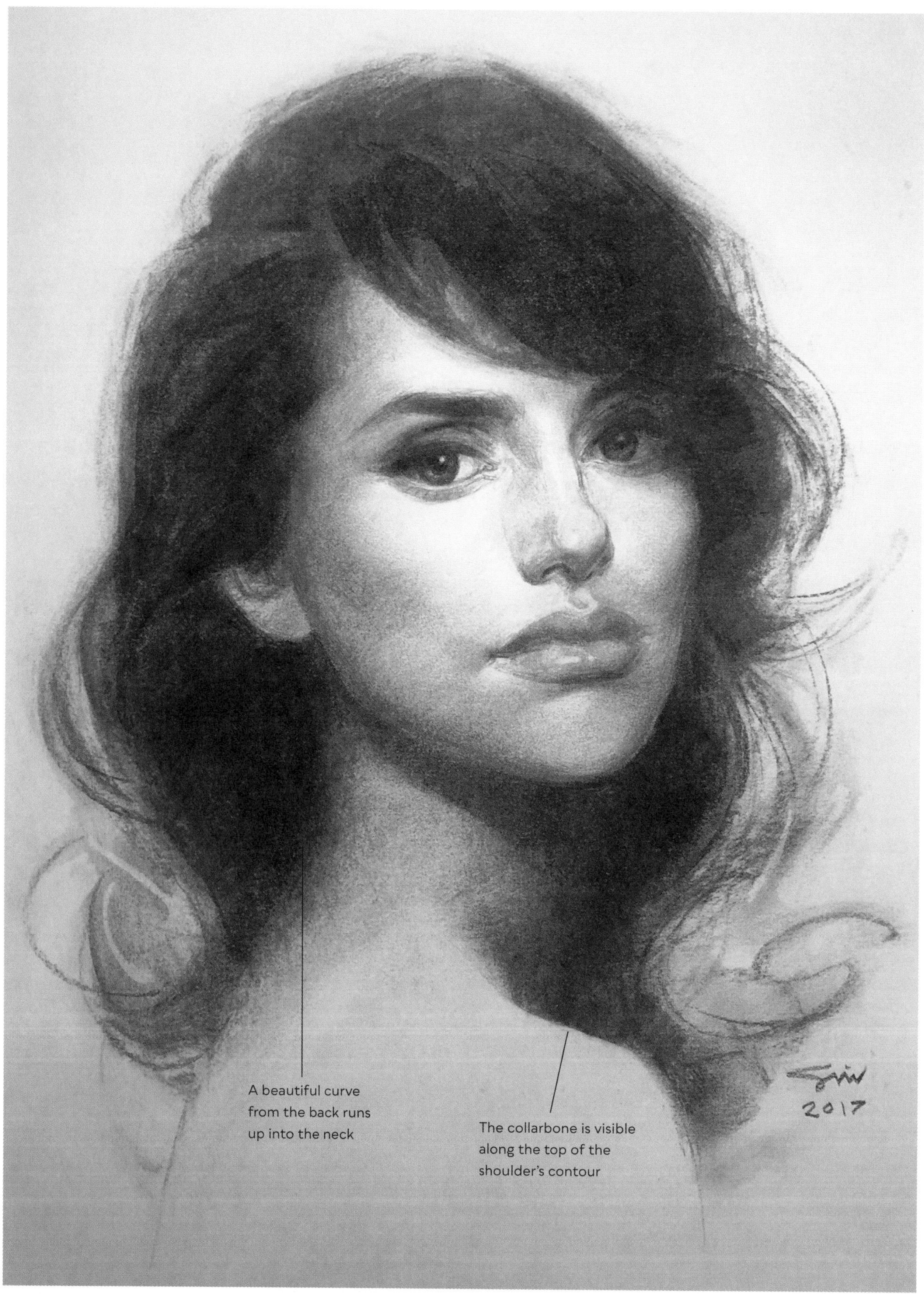

▲ The attitude communicated in this model's pose is lovely indifference. The stretch of her neck as she tilts her head back slightly expresses pride, while her direct gaze conveys a sense of seduction.

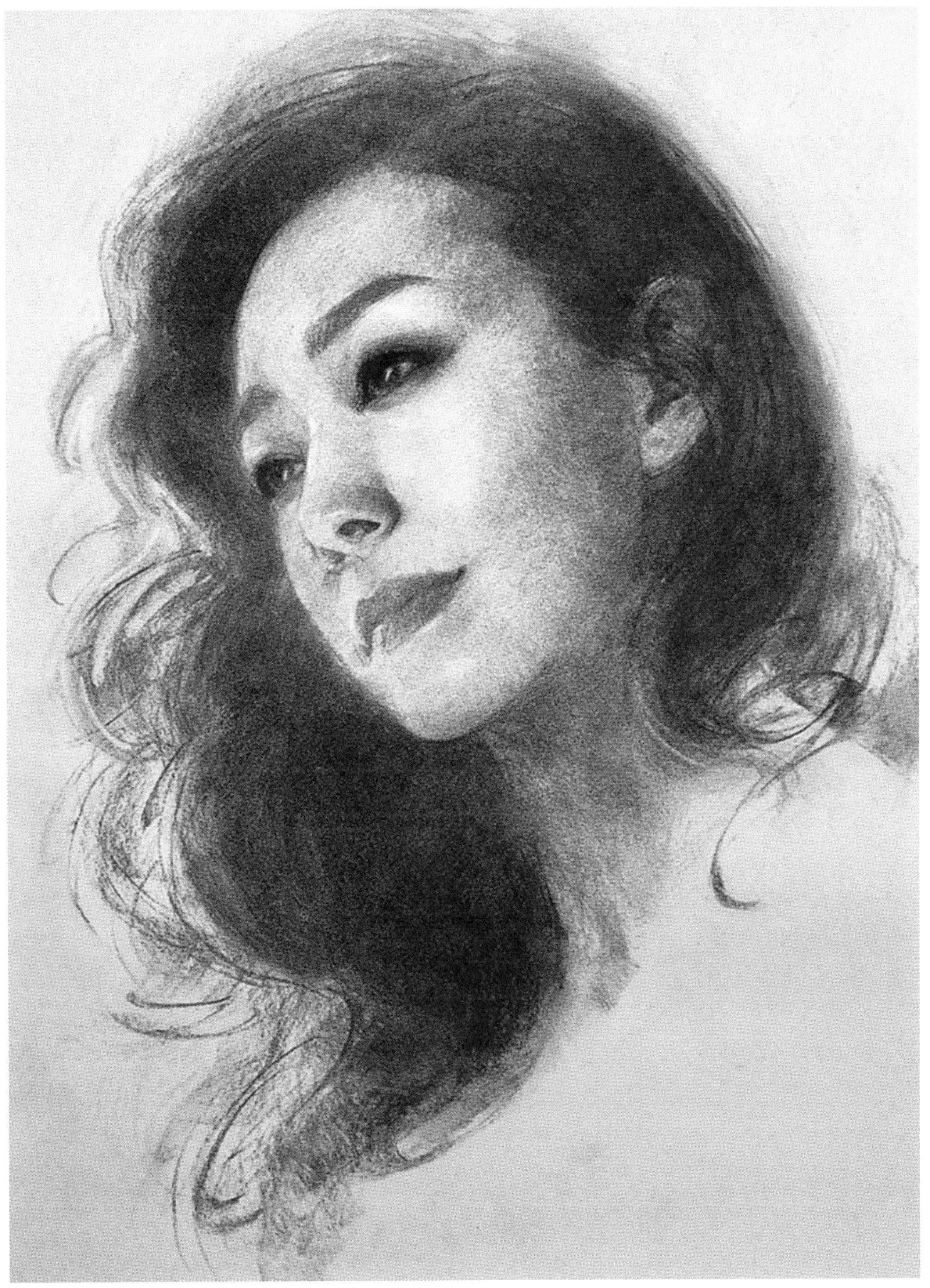

HATS, SCARVES & COLLARS

Hats

When drawing any type of head covering, it's important to be aware of the form beneath, even if the hat is made of stiff material, because you need to draw a hat to fit the head. Think of the crown of the hat like a narrow band that wraps around the head. Locate the placement of that band, ignore the brim, and draw the crown upward. Finish by drawing the brim, which adds style and design. A hat can convey various attitudes, depending on the style and how the model wears it.

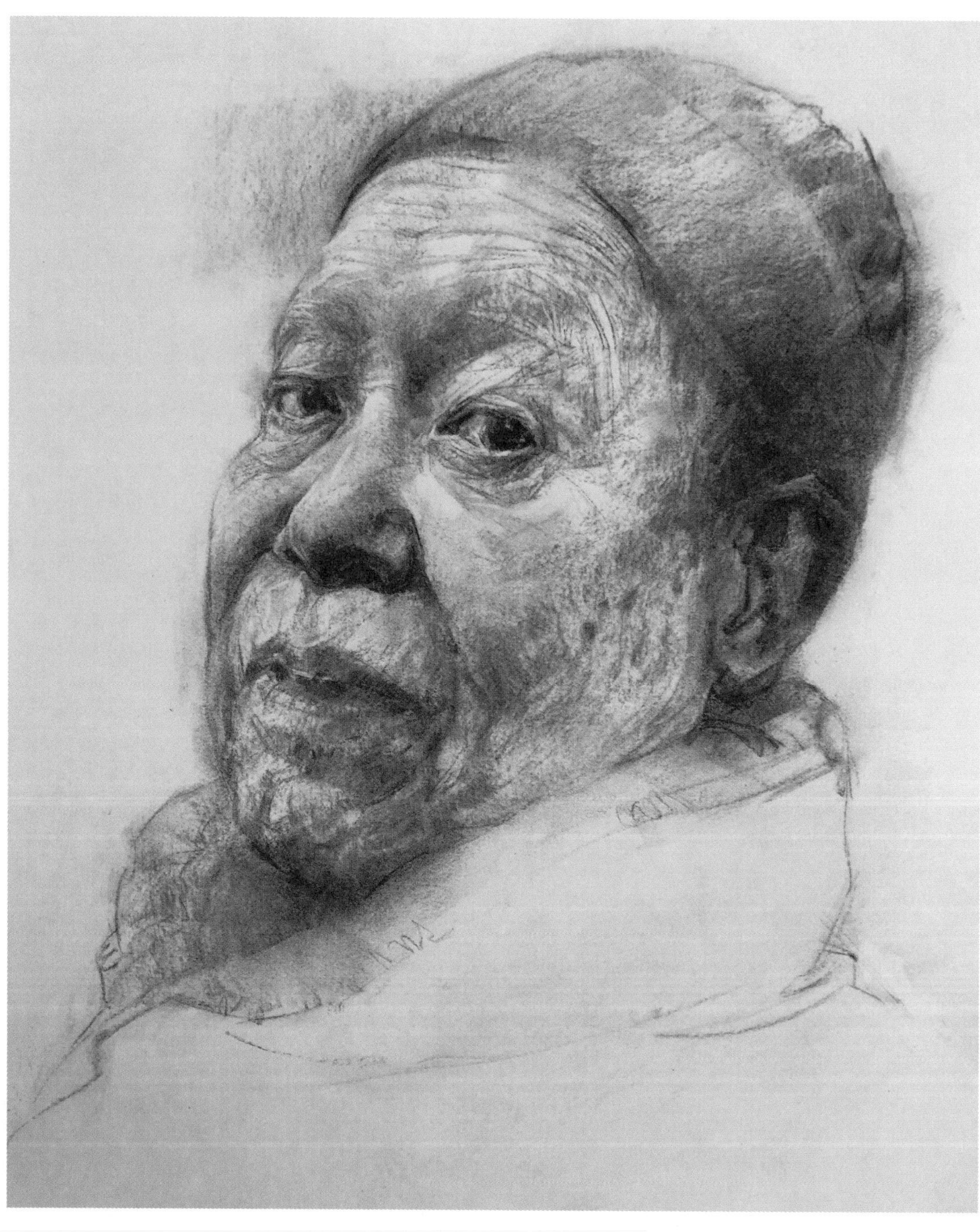

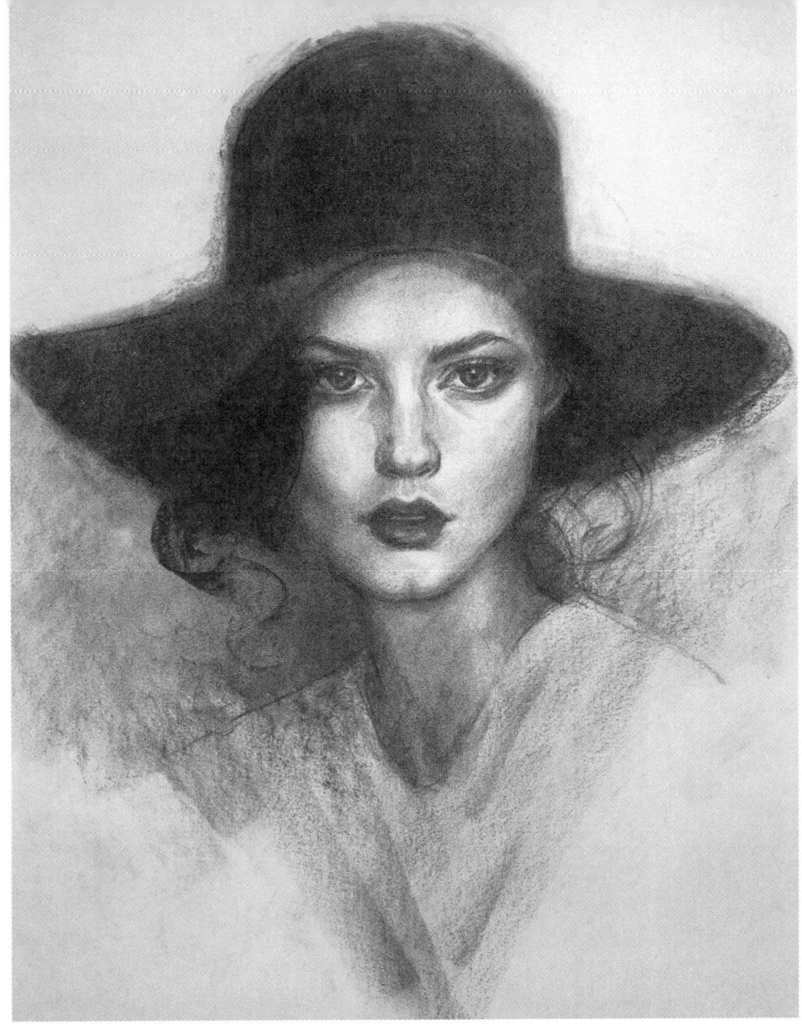

Knit hats (opposite) hug the shape of the head, while wide-brimmed hats add drama and create contrast and shadow on the face and shoulders.

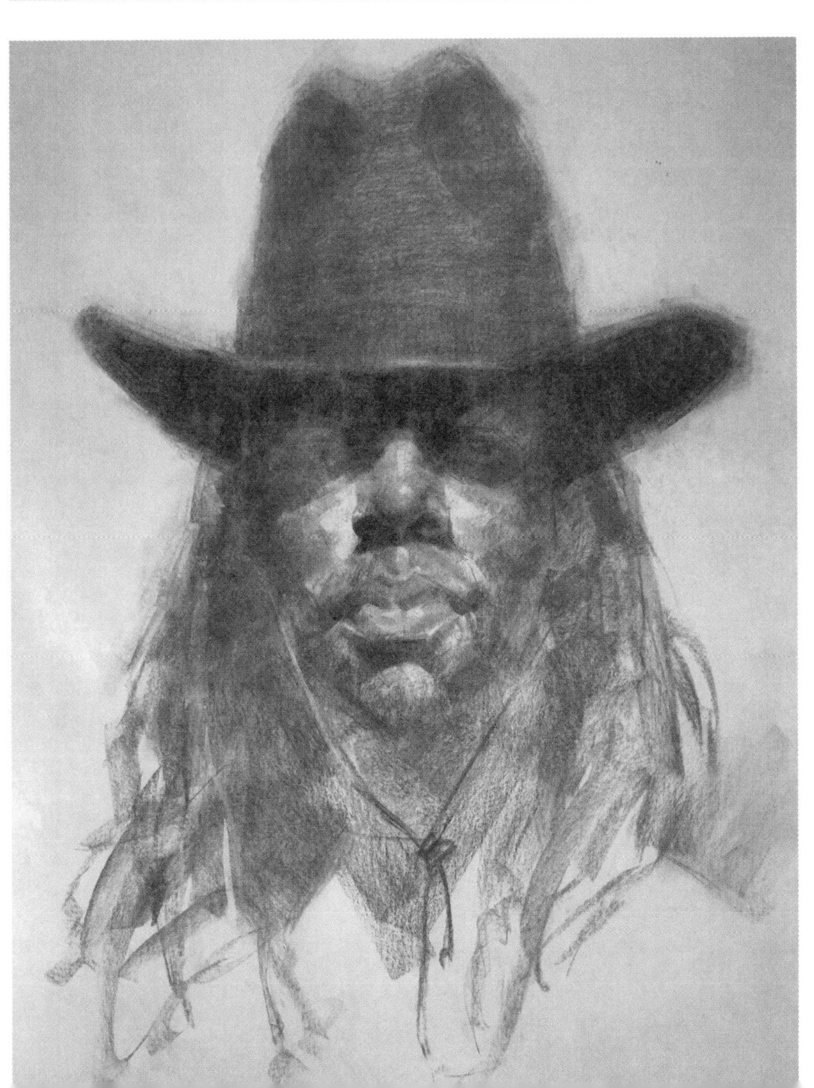

Scarves

When drawing a model wearing a scarf,
it's especially important to be conscious of
what is underneath. The shape of the head
affects the shape of the wrapped scarf.

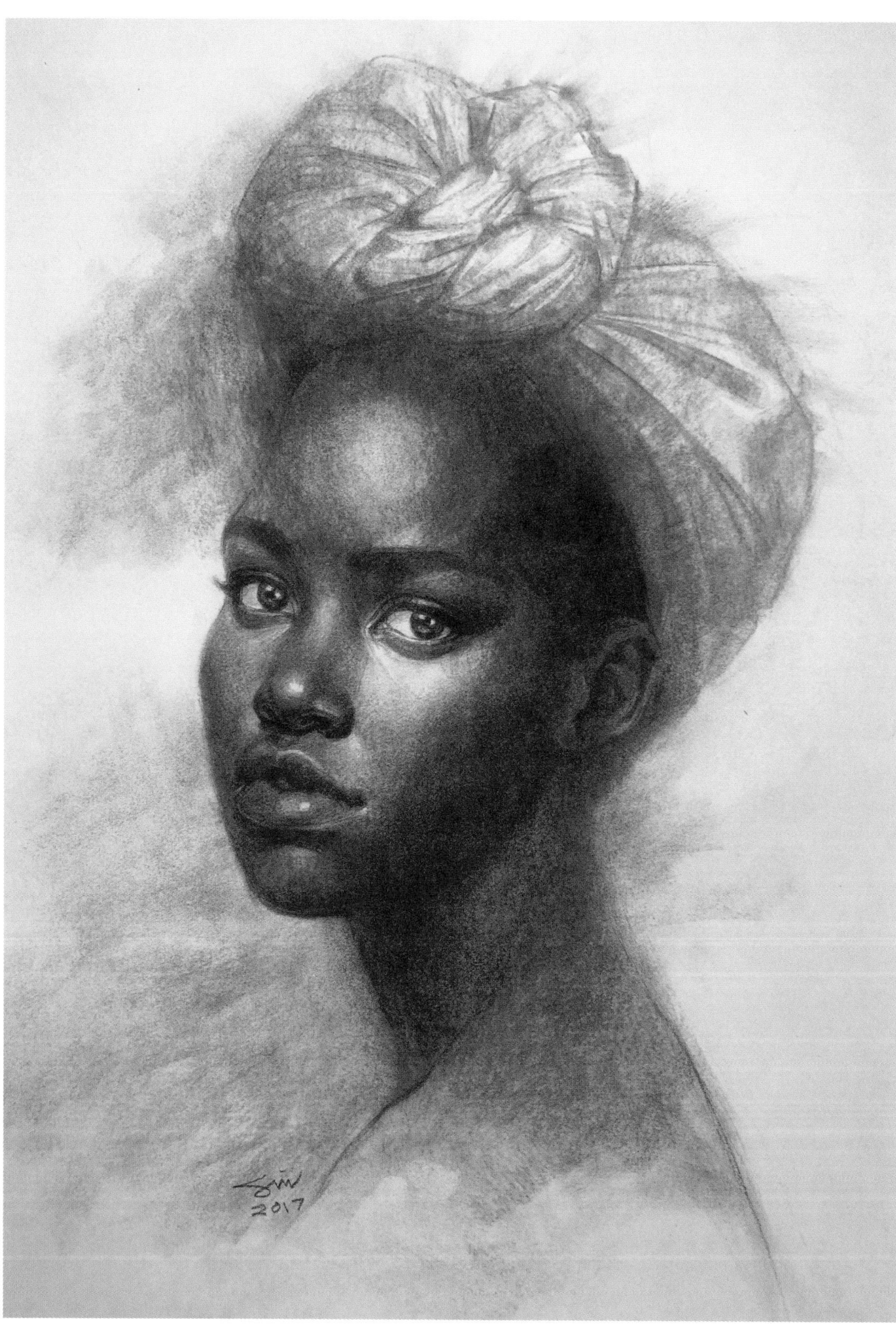

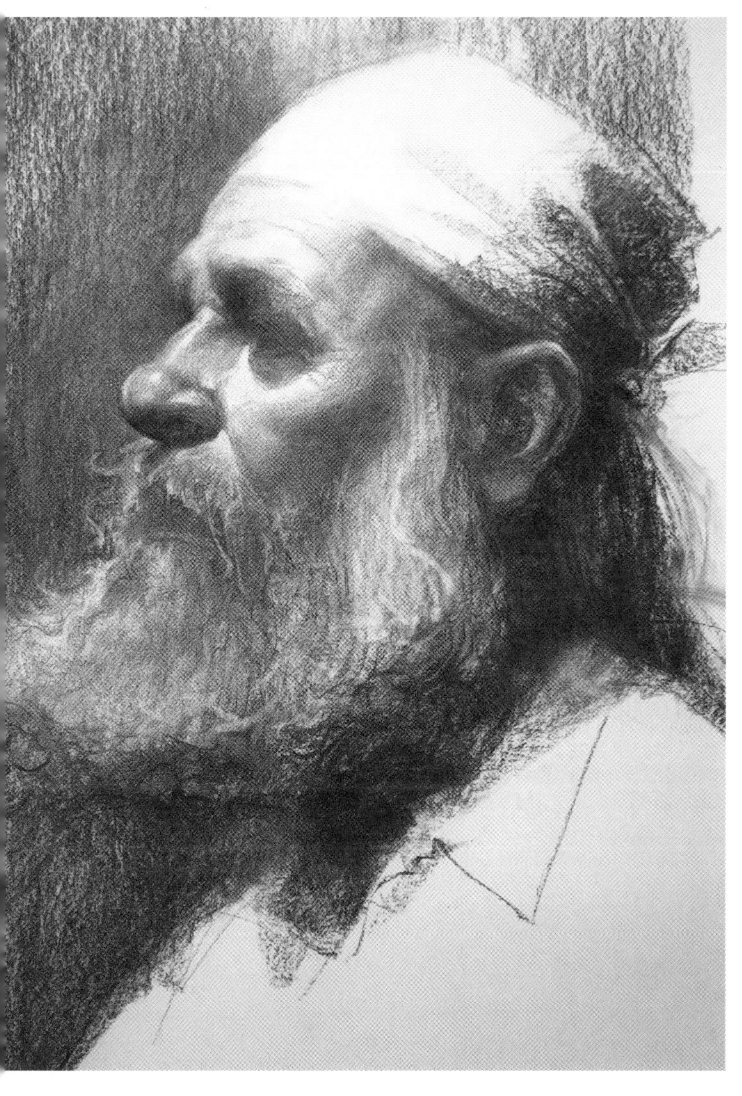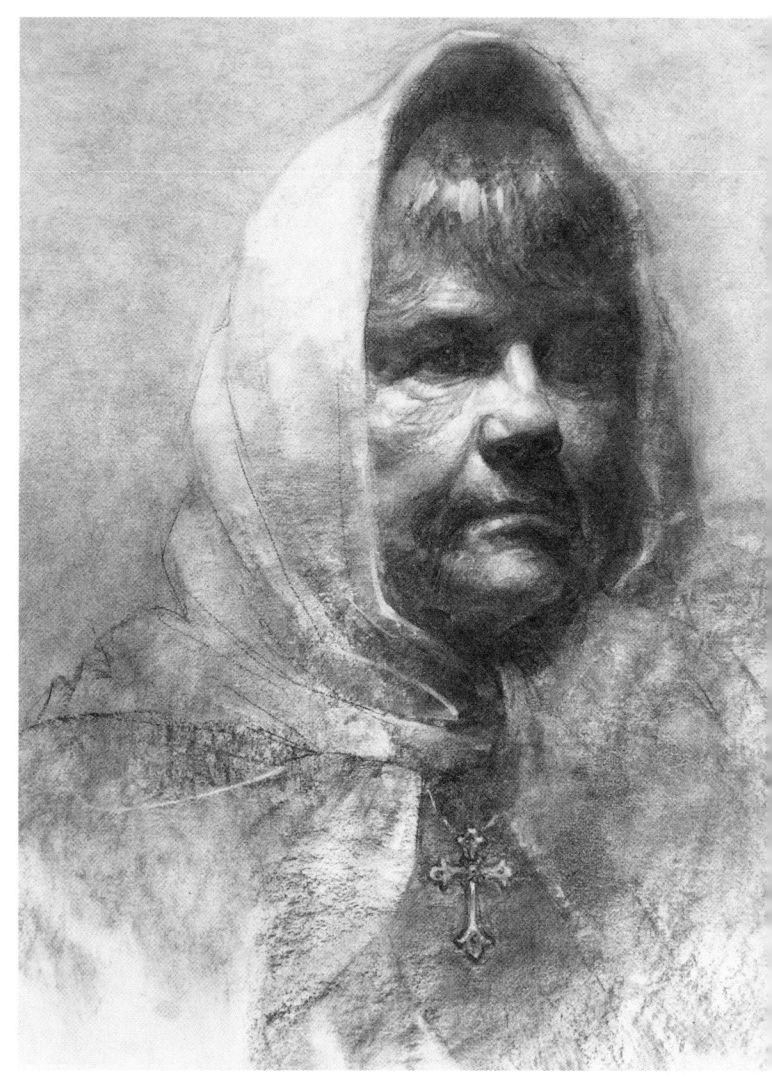

Collars

Shirt collars wrap around the neck. Be sure to create dimension and the illusion of space between the neck and the collar so they don't appear as one fused piece.

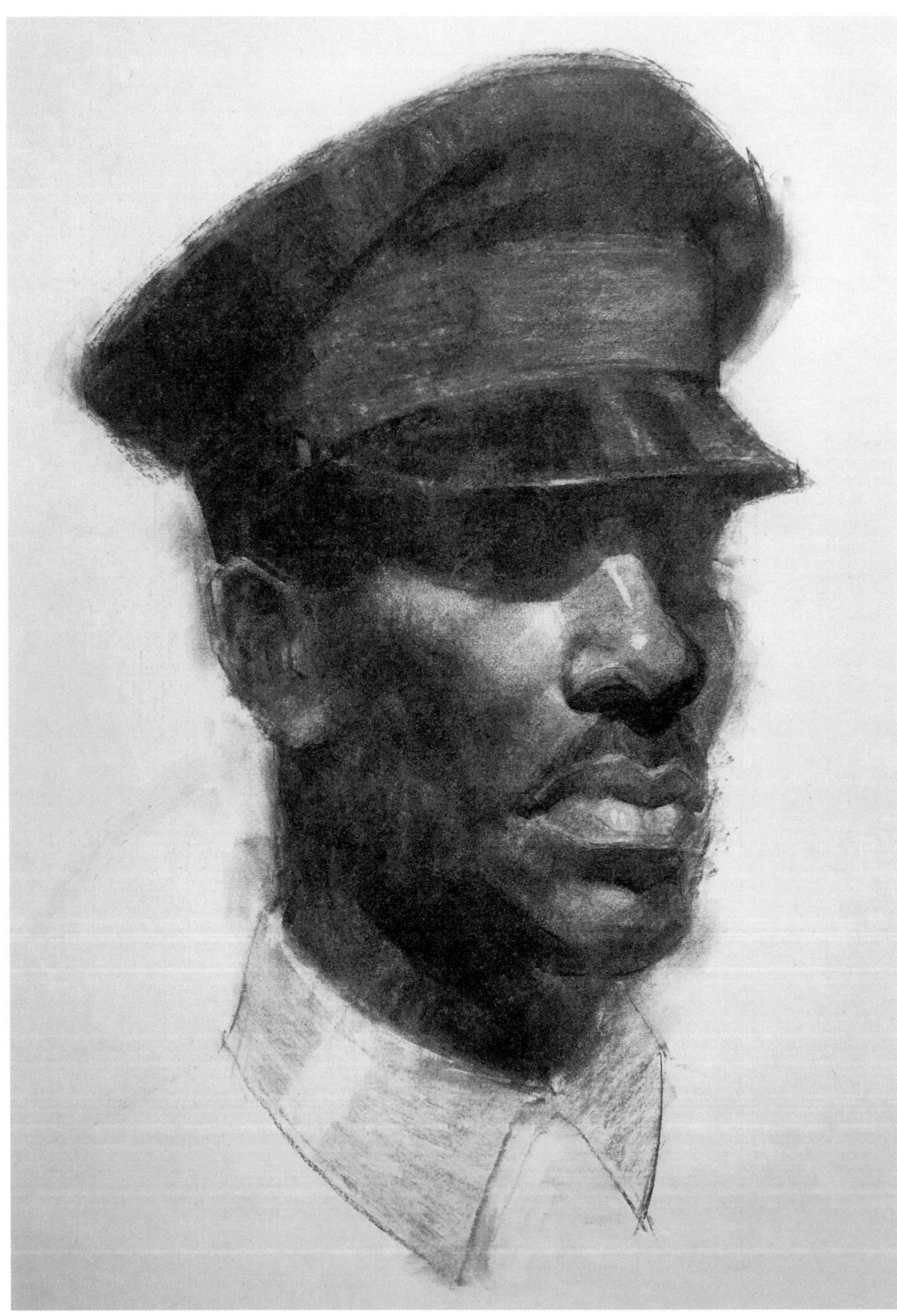

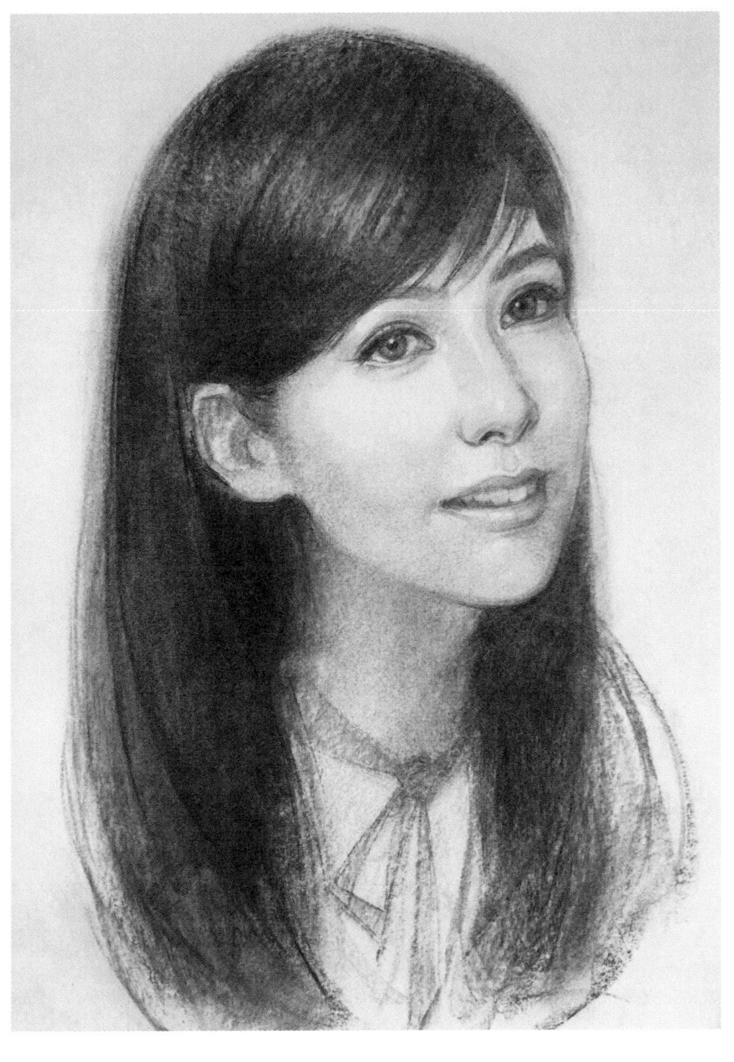
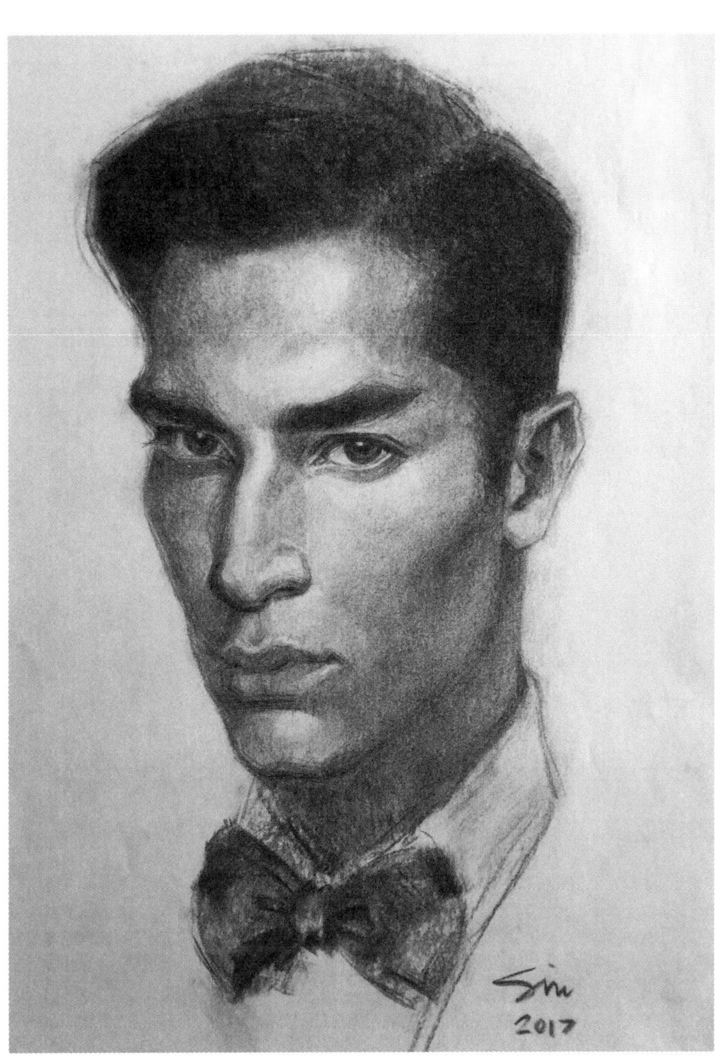

EXPRESSING MOOD WITH THE HANDS

Hands add emotion and feeling to a drawing. Including the hands can turn a regular portrait into a character study, a candid, unposed approach that reveals the subject's personality.

Drawing hands is difficult for many artists, including myself, but they can enhance the visual impact of your artwork. Often the most expressive and revealing portraits incorporate the hands and props.

On a philosophical level, hands represent the way we touch and feel objects, or even other people, how we "connect" with the outside world. They deserve a place of honor in a portrait drawing.

In these portraits, the expressive eyes grab the viewer's attention, while the pose of the hands tells a story and establishes the serious mood.

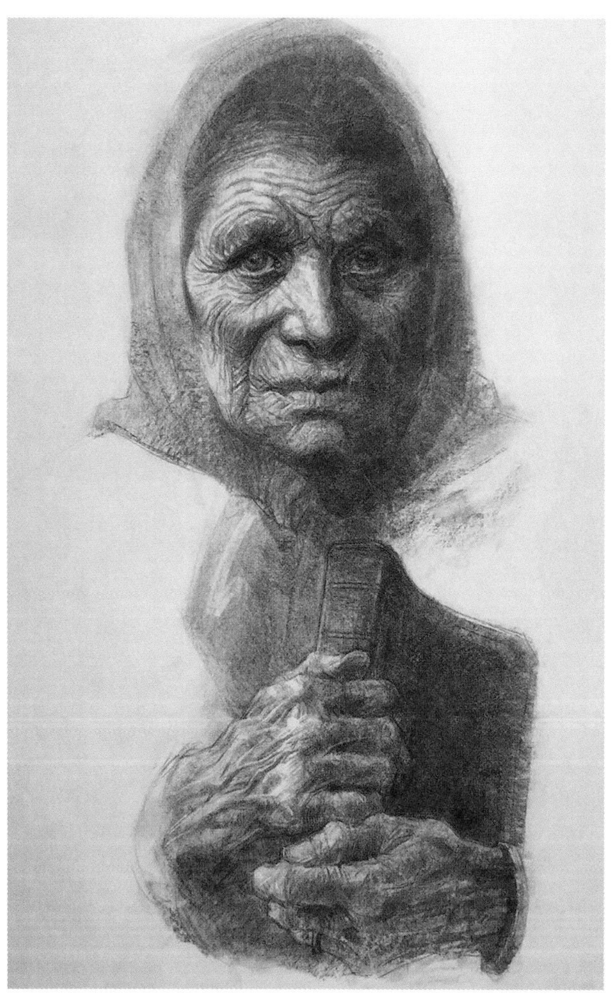

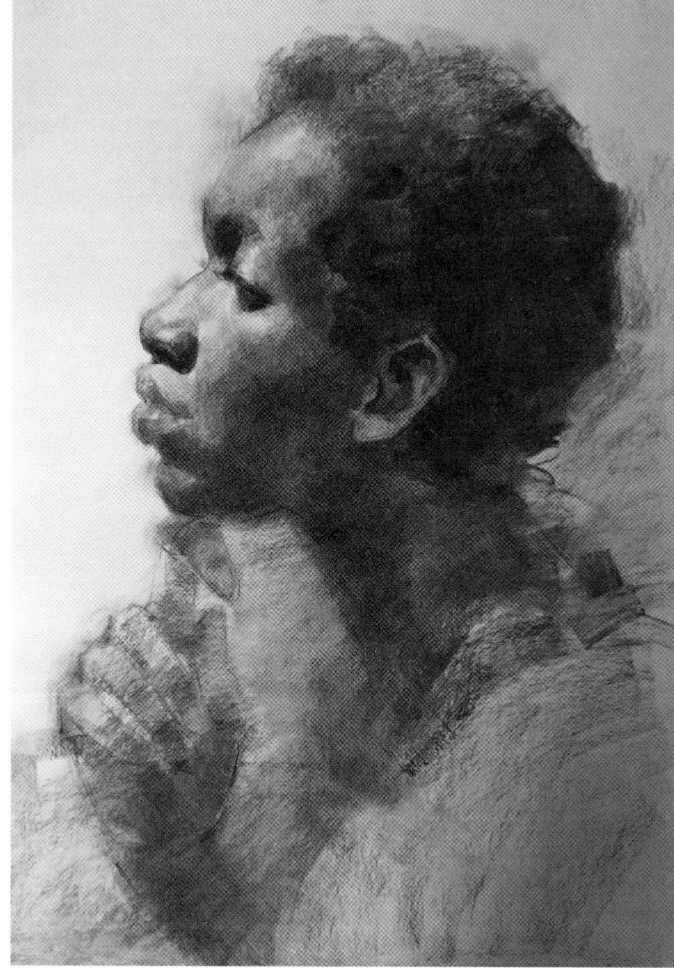

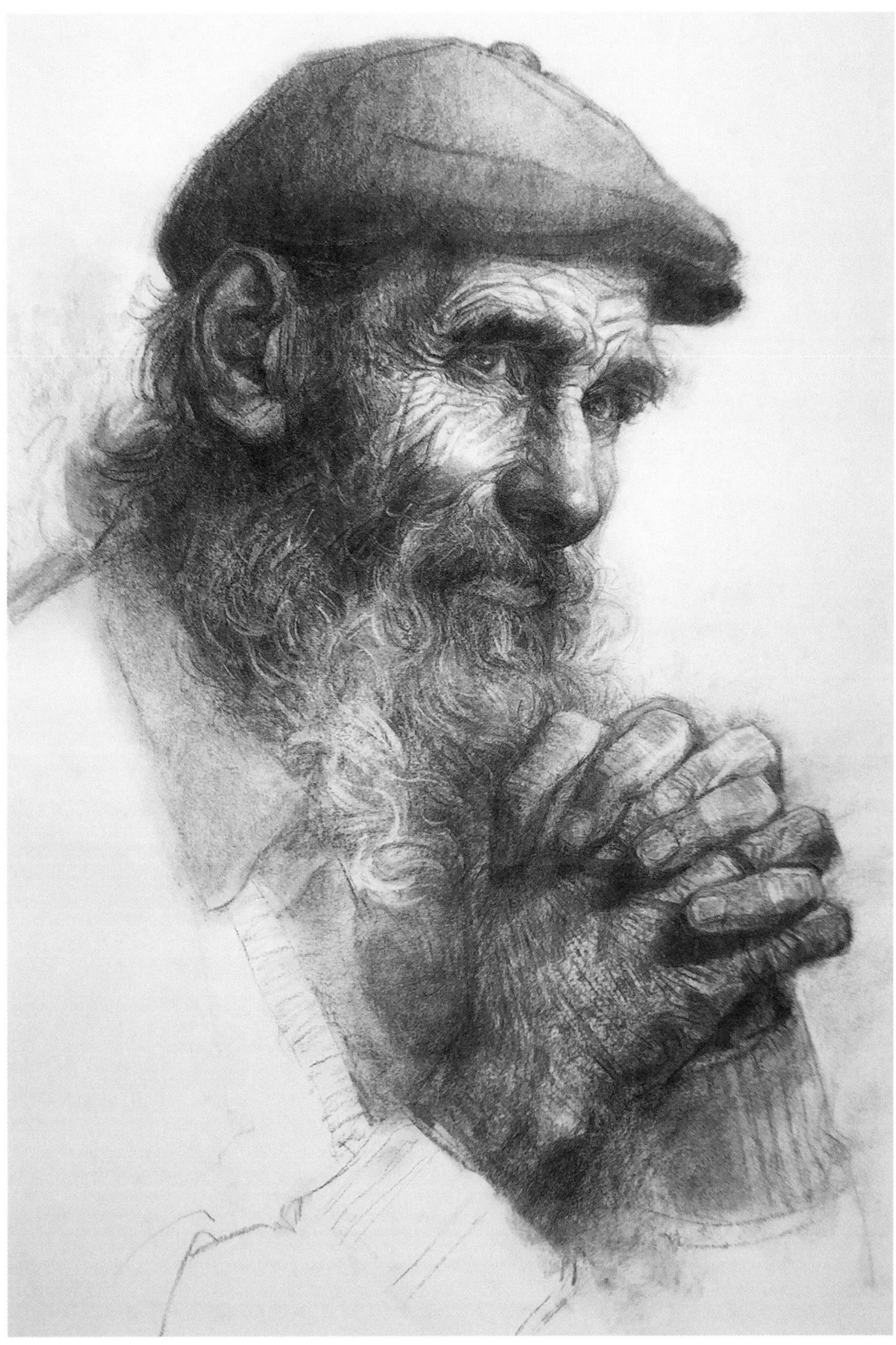

▲ Drawing hands may require more time to finish the portrait, but an unfinished study of the hand can be more attractive than the completely executed drawing. Hands are a contributing but subordinate element of the drawing and shouldn't detract from the portrait. The face remains the focal point, while the hands are rendered with softer tones and less defined shape and form.

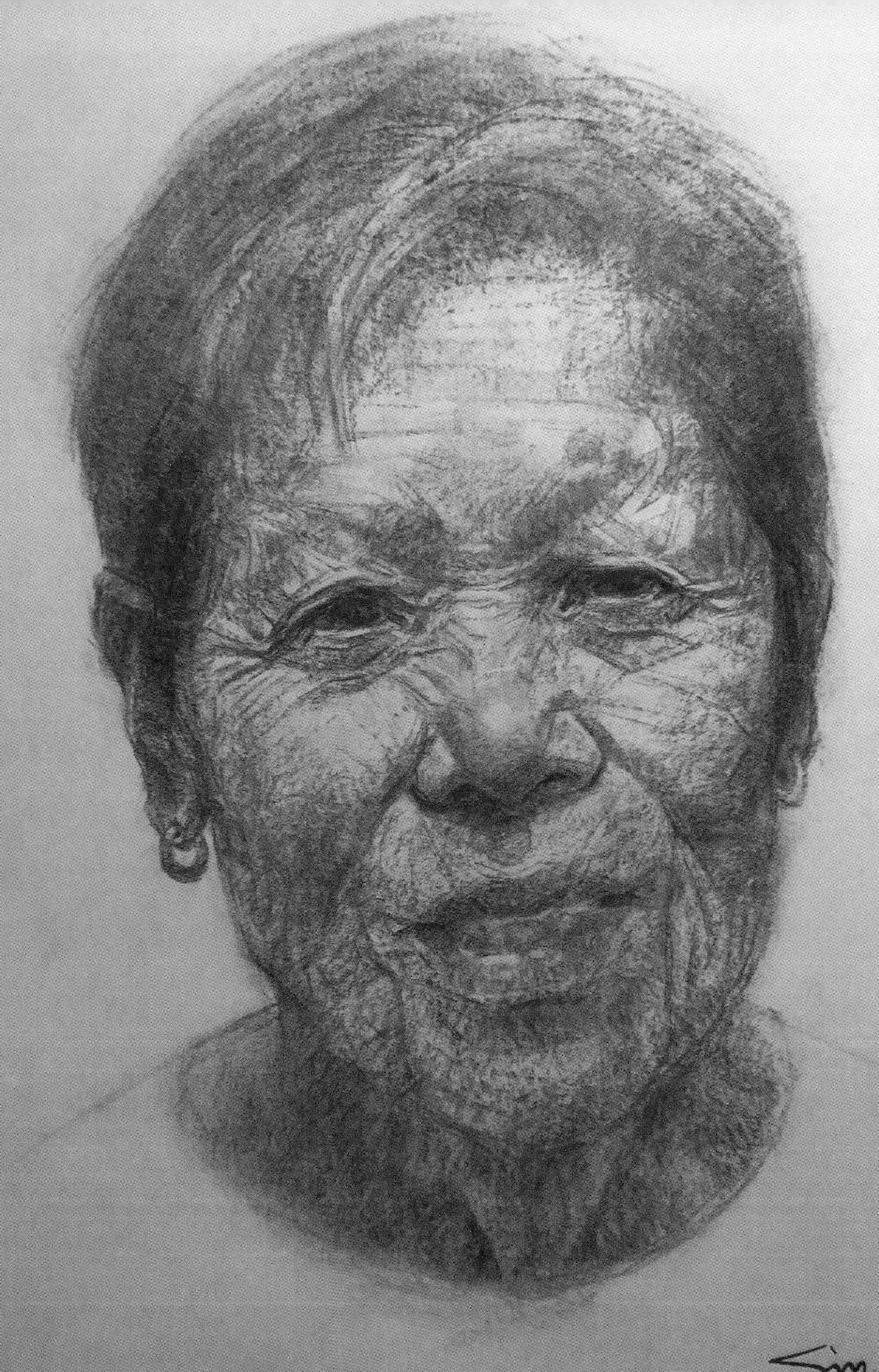

Sim
2017

6

DRAWING CHILDREN & ELDERLY PEOPLE

DRAWING CHILDREN

Children have distinctive characters and personalities. They register as many feelings and emotions as adults, but much more freely and obviously. As we age, we learn to hide our real emotions, sometimes too deeply. Most children are much more truly themselves than adults are.

Although the principles and objects of drawing the head apply to children as well, the proportions are different than those of adults.

A child's head is shaped more like a rounded egg than the elongated egg shape of an adult's head, and the face is smaller in proportion to the rest of the head.

The ears are usually proportionately larger than the rest of the features.
The space between the eyes is larger.
The bridge of the nose is shallow; avoid applying too much tone between the eye and the bridge. Keep the bridge of the nose low and concave. The nostrils are widely spaced.
The mouth is more indented at the corners.
The chin is less prominent and the cheeks are rounder, higher, and fuller.
The eyebrows tend to be lighter, and the hair is wispier.
Look for baby fat in the face, body, hands, arms, belly, feet, and legs.

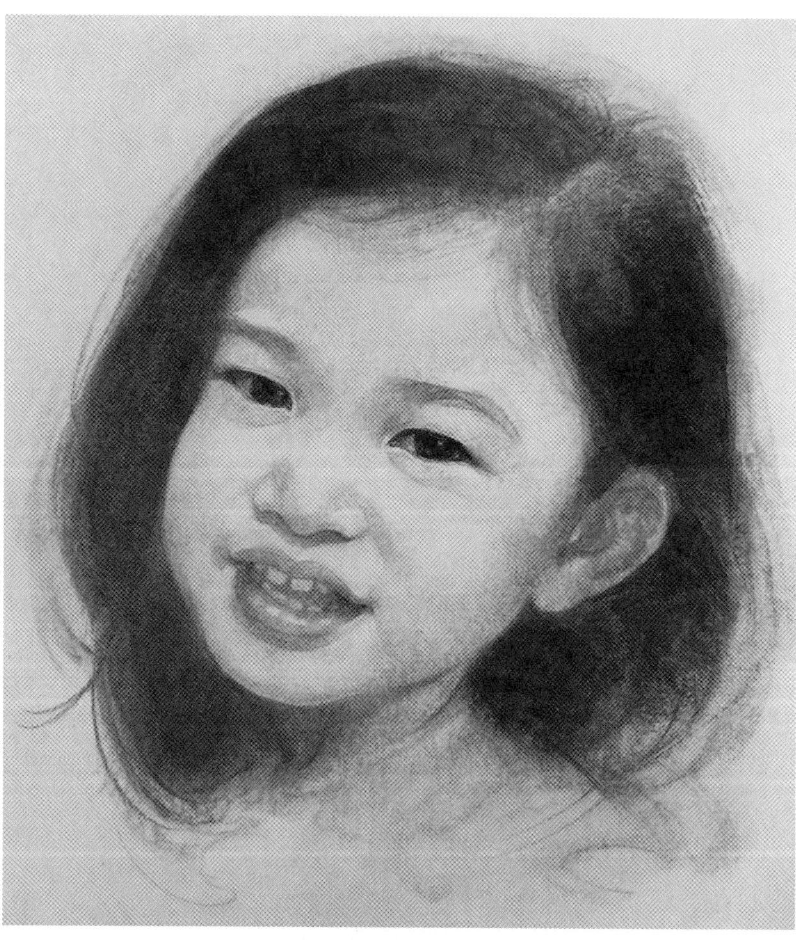

In addition to varying proportions and the placement of the features, children's faces are generally rounder and more curved than adult faces. Even at the brow and cheek, the shapes are curved instead of angular.

Children also have more slender, shorter necks. When you draw children, make sure the neck is slender to bring out the round shape of the cranium.

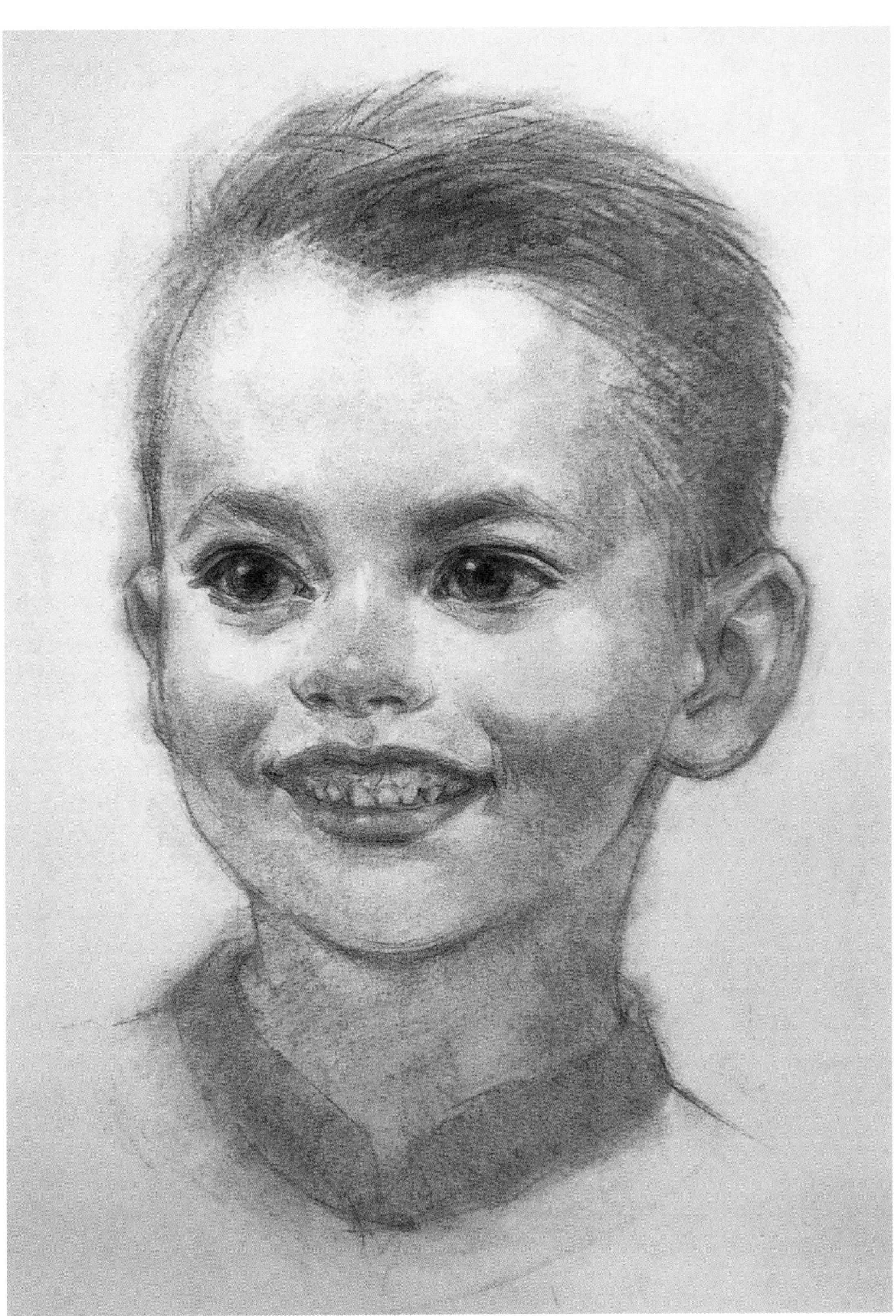

Sketching Children with Gesture Drawings

Gesture drawings are done from life and might take five to ten minutes to finish. These quick drawings capture the essential pose and action of the subject with loose, sketchy lines and are perfect for capturing on-the-go children.

Beginning artists may not be able to finish many gesture sketches, and that's okay. The important thing is to observe and learn.

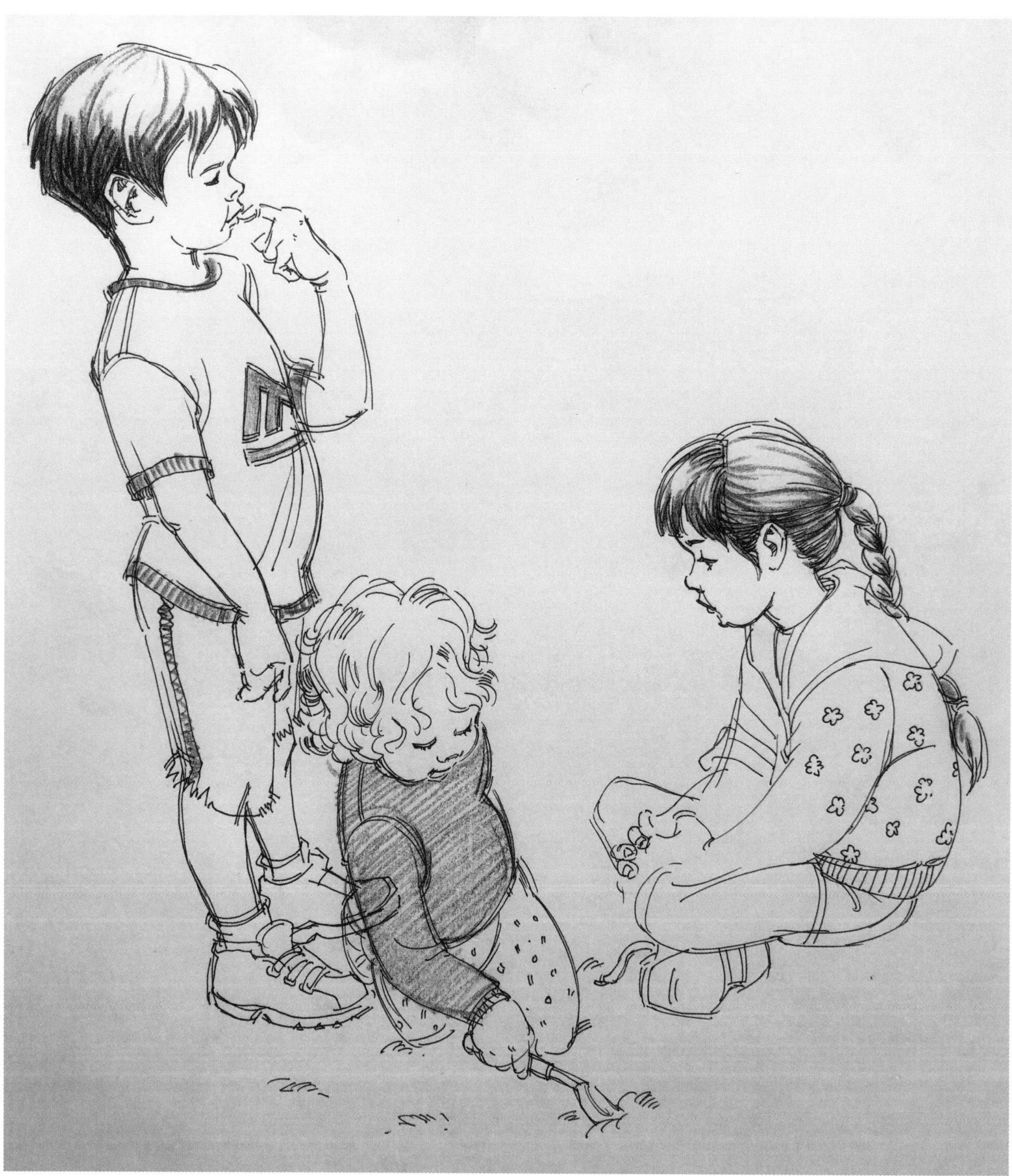

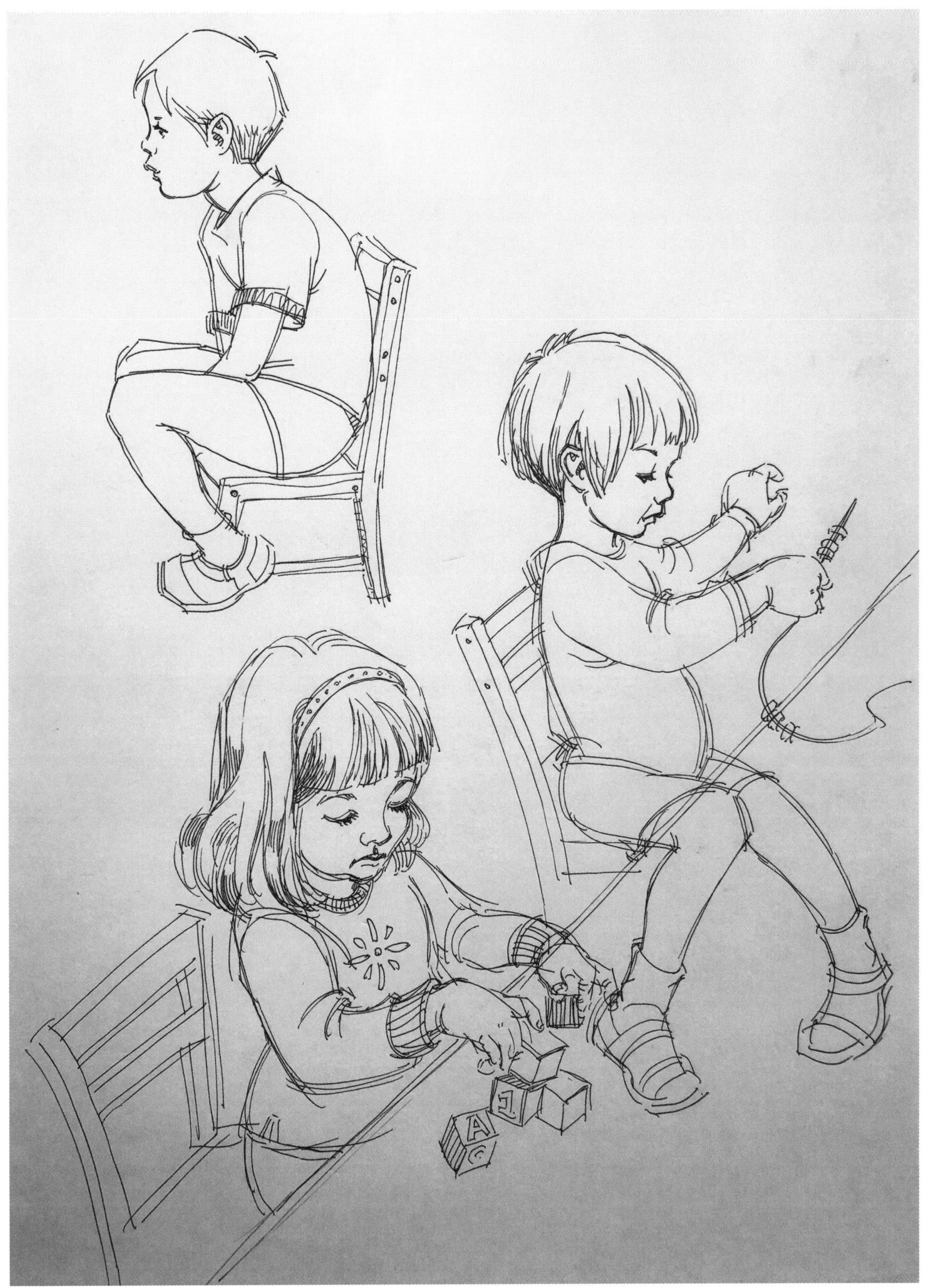

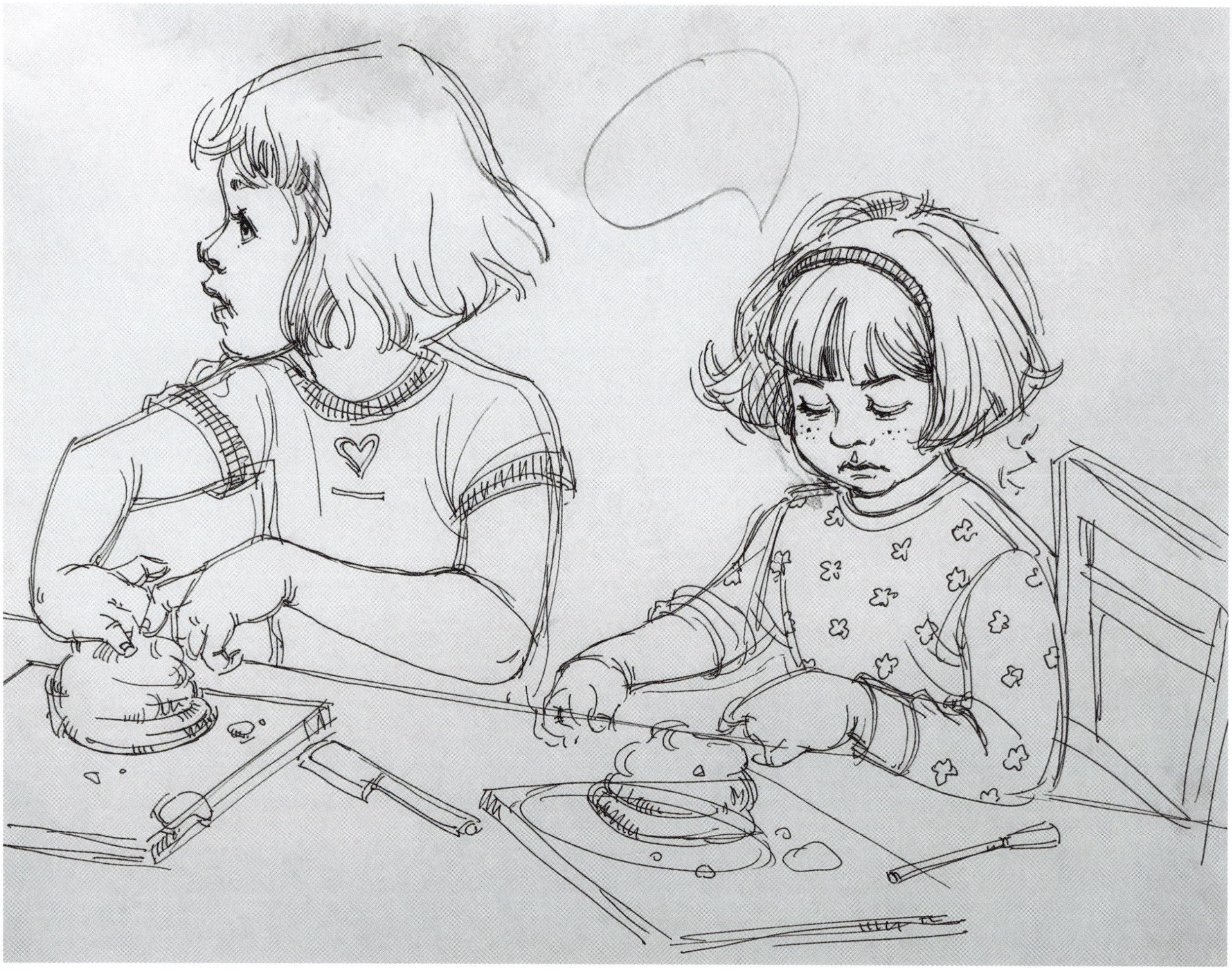

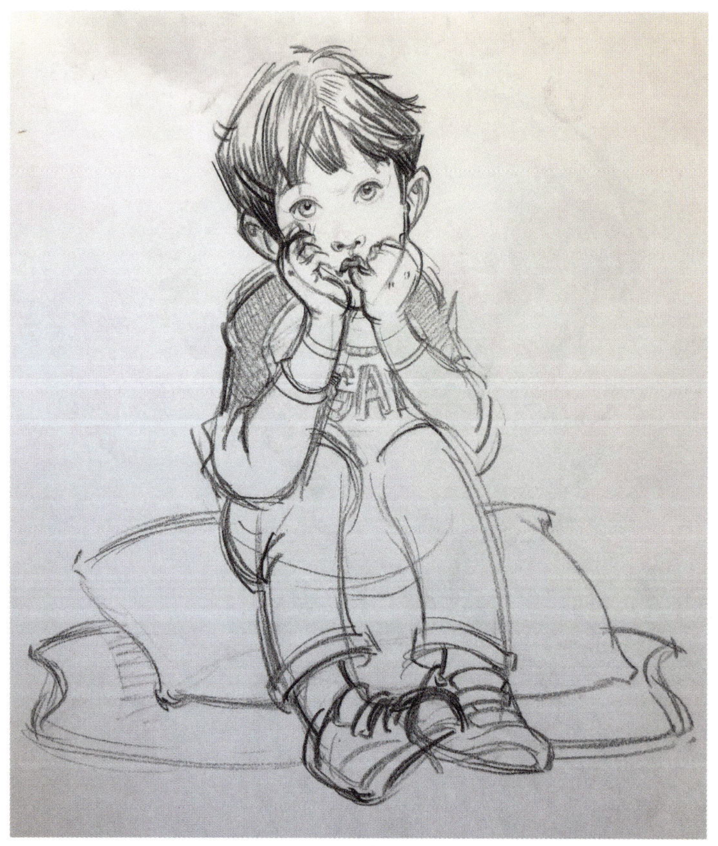

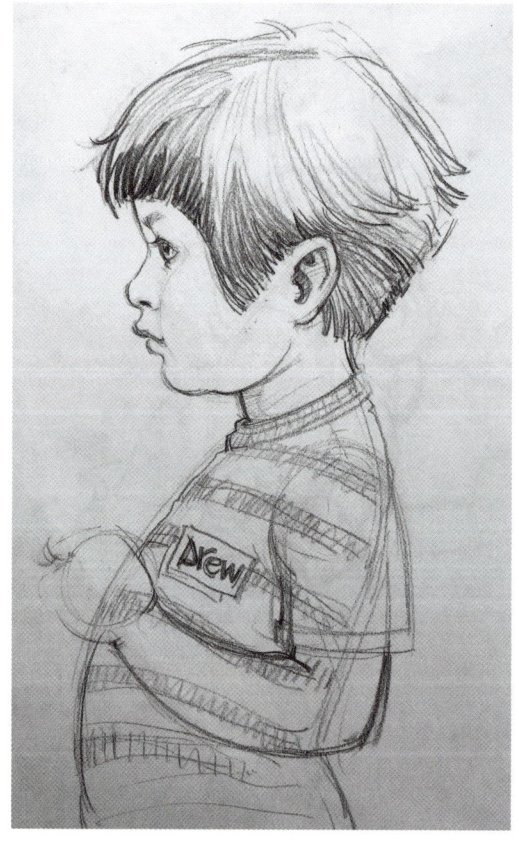

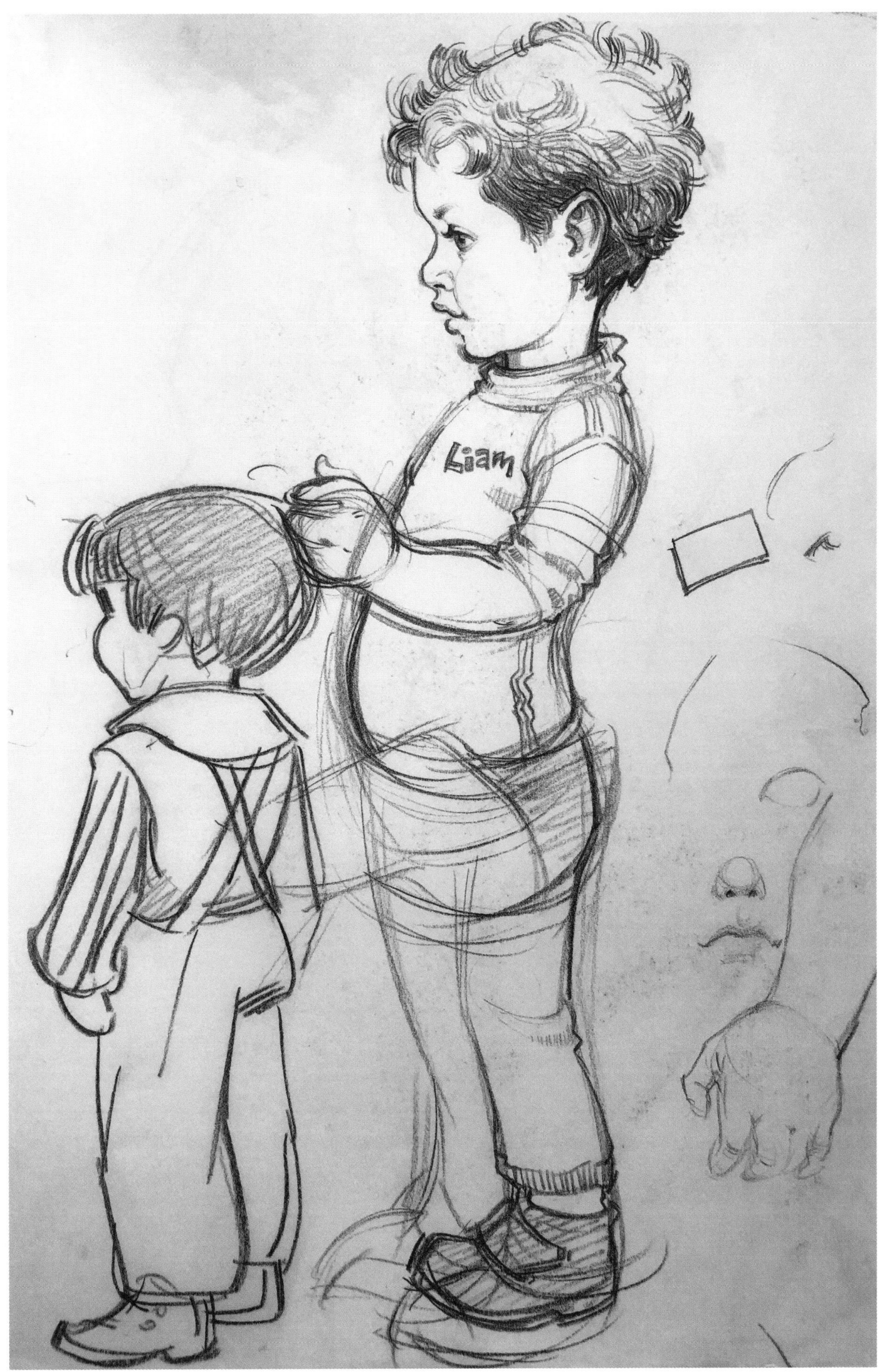

Liam

DRAWING ELDERLY PEOPLE

The faces of elderly people give the artist more to study and capture in the way of forms and lines. Wrinkling is a normal part of aging, but you can achieve the impression of age with minimal rendering of wrinkles by working the main lines and forms of the emaciating muscles and the creases between them. The cheekbones, the corners of the jaw, and the bone of the chin all become more evident in the aging process. Other points to remember when drawing elderly people include:

The hair thins or turns noticeably white, and the eyebrows may become sparse or scraggly.

Defined lines remain in the forehead, and the temples deepen.

The eyelids tend to droop and the socket bone protrudes as the eyes sink back. Wrinkles form around the lower lid.

The cheekbones become prominent and the chin bone protrudes as well.

The ears lengthen and the lobes hang, pendant-like.

The ball of the nose may appear to swell.

The neck becomes gaunt, and the skin drapes. The wrinkles around the ear merge with those of the jawline and neck.

Most noticeable are the changes in the cheeks and around the eyes and mouth. The flesh sags at the sides of the chin and along the jaw. Pouches form under the eyes, and deeper lines form at the corners. The mouth sinks back and wrinkles run from the lips. The lines at the corners of the mouth deepen down the sides of the chin.

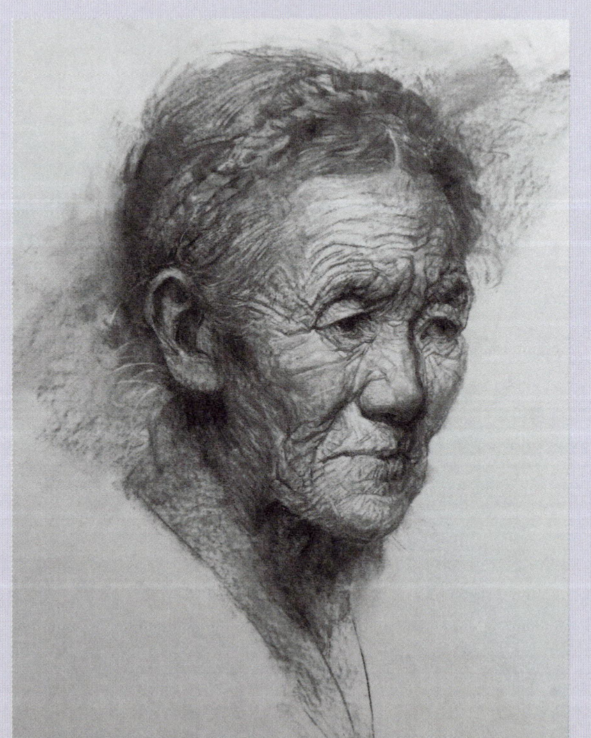

UNDERSTANDING WRINKLES

Wrinkles are one of the more obvious signs of aging. However, much of the time you can safely eliminate most of the wrinkles and instead concentrate on the lines, bones, and soft forms of the flesh beneath the surface. These subtler characteristics give the impression of age and an accurate likeness without having to painstakingly draw each wrinkle. Remember that wrinkles are not actual lines on the face, but very delicate valleys of shadow that can be seen only from a few feet (a meter) away.

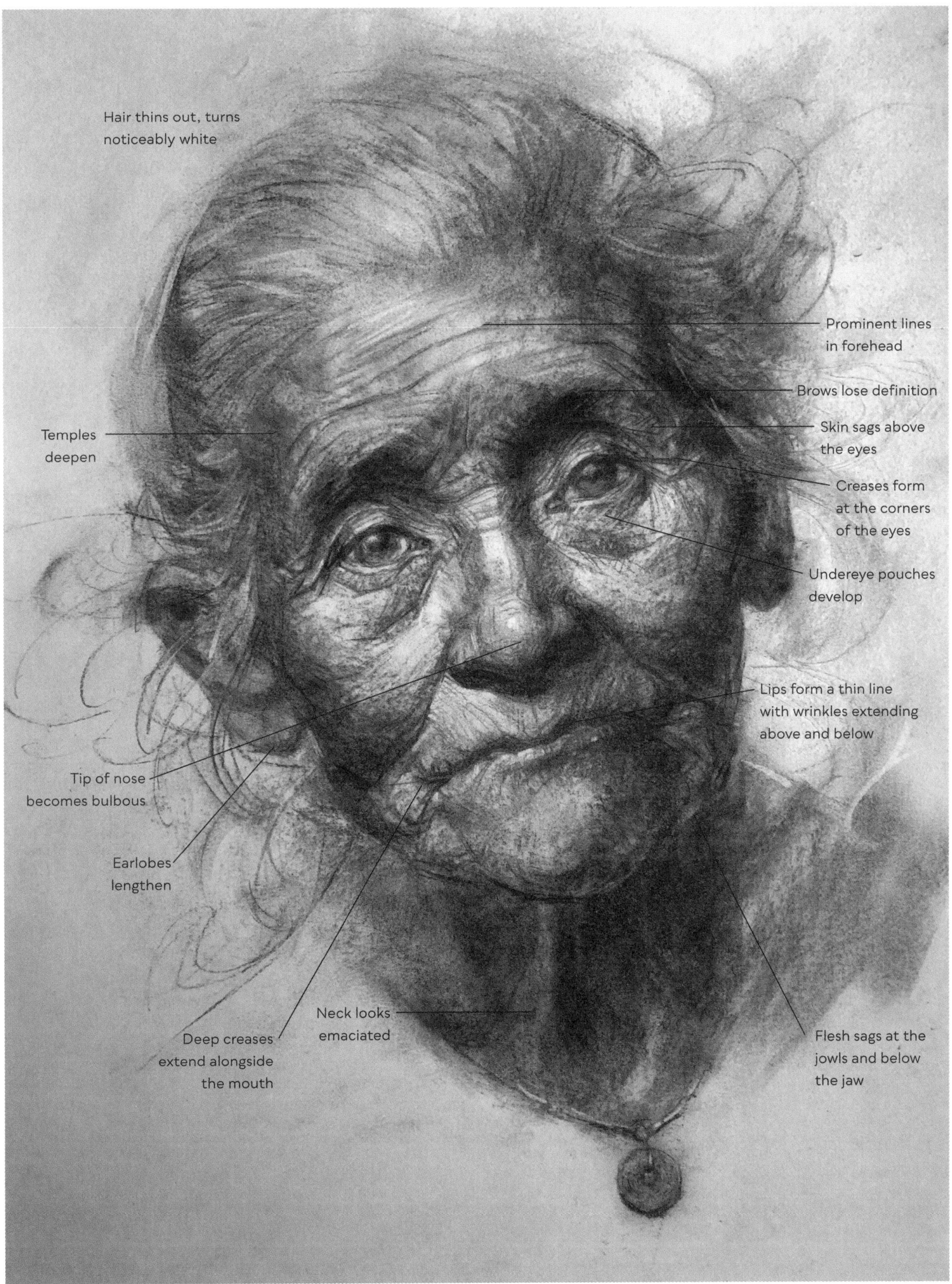

Hair thins out, turns noticeably white
Temples deepen
Tip of nose becomes bulbous
Earlobes lengthen
Deep creases extend alongside the mouth
Neck looks emaciated
Prominent lines in forehead
Brows lose definition
Skin sags above the eyes
Creases form at the corners of the eyes
Undereye pouches develop
Lips form a thin line with wrinkles extending above and below
Flesh sags at the jowls and below the jaw

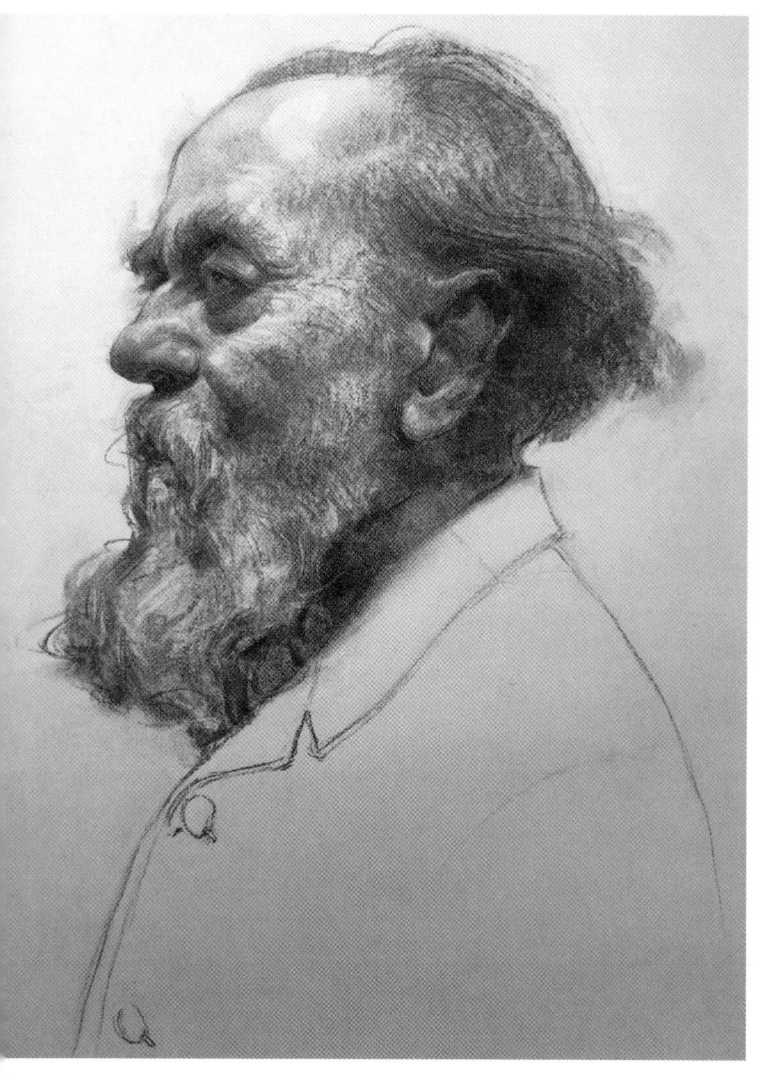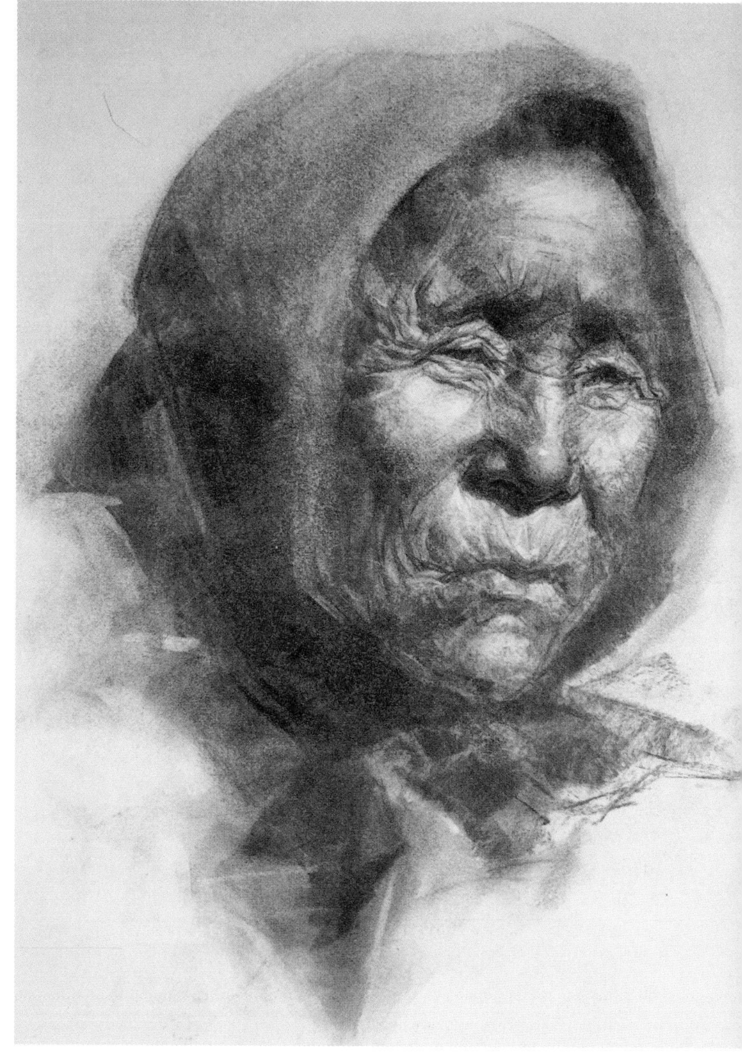

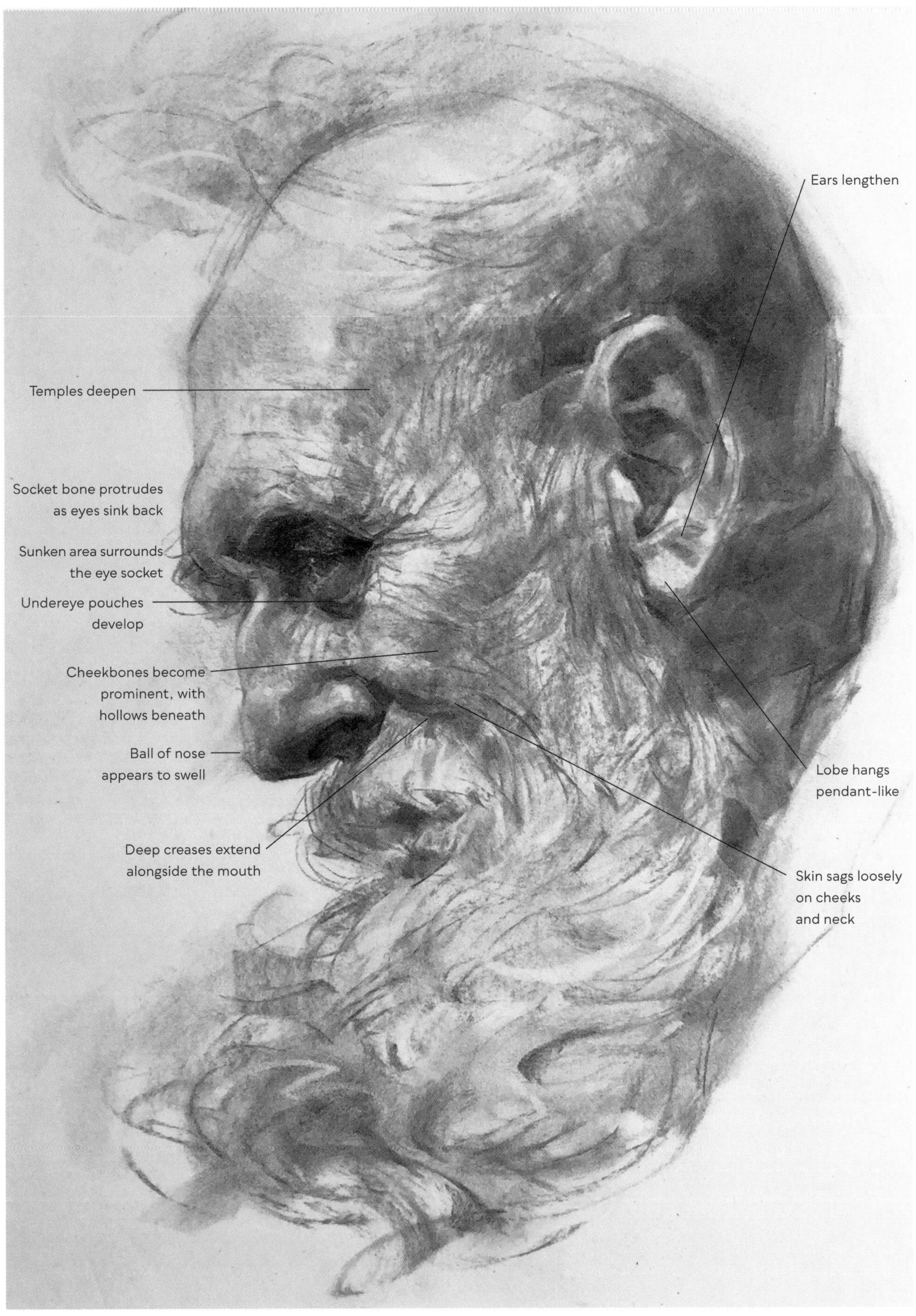

Ears lengthen
Temples deepen
Socket bone protrudes as eyes sink back
Sunken area surrounds the eye socket
Undereye pouches develop
Cheekbones become prominent, with hollows beneath
Ball of nose appears to swell
Deep creases extend alongside the mouth
Lobe hangs pendant-like
Skin sags loosely on cheeks and neck

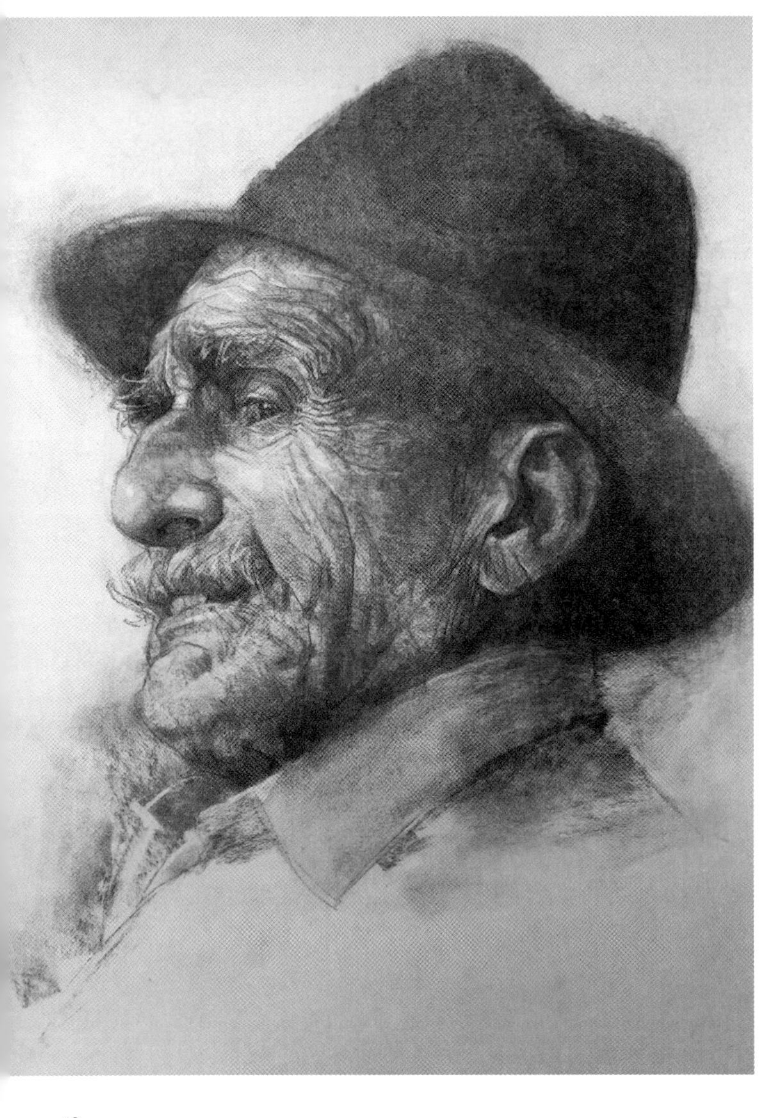
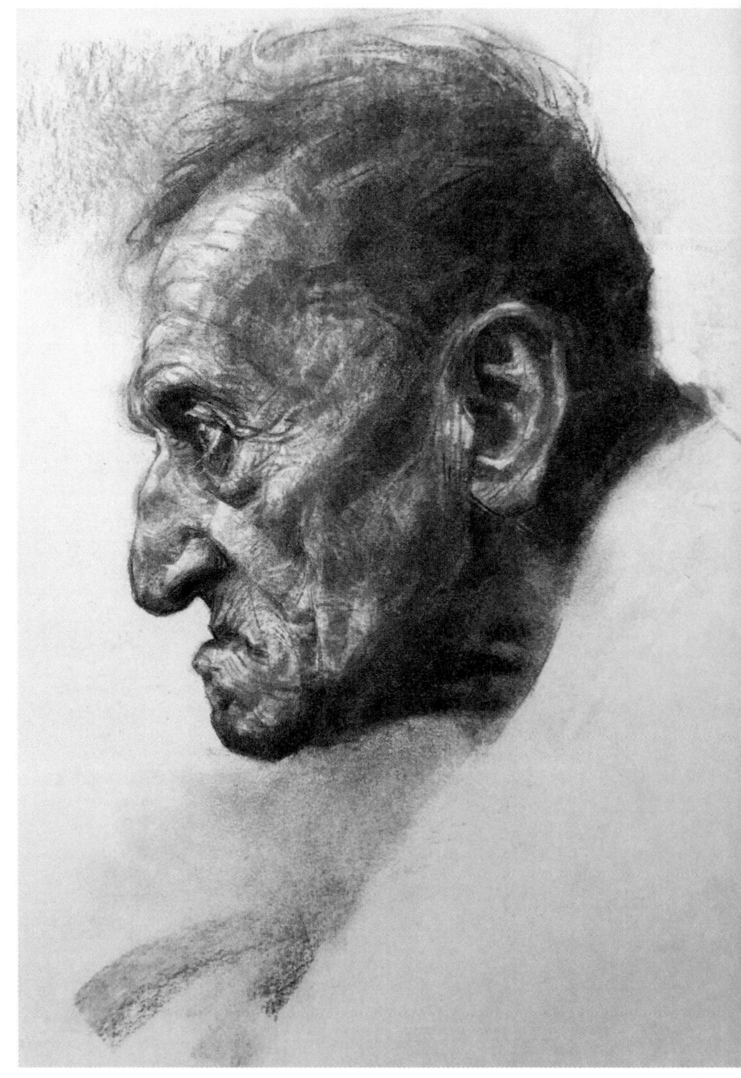

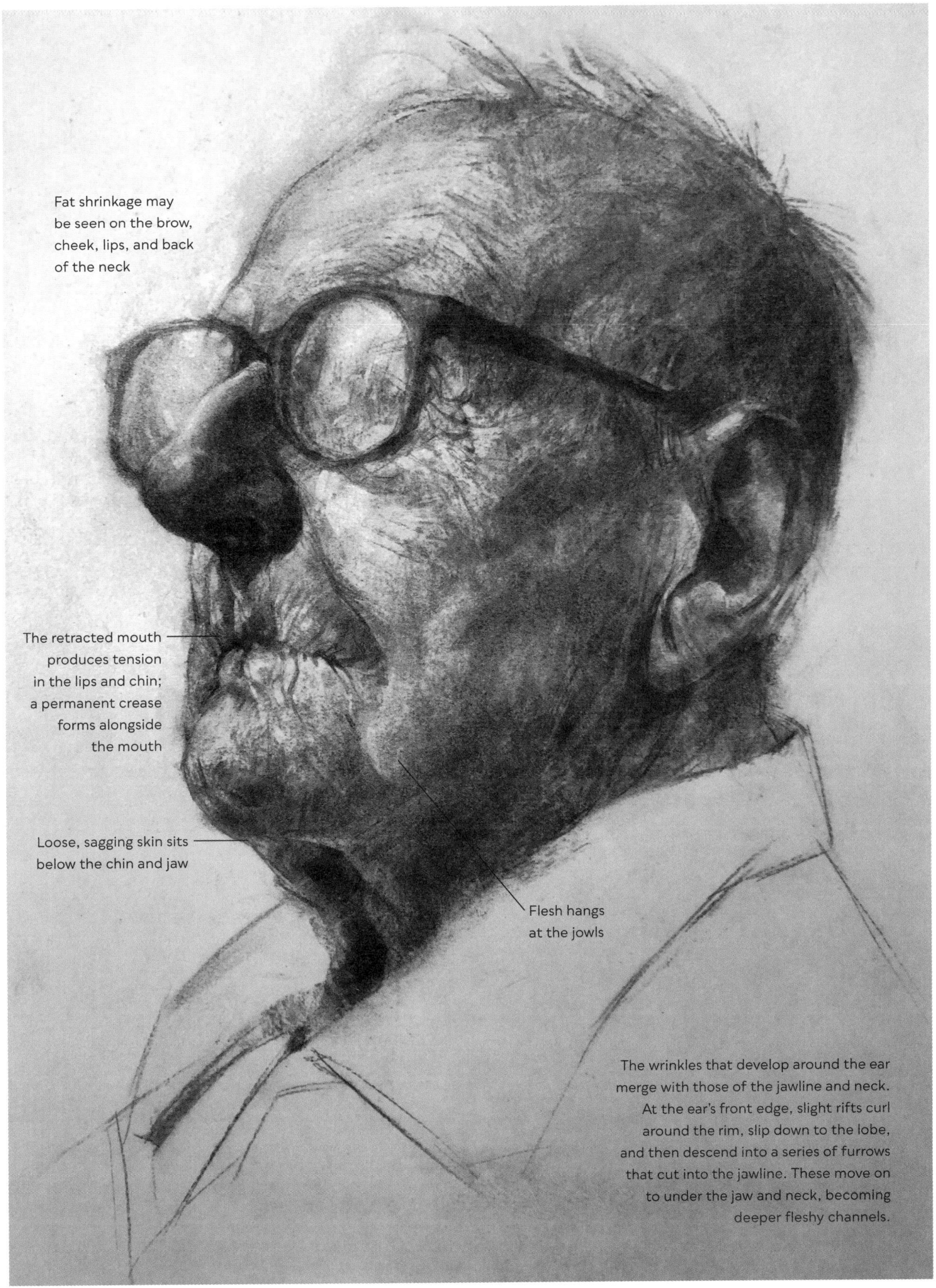

Fat shrinkage may be seen on the brow, cheek, lips, and back of the neck
The retracted mouth produces tension in the lips and chin; a permanent crease forms alongside the mouth
Loose, sagging skin sits below the chin and jaw
Flesh hangs at the jowls
The wrinkles that develop around the ear merge with those of the jawline and neck. At the ear's front edge, slight rifts curl around the rim, slip down to the lobe, and then descend into a series of furrows that cut into the jawline. These move on to under the jaw and neck, becoming deeper fleshy channels.

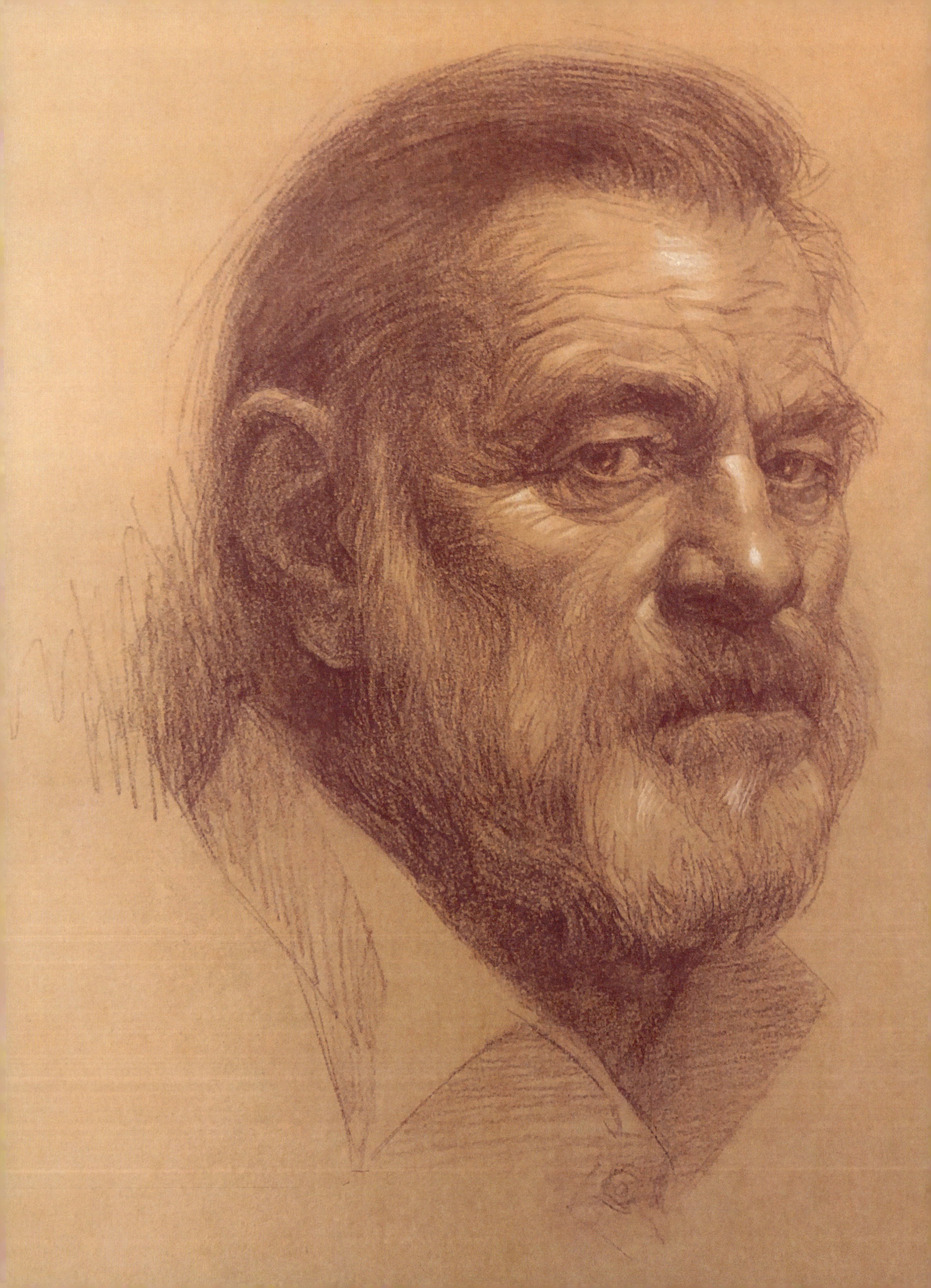

7

ALTERNATE APPROACHES

STARTING WITH A CREATIVE BACKGROUND

In this approach, charcoal is applied to white paper to establish a toned surface, and then a portrait emerges through manipulation and lifting to create value and highlights.

The background can play an important role in the visual statement of a drawing. A background can give artwork a soft, calm look, or liven a piece with an energetic, striking approach. Incorporating a creative background in your artwork shouldn't take the focus away from the subject. Concentrate on the lights and darks of the subject when selecting a background treatment. If the subject is very light on one side, a dark tone behind will show the contours more clearly. Use the background to show off the contrast and enhance your work, not compete with it.

Paper texture and abstract backgrounds can help convey feeling in artwork, acting as an indirect expression of the artist's emotion. There's no formula for achieving creative backgrounds. Use your imagination, and explore different papers, mark making, and techniques to discover what inspires you and captures the emotion of the portrait.

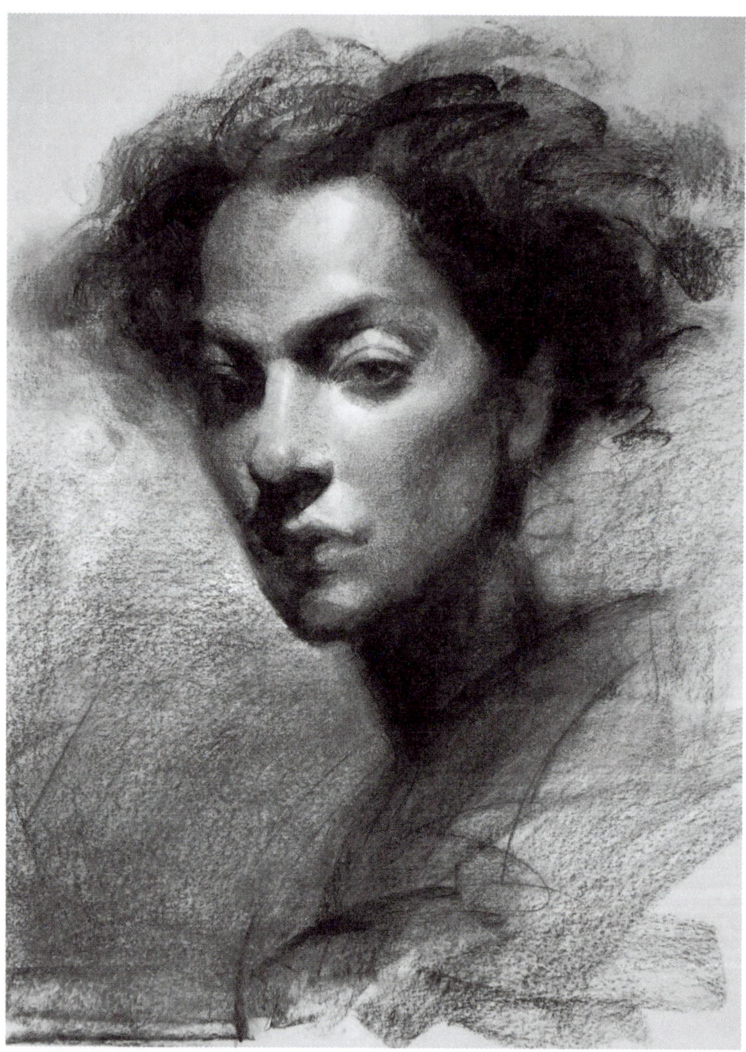

◀ Creative backgrounds can lend a painterly appearance to the drawing and bring more expression to the portrait.

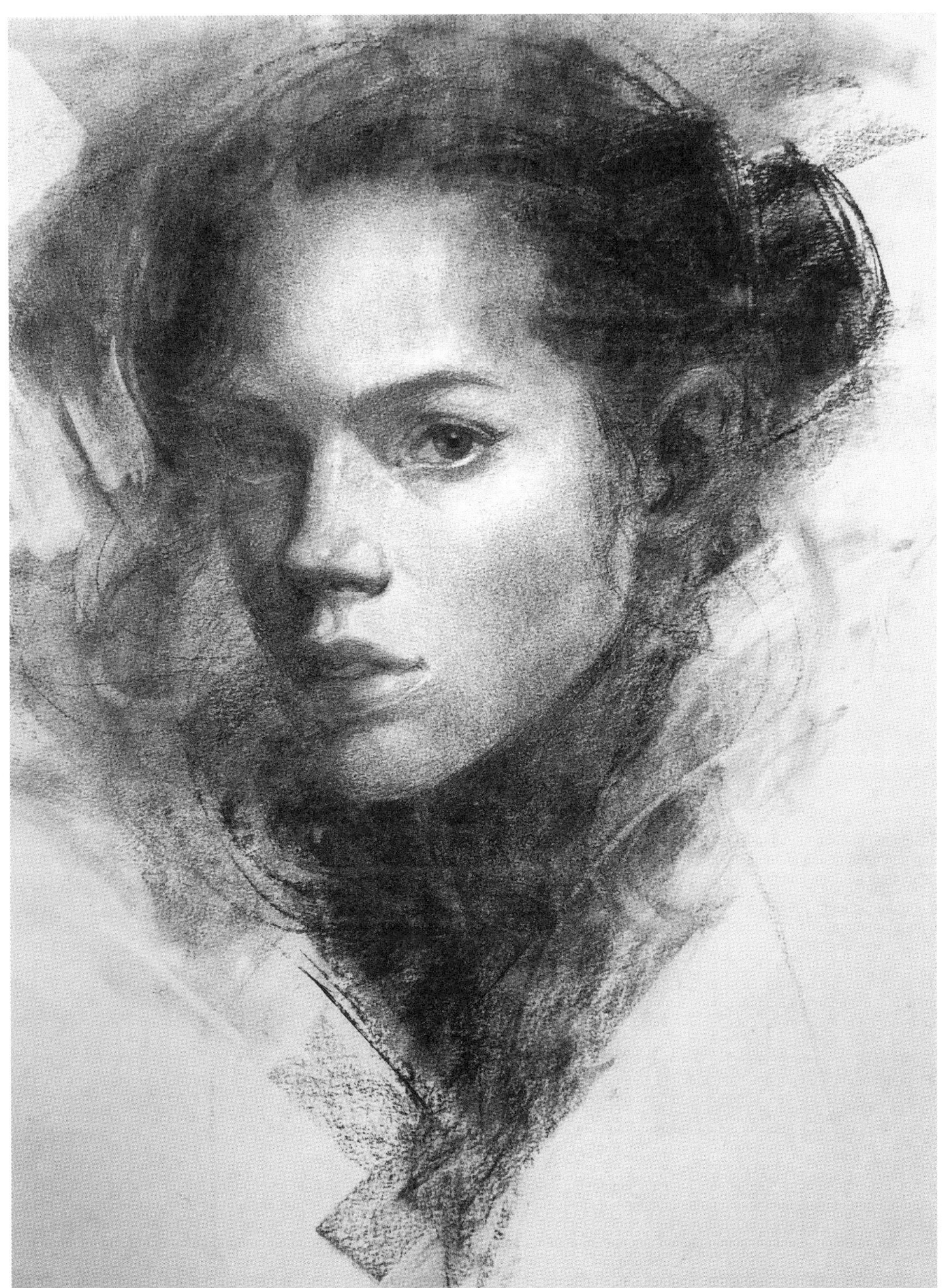

▲ You can use a variety of interesting materials to draw creative backgrounds. I usually smear the shading with my fingers and then use either a kneaded eraser or clean fingers to remove tone in areas of delicate shading. I like to add heavy, raw strokes and make broad sweeps with the sides of the charcoal to add life. Sometimes I rub my fingers over the zigzag shading to blend it.

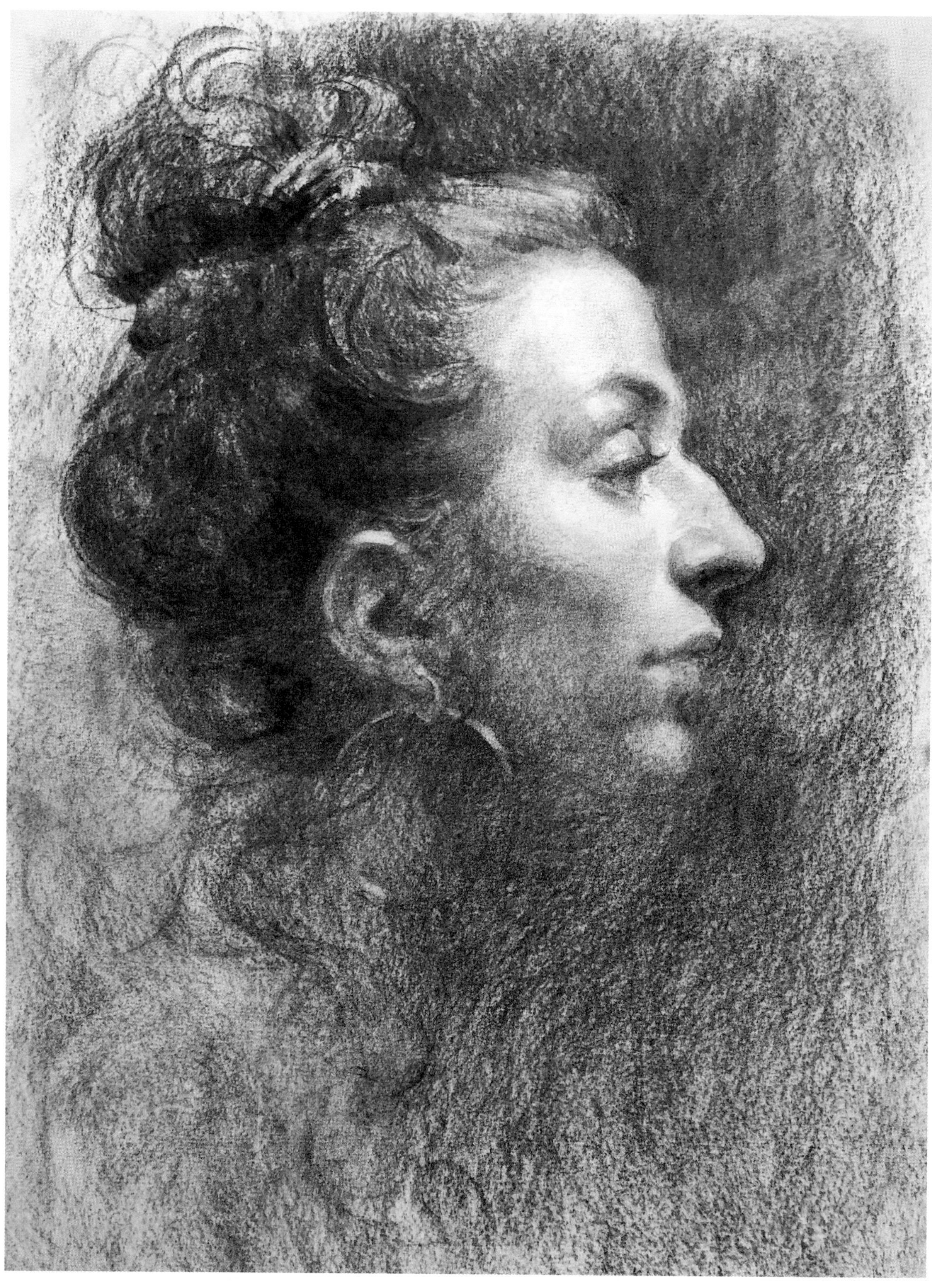

▲ The front side of the face is facing the light. By applying a dark tone to the background of this area, the contours of the face are more visible. Similarly, the back of the head is in shadow. A lighter background tone against the dark hair helps define the shape and form and increases the contrast.

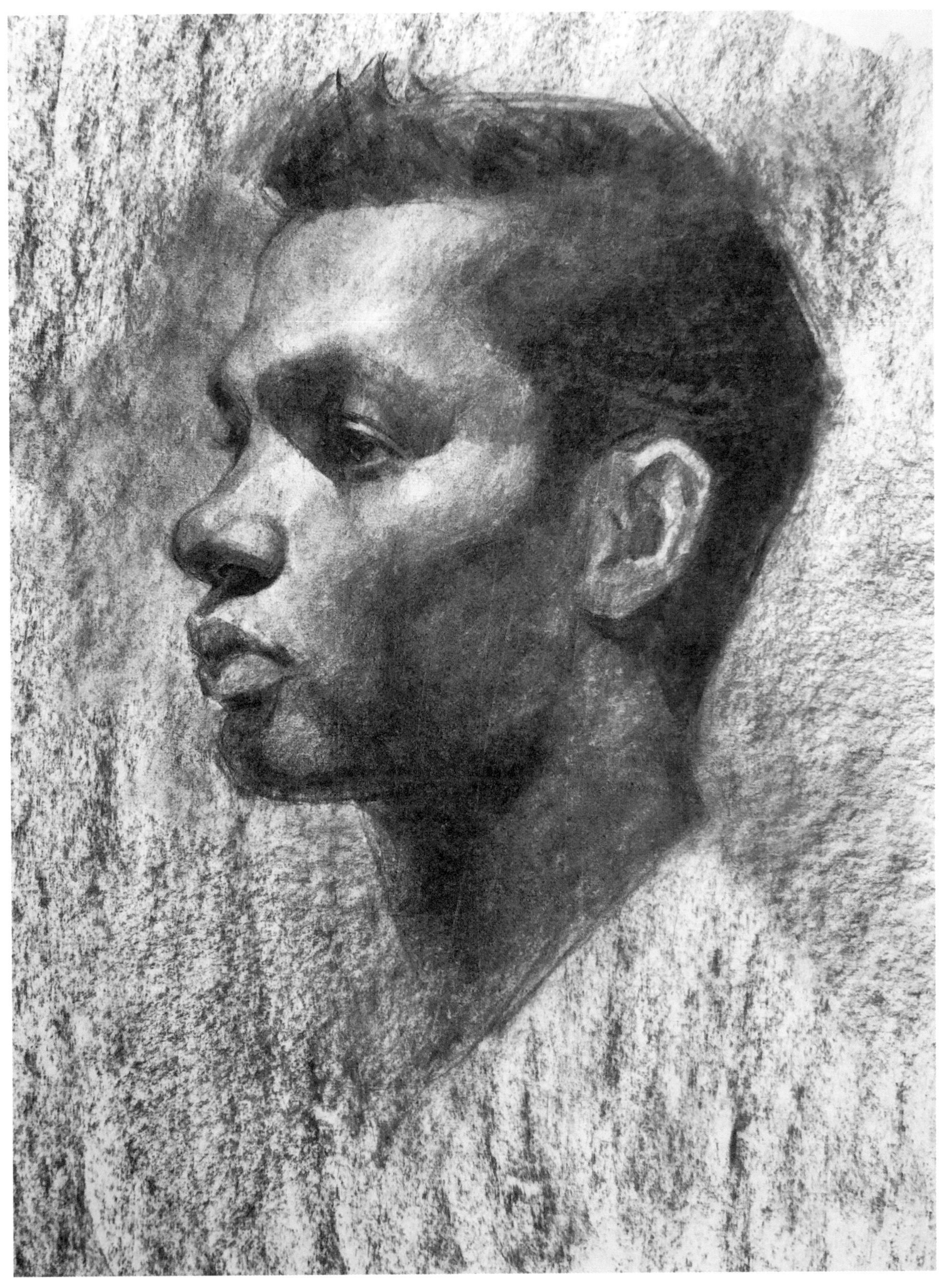

▲ I used the broad side of the vine charcoal for this bold, streaked background, which gives this portrait life and a rugged, masculine look.

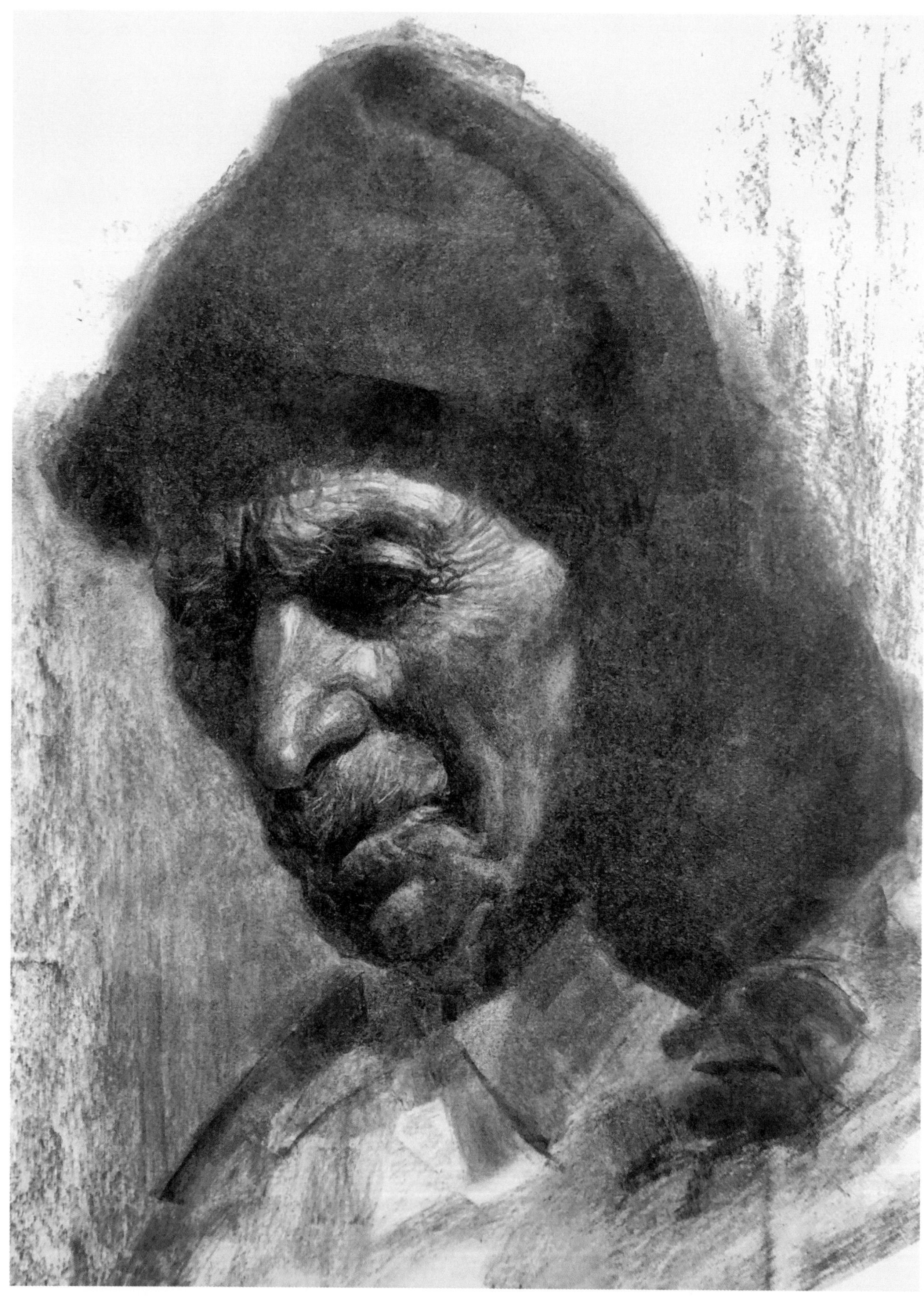

▲ For a background with more grain, cold-pressed illustration board is an interesting surface to use. Compressed charcoal on layout bond paper is also pleasing, resulting in a fair amount of texture while also blending nicely.

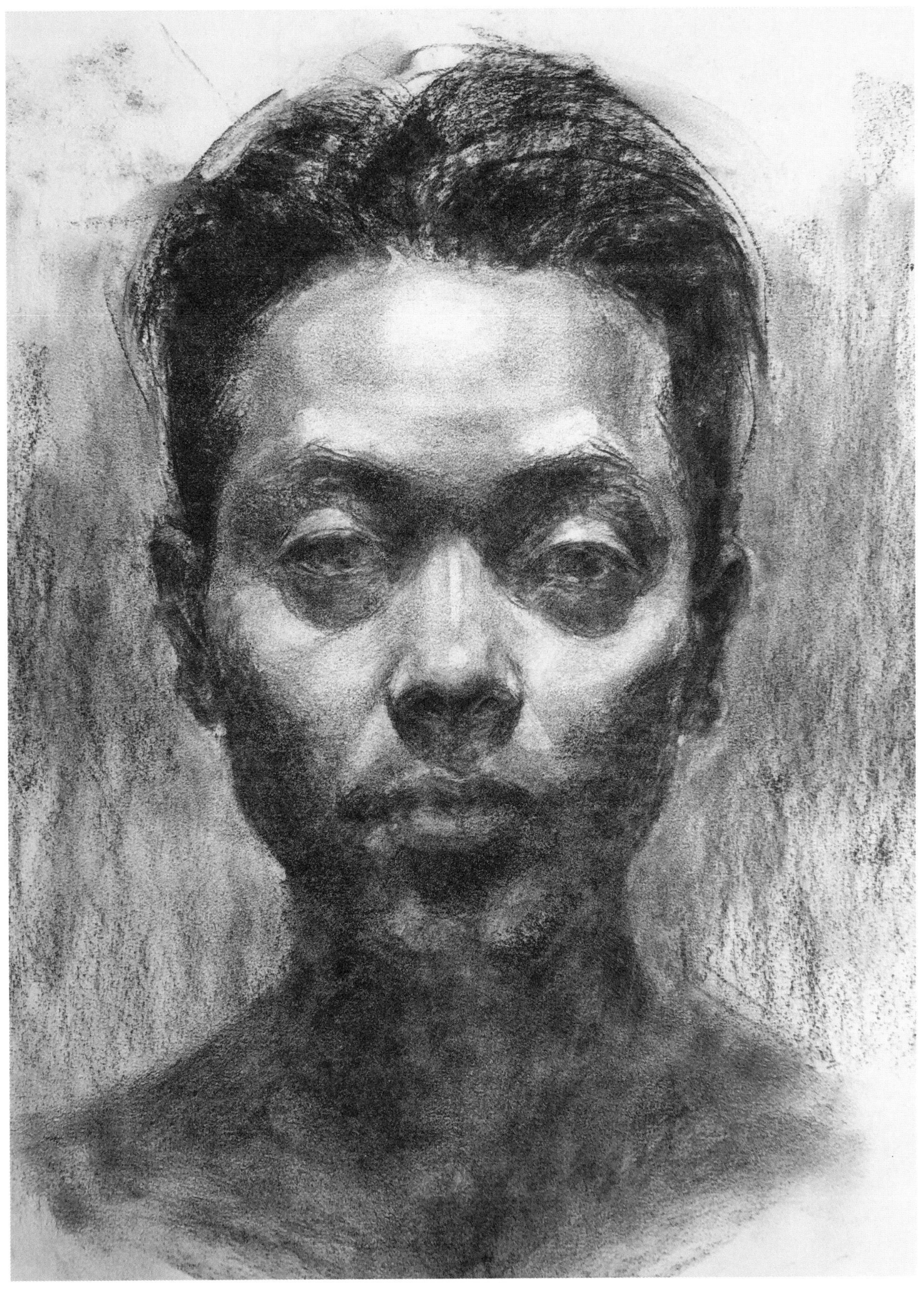

WORKING WITH TONED PAPERS

For colorful portrait work, I like to use pastel pencils on toned paper, with the addition of white pastel pencil for highlights.

Working on toned paper saves time because the artist shades the darks areas, applies white for highlights, and allows the paper to act as the midtone value. When artists draw on white paper, they mostly work from light to dark because the paper establishes one extreme of the value scale. When painting, however, the artist begins with a range of values and colors on the palette and makes light and dark marks simultaneously. Drawing on toned paper is a valuable bridge between these two approaches to rendering light and form. Experiment with different colors of toned papers, and have fun with the process!

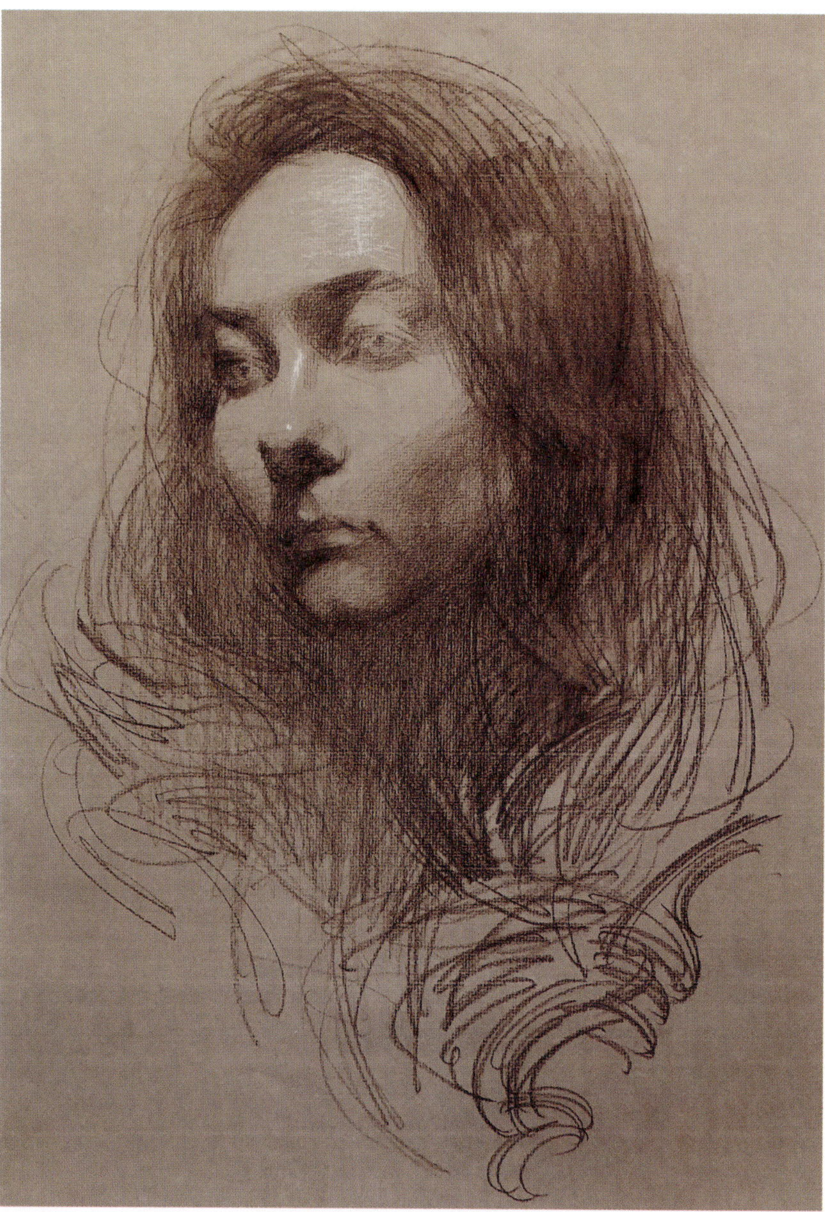

◄ *Mediums:*
CarbOthello pastel pencils in Caput Mortuum Red (#645) and Titanium White (#100) for highlights

Surface:
Strathmore 500 Series charcoal paper in Peachblow

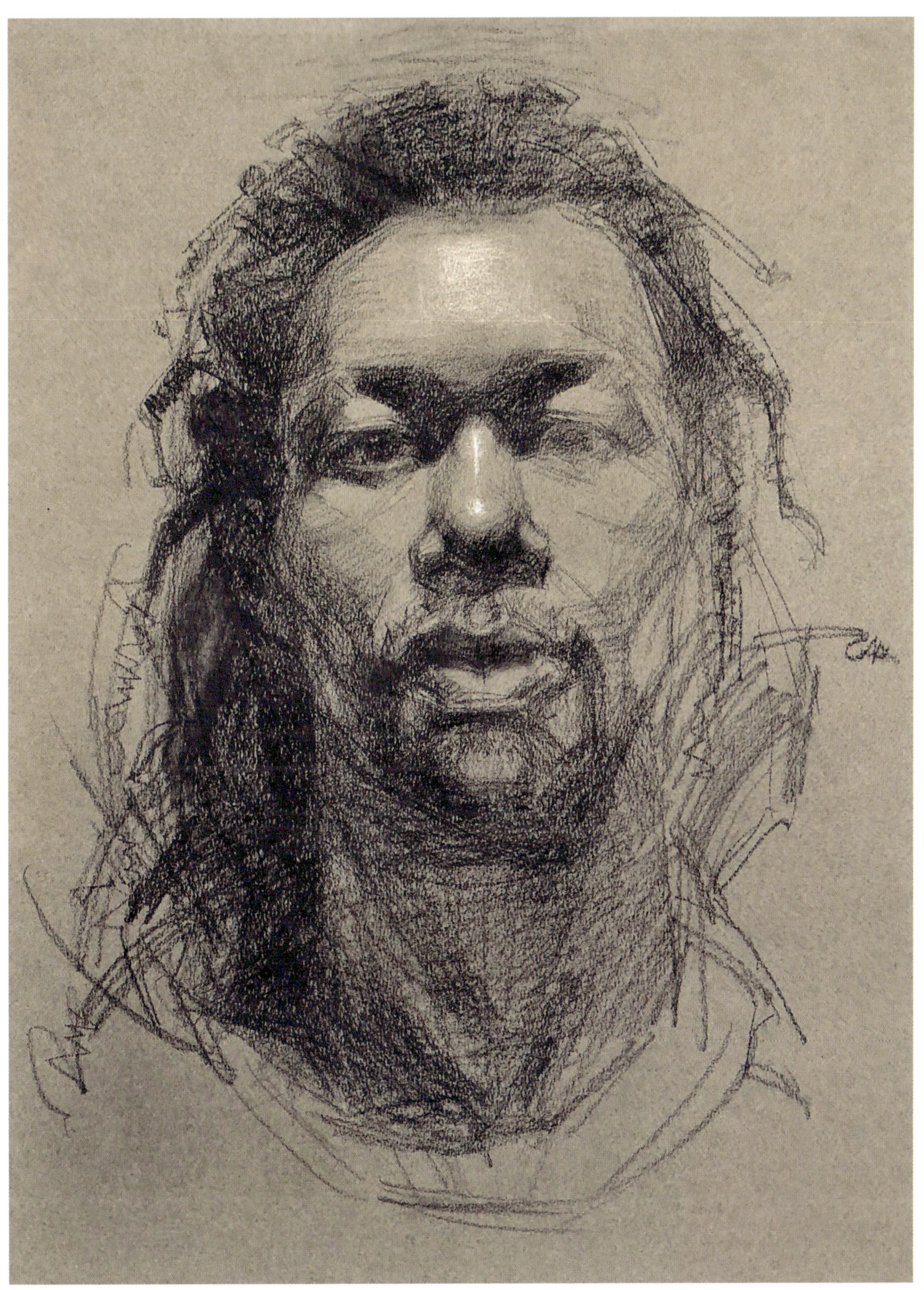

▲ *Mediums:* General's charcoal pencils in 2B, 4B, and 6B, and General's charcoal white pencil for highlights

Surface: Canson Mi-Teintes drawing paper in Felt Gray

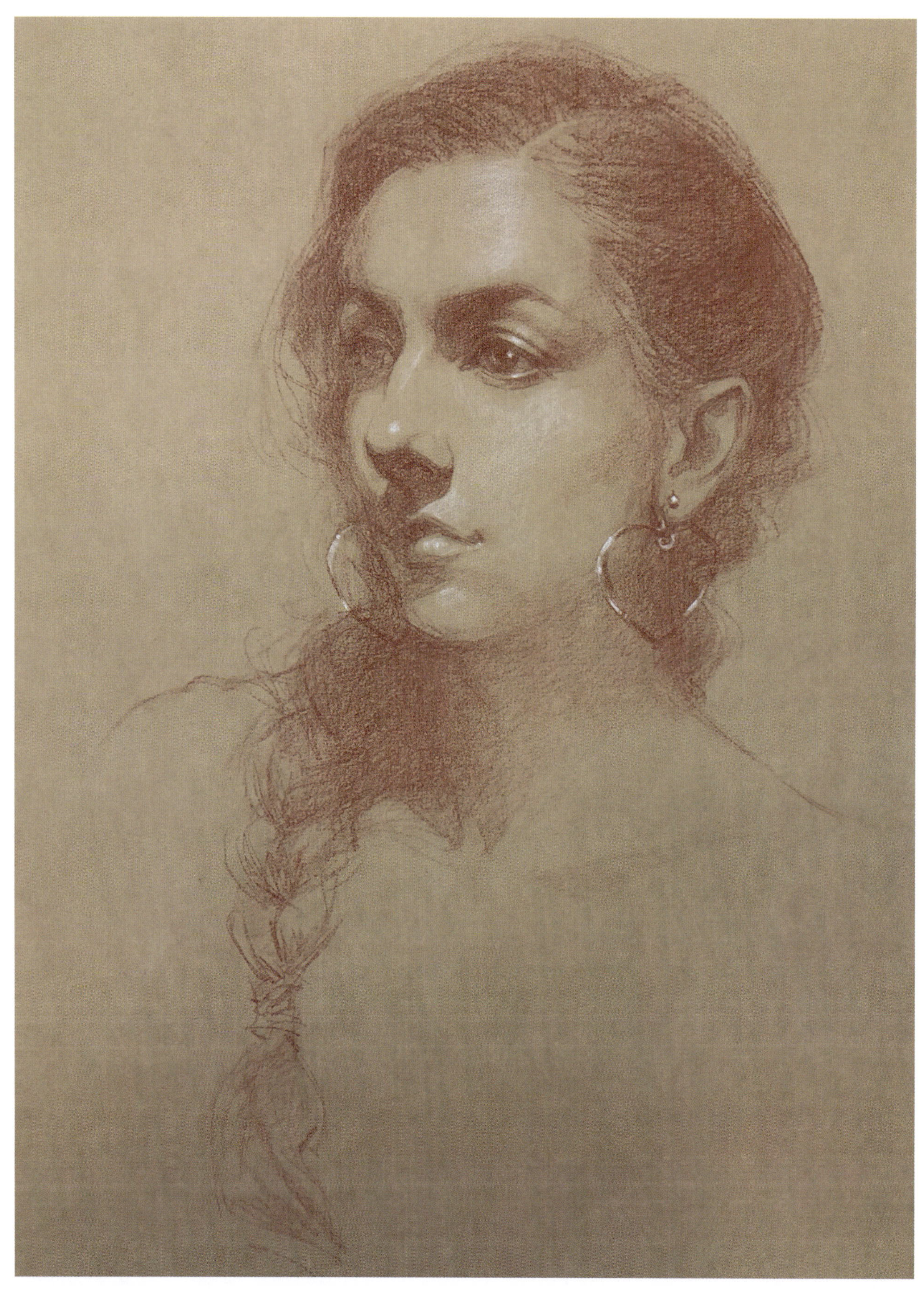

▲ *Mediums:* CarbOthello pastel pencils in English Red Deep (#655) and Titanium White (#100) for highlights
Surface: Strathmore 500 Series charcoal paper in Golden Brown

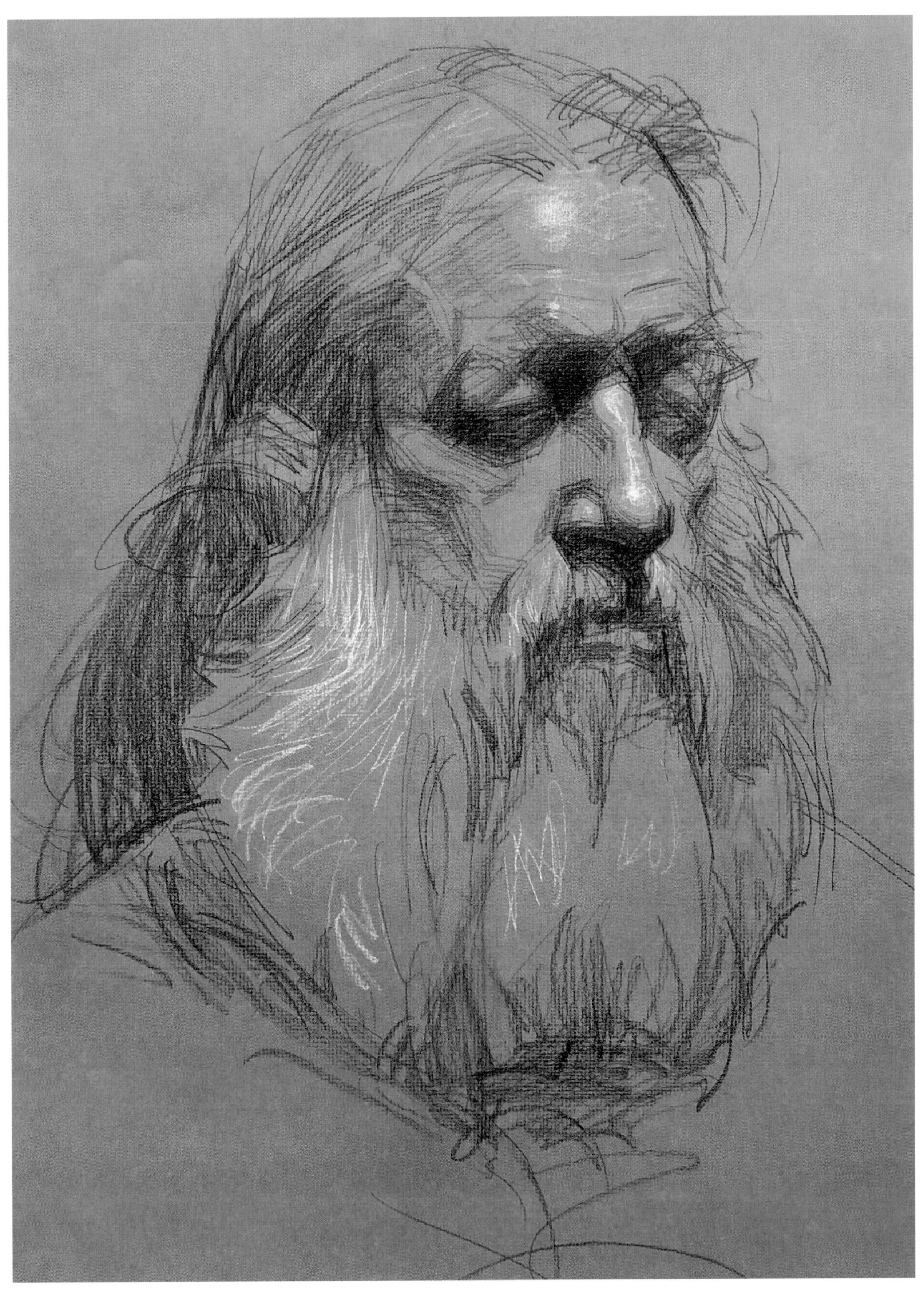

Mediums: Charcoal 6B pencil with CarbOthello pastel pencil in Titanium White (#100) for highlights

Surface: Strathmore 500 Series charcoal paper in Cadet Blue

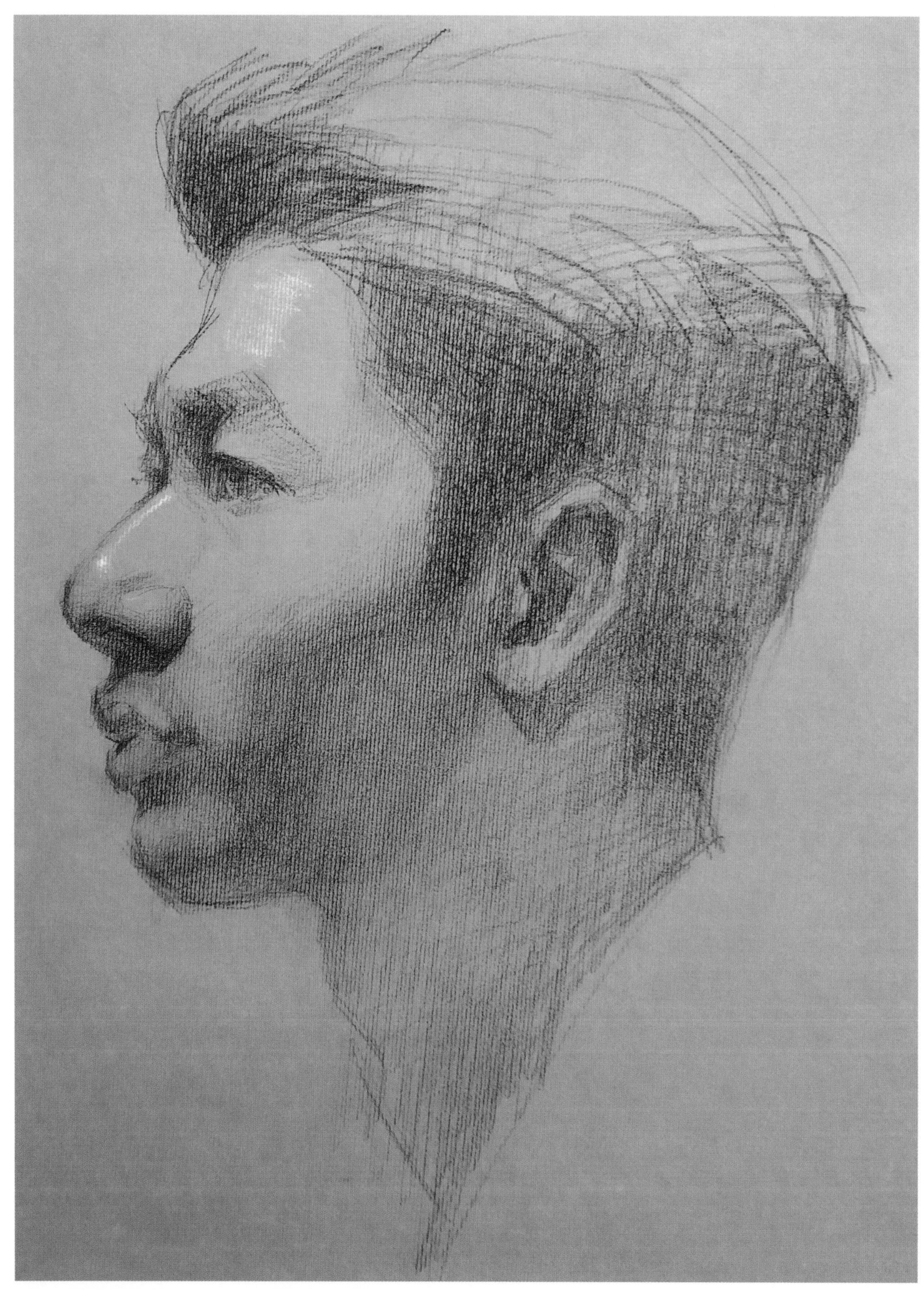

▲ **Mediums:** Charcoal 6B pencil with CarbOthello pastel pencil in Titanium White (#100) for highlights
Surface: Strathmore 500 Series charcoal paper in Storm Gray

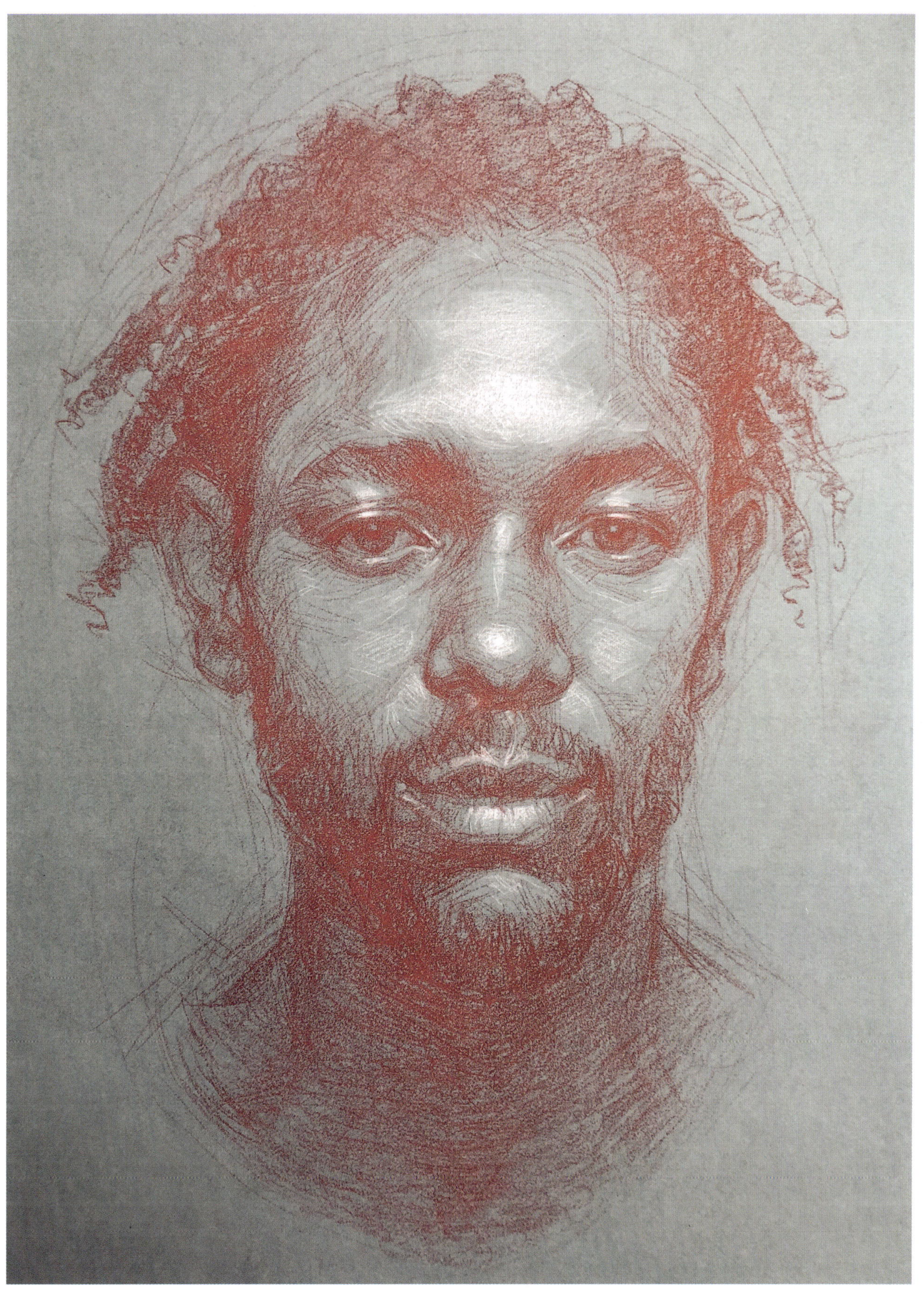

▲ *Mediums:* CarbOthello pastel pencils in Caput Mortuum Red (#645) and Titanium White (#100) for highlights

Surface: Strathmore 500 Series charcoal paper in Pottery Green

Developing a Portrait on Toned Paper

All objects have light, middle, and dark values when exposed to light. When an artist works on toned paper, the paper acts as the middle value. For this portrait of Emily on gray-toned charcoal paper, I used a sanguine pastel pencil for the dark values and a white pastel pencil for the light values. At this stage of the drawing, I have blocked in the shapes of the head with a loose contour drawing and established the perspective and shapes of the facial features.

1 | Blocking-in builds the structure of the head. Start by darkening the shadow shapes. Avoid going too dark initially, so that you can refine the shadows as you work. Ignore details for now, and hatch all the dark areas at one time. Don't darken the light areas of the head; because the toned paper serves as the middle value, the paper automatically does much of the work for you.

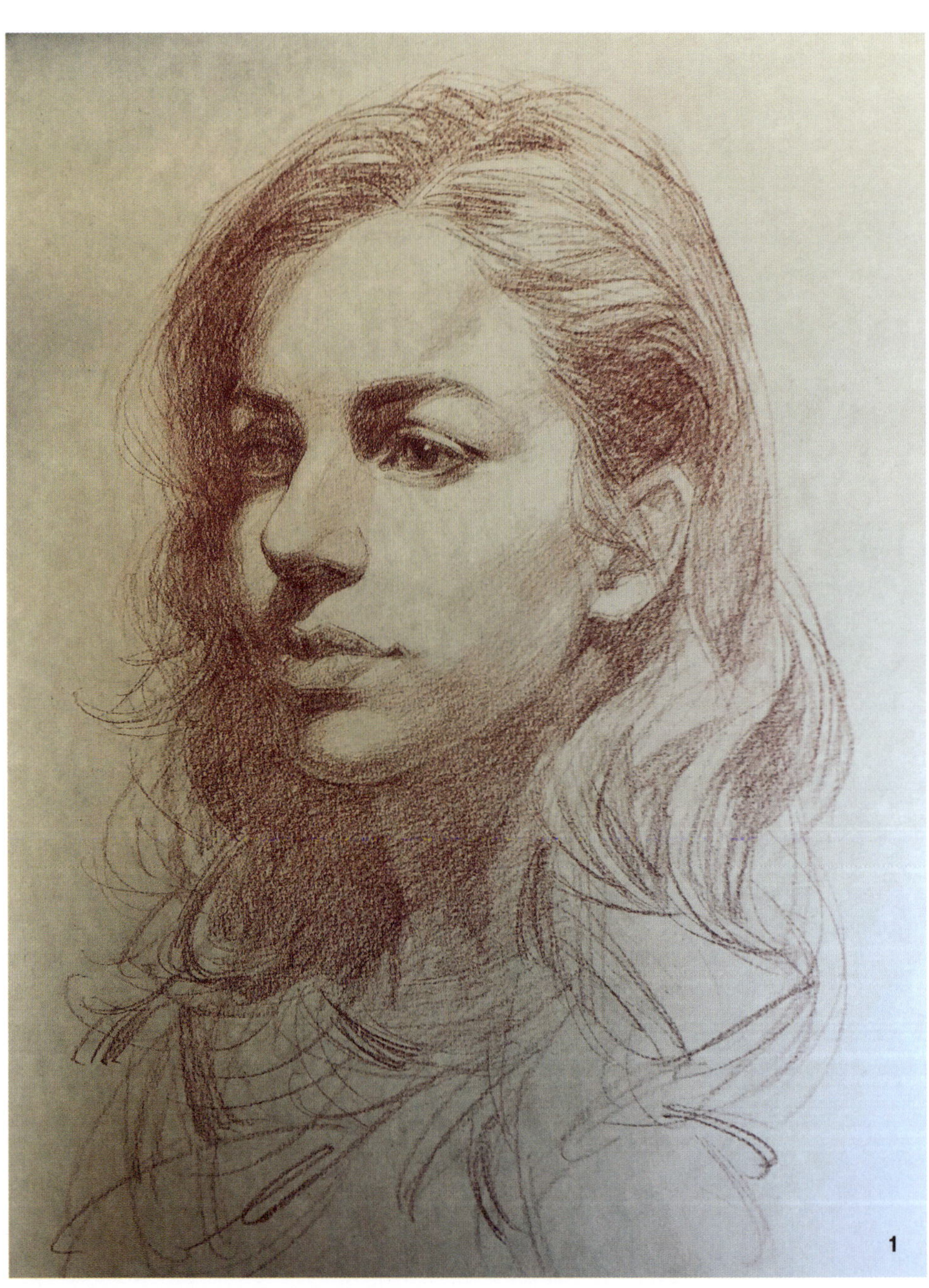

1

2 | Define the hair, and strengthen all the darks within the shadow planes of the face by applying more pressure with the pencils. At this stage, I also recommend revisiting the shadows of each feature, studying the distance between shapes for accuracy. For example, I add dark accents within the shadow triangular depression below the eyebrow. Add dark accents on the pupil and define the brow and outer corner of the lids.

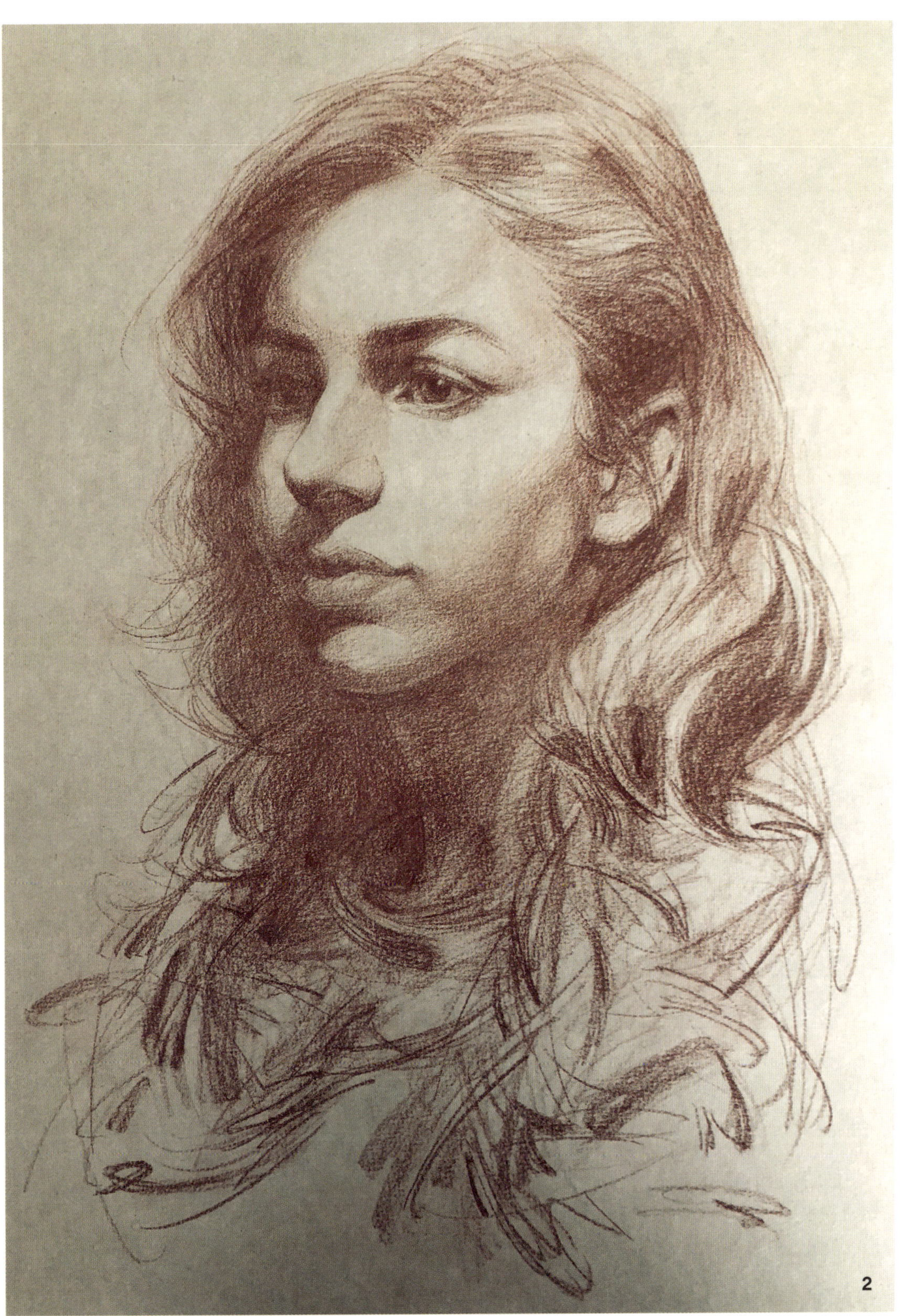

2

3 | To add dimension and truly make the portrait seem three-dimensional, use a white pastel pencil to add highlights to the forehead, the bridge of the nose, and the tip of the nose. Make sure the paper is completely clean before applying any highlights, using a kneaded eraser to clean the surface if needed. Blending the white and sanguine pencils together results in an unattractive pink tone. Fade the highlights into the midtones of the paper and then add highlights along the hard edges of the cast shadows: the bridge of the nose, under the left eyelid, on the lower lip, and on the chin.

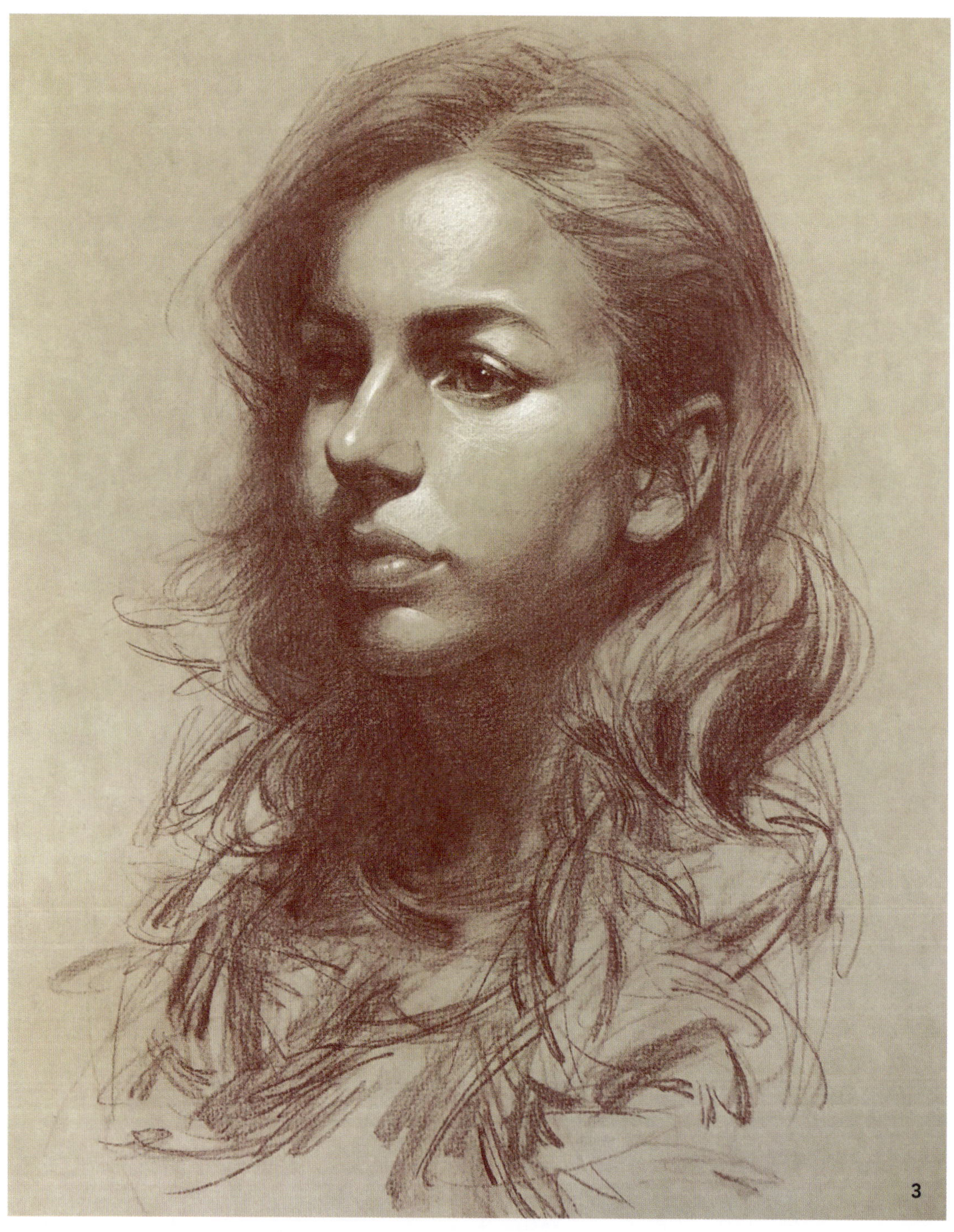

▲ *Mediums:* CarbOthello pastel pencils in Caput Mortuum Red (#645) and Titanium White (#100) for highlights
Surface: Strathmore 500 Series charcoal paper in Velvet Gray

Rendering a Full Beard on Toned Paper

The subject of this portrait, John, served in the U. S. Navy for a decade. He joined the Navy when he was young, hurt his spine during a dive, and has been paralyzed since. John is always very grateful, uttering many words of thanks and exuding positive energy, and I drew this portrait full of respect for him and his service. Remember that portraits are not just a study of the physicality but also the character of the sitter.

To create John's full beard, I worked on toned charcoal paper. The color of the blue toned paper is a perfect middle value between my white pastel pencil (light value) and black charcoal pencils (dark values).

For this portrait, I used the smooth back of the toned paper, because the textured side produces a checkerboard look that tends to overpower any subtlety in a drawing.

1 | Lightly block in the shapes and define the boundaries of the head, mustache, and beard on toned charcoal paper. I recommend a 2B charcoal pencil, as it's light in value and not too soft. Use light, scribbly lines to draw the contours of the facial hair shapes. The nose casts a shadow in the middle of the mustache, dividing the shape in half. For the beard, define the overall shape first, and then break it down into front, left, and right shapes.

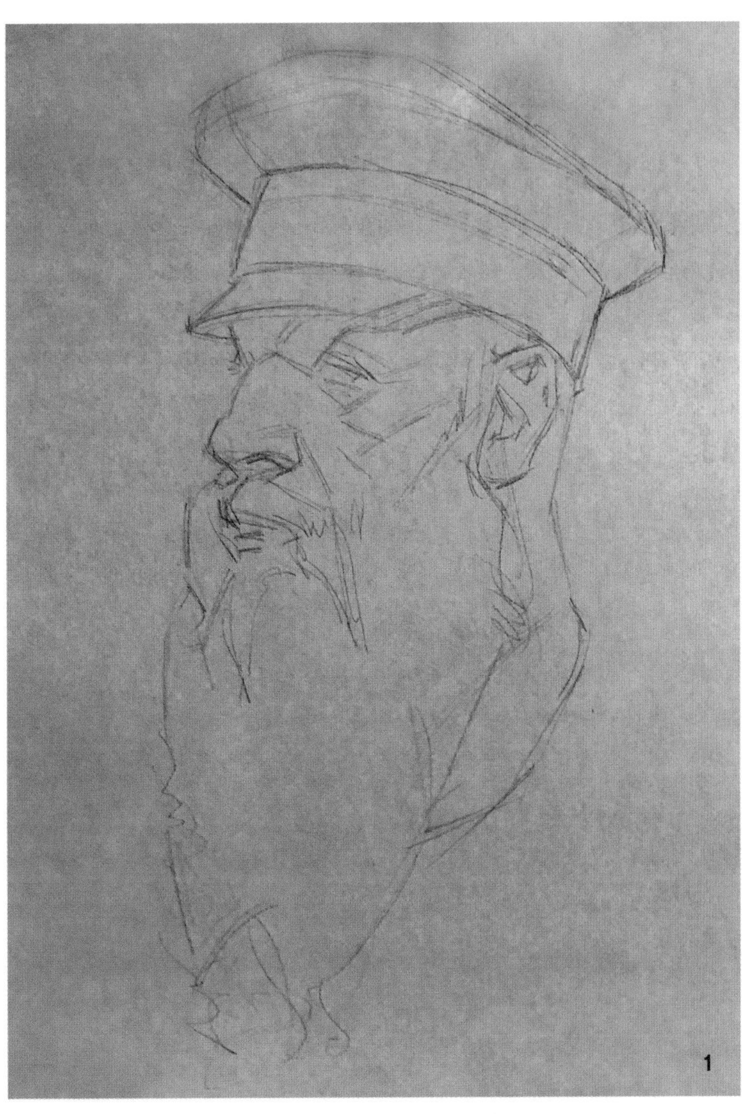

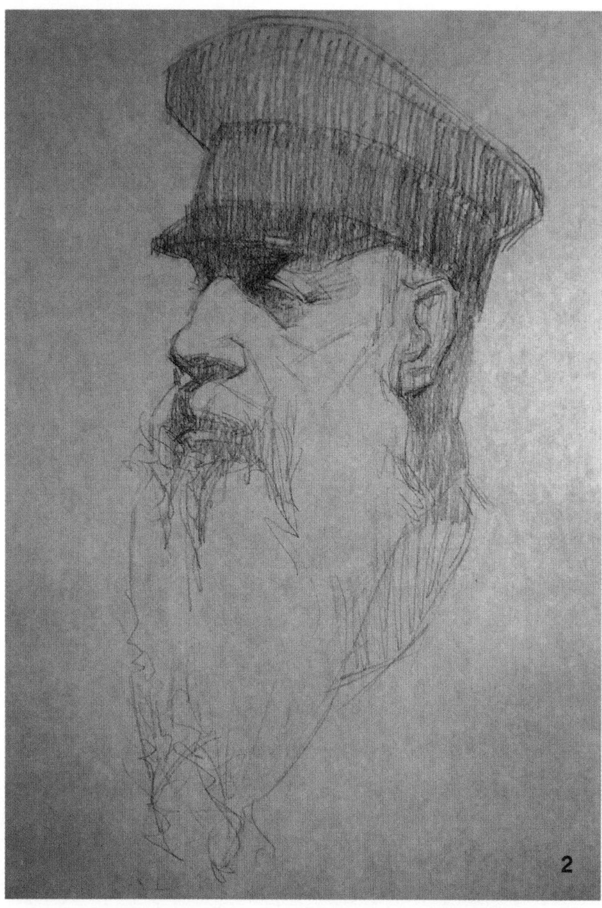

2 | Darken the darkest shadow shapes, such as the cast shadows of the nose and mustache, with a 4B charcoal pencil. Use the side of the pencil to apply soft pressure, as if you are caressing the drawing surface, creating soft edges. Hatch vertically to shade the shadow shapes. Defining the dark areas sets the foundation of the drawing and places the full white beard as the focal point.

3 | After building up the details in the face, harden all the edges of the cast shadows before moving on to the beard. Use a white pastel pencil to add highlights on the face and to begin developing the facial hair, letting the toned paper serve as the shadow. Remember, instead of simply drawing the mustache, think of it as a mass of planes of different values.

Study the shape, fullness, and hair growth pattern. Each shape should have areas of light and shadow. Use scribbling lines with the white pastel pencil for the light areas, and reserve the blue toned paper for the shadow areas. A great tip is to squint your eyes as you look at the subject. Squinting helps you easily see the light and dark areas so you can make adjustments as you work.

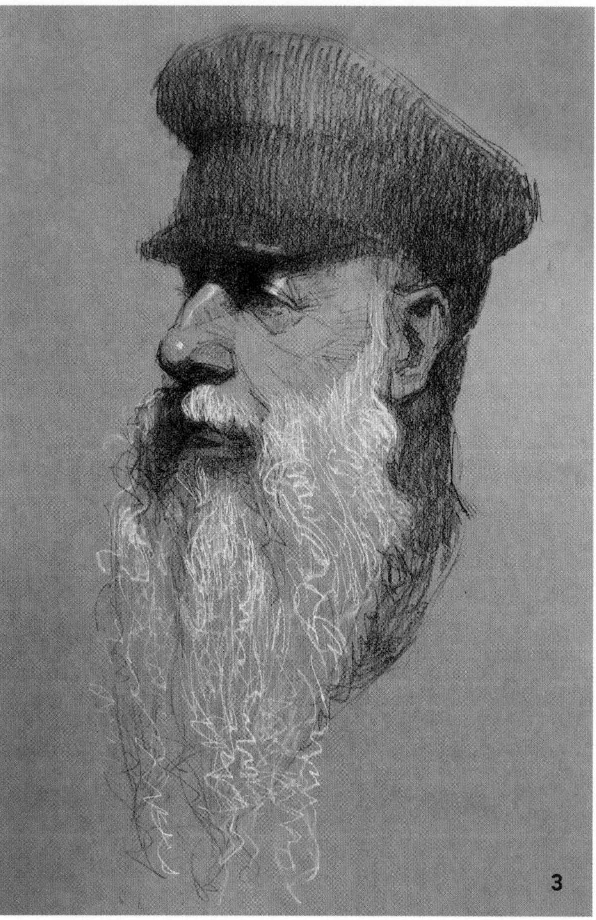

4 | Developing the fullness and depth of the beard requires layers of white pastel pencil. Continue applying scribbling lines to build the form of the facial hair, paying attention to the volume of the beard's shape as you work. The more pressure you apply with the white pencil, the brighter the value.

Try not to press too hard initially; instead, take your time to build up the brightest values, using a kneaded eraser to soften the edges and erase mistakes as needed. Use the direction of the light source on the forehead as a guide for placing the brightest highlights on the facial hair.

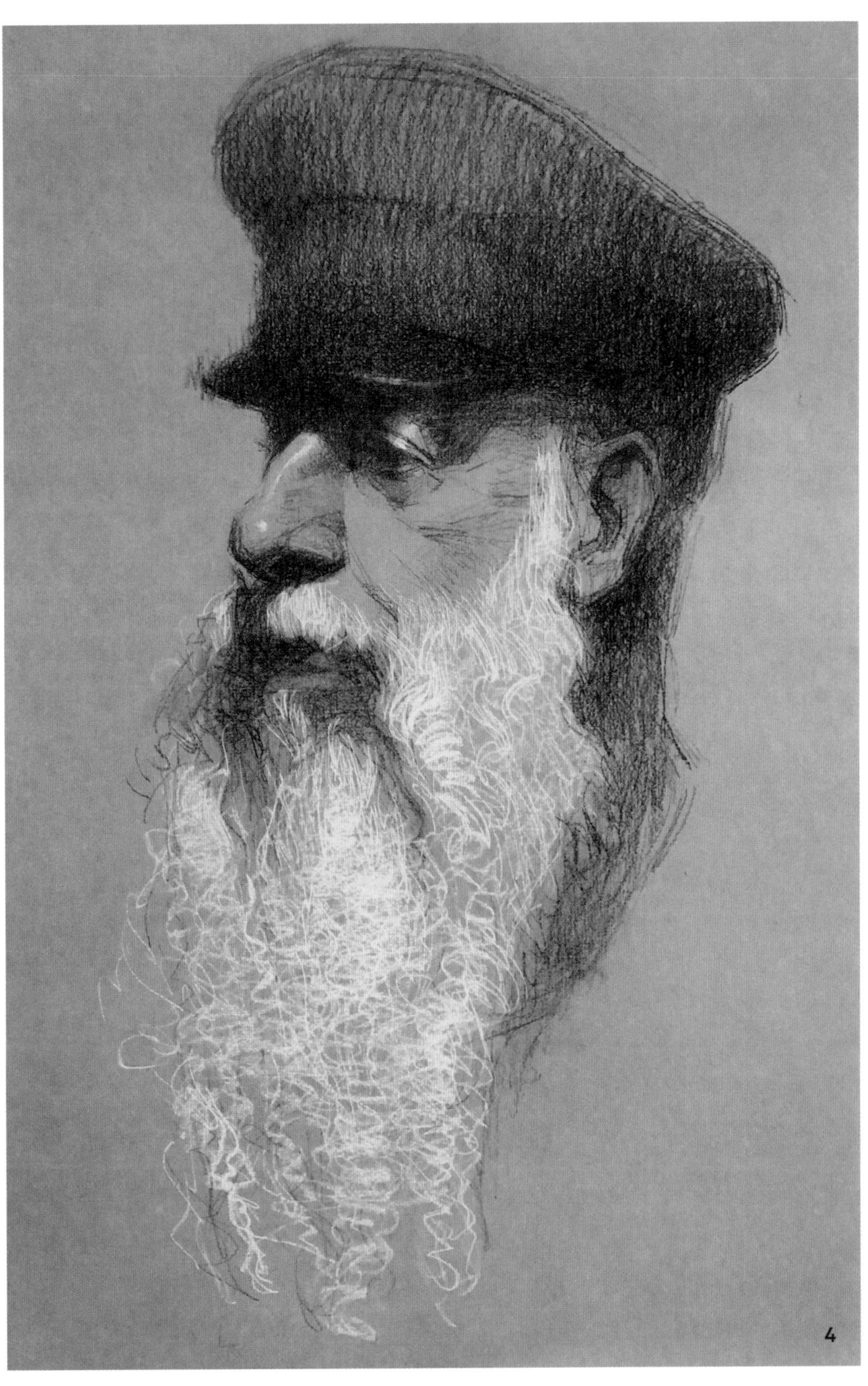

4

5 | Try to avoid being overly meticulous as you develop the details. Observe your drawing with squinted eyes, feel the rhythms in the details, and then render them with a variety of strokes to bring the work to life. Keep the outer contours of the facial hair soft and out of focus, as though there's no definable edge. This technique, called *sfumato*, which is Italian for "smoke-like," is common in painting. Artists use this technique to soften the transition between values or colors and mimic an out-of-focus plane.

Reinforce the shadow areas, making some darker and some lighter. Examine the drawing as a whole to determine whether anything is missing or whether there are unnecessary details. If needed, add more volume to the beard, using a 2B pencil to darken the shadow value on the bottom plane.

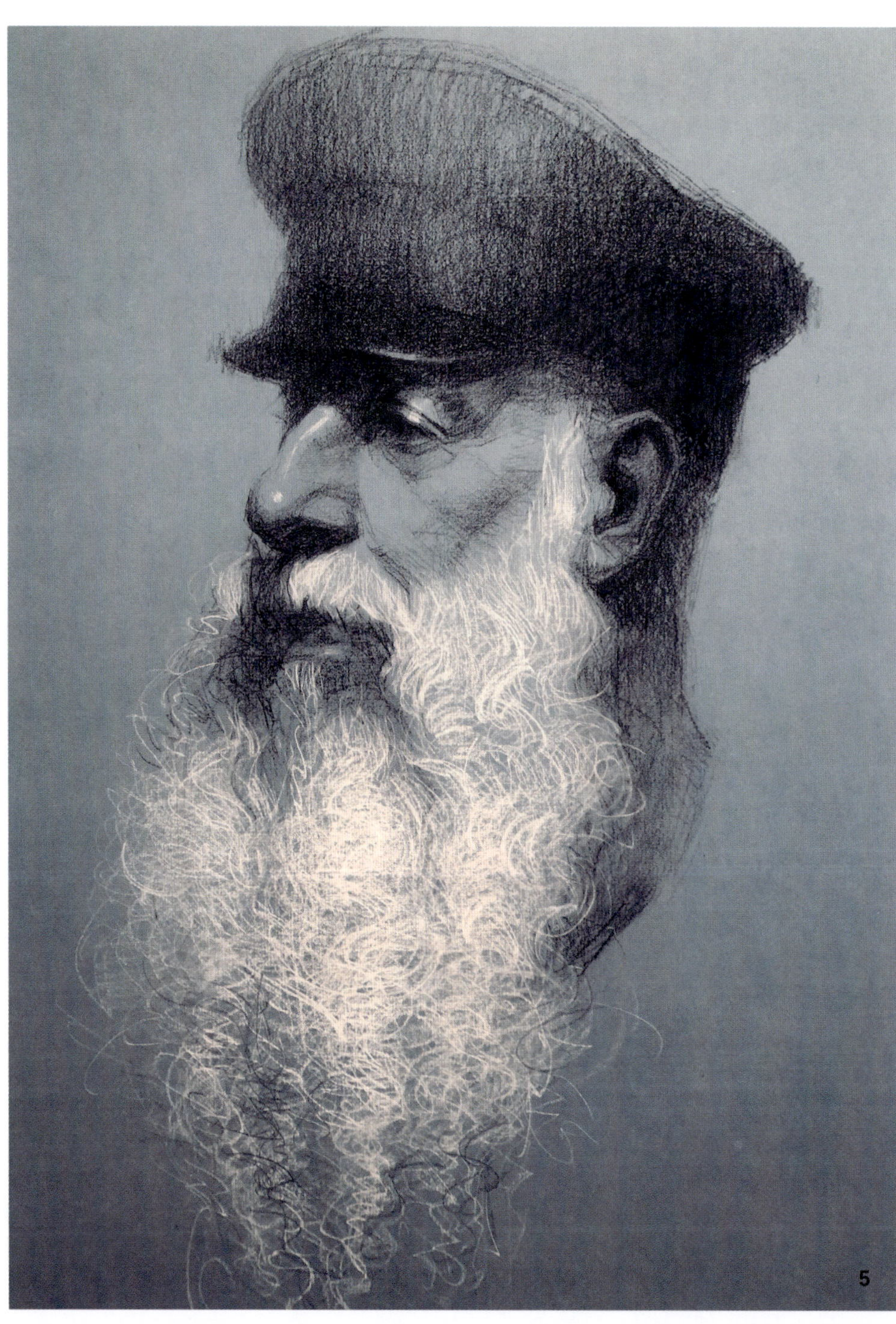

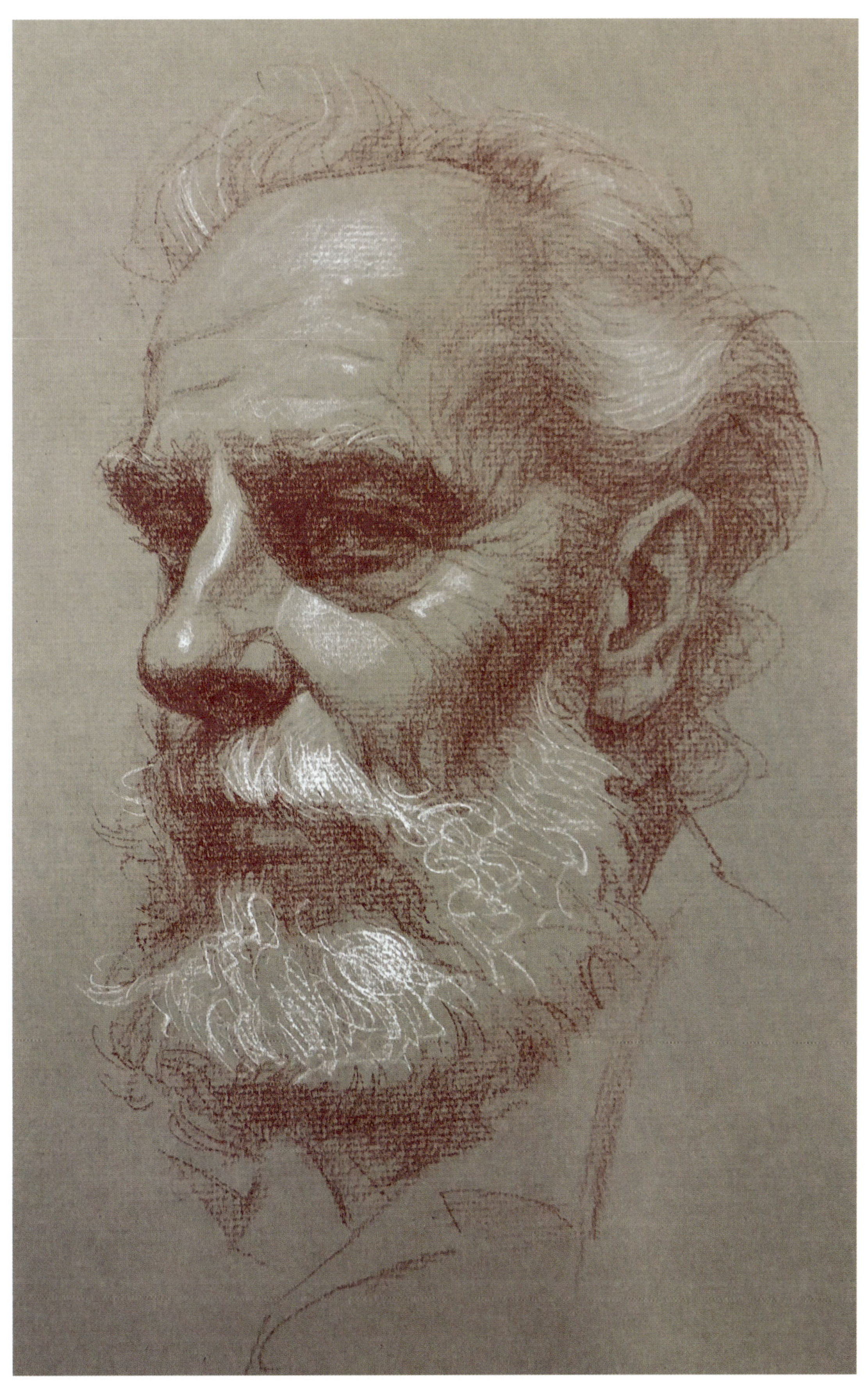

▲ **Mediums:** CarbOthello pastel pencils in English Red Deep (#655) and Titanium White (#100) for highlights

Surface: Strathmore 500 Series charcoal paper in Velvet Gray

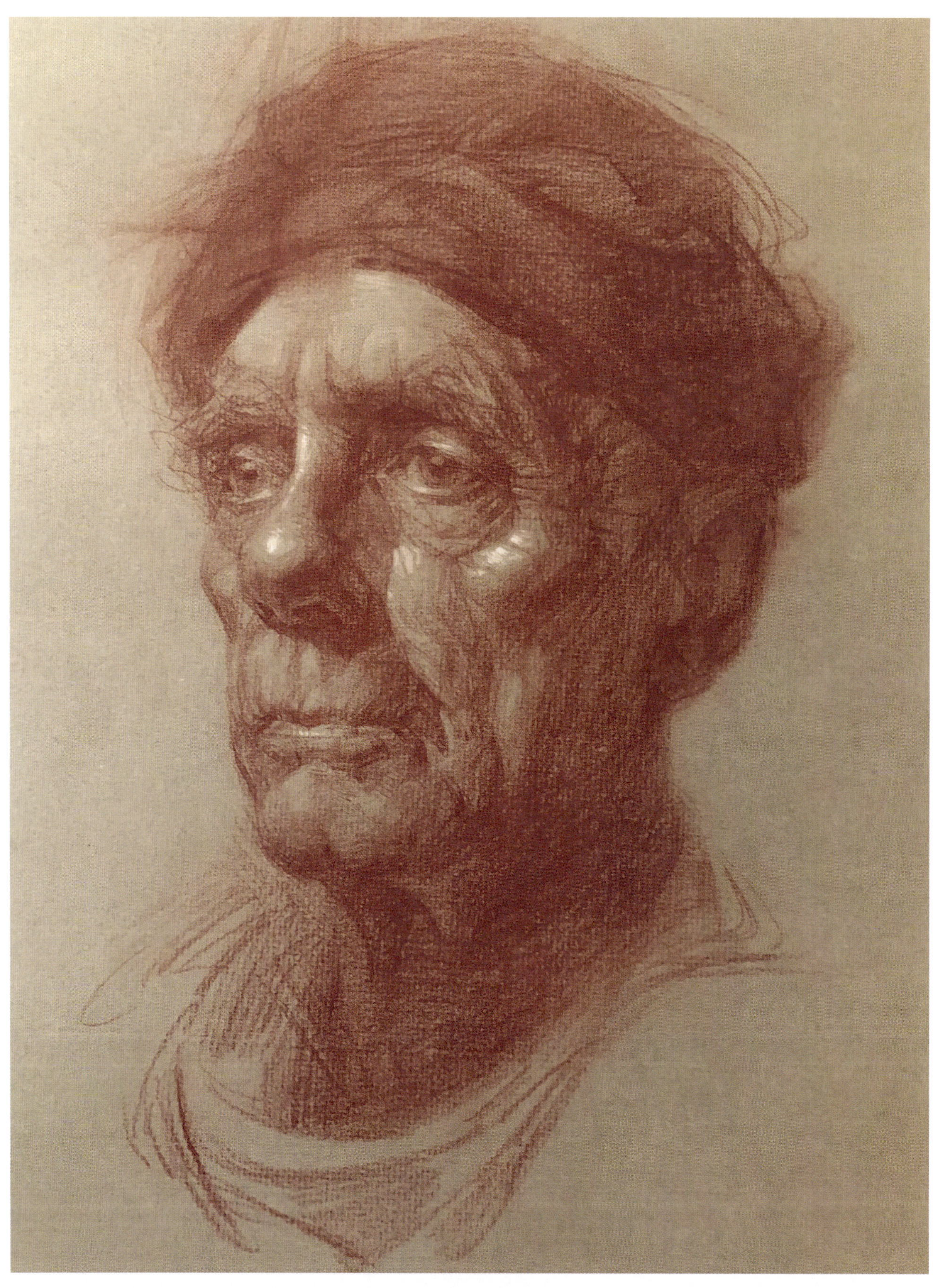

▲ *Mediums:* CarbOthello pastel pencils in Caput Mortuum Red (#645) with Titanium White (#100) for the highlights

Surface: Strathmore 500 Series charcoal paper in Golden Brown

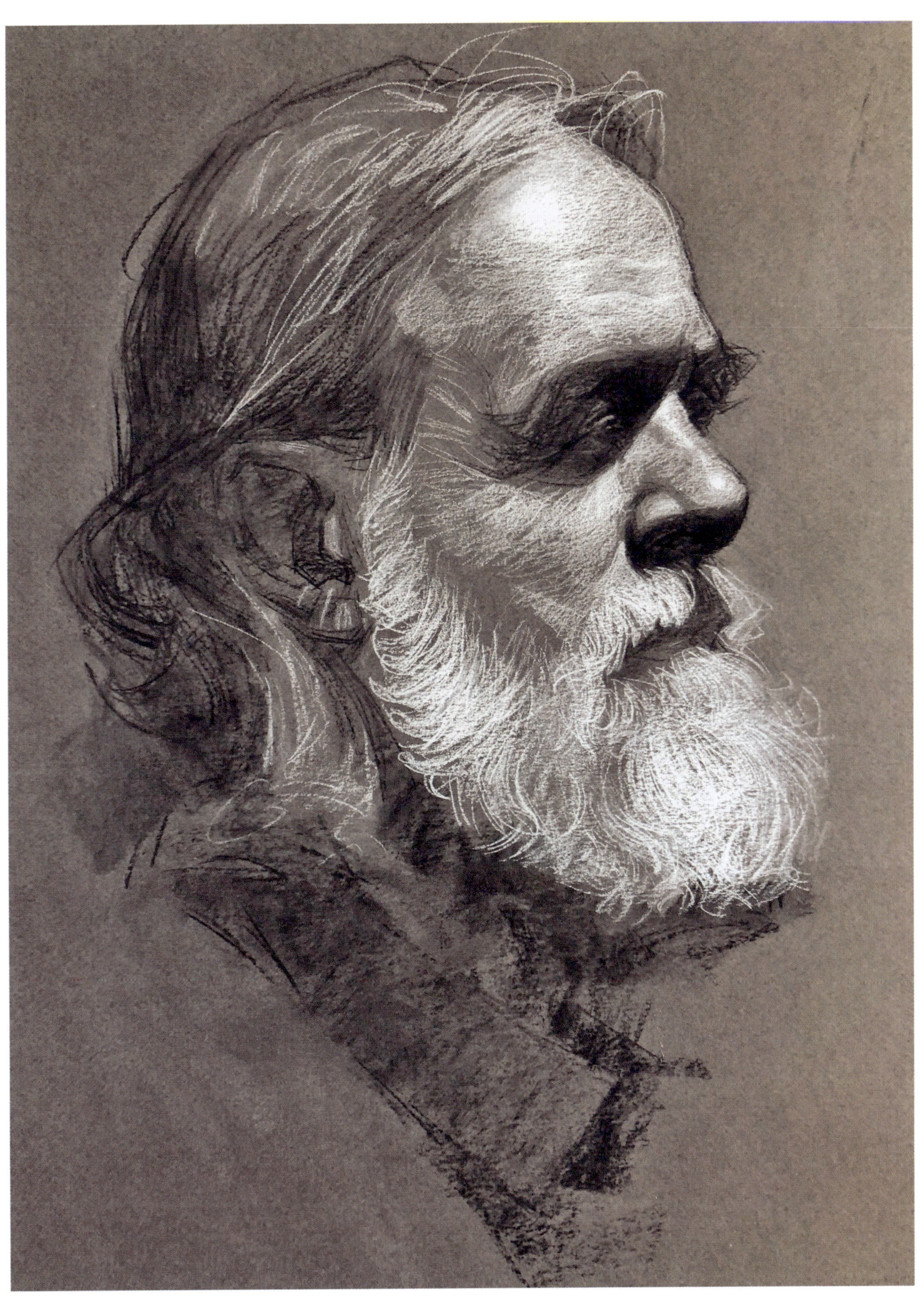

▲ *Mediums:* Vine charcoal and CarbOthello pastel pencil in Titanium White (#100) for highlights

Surface: Canson Mi-Teintes drawing paper in Dark Gray

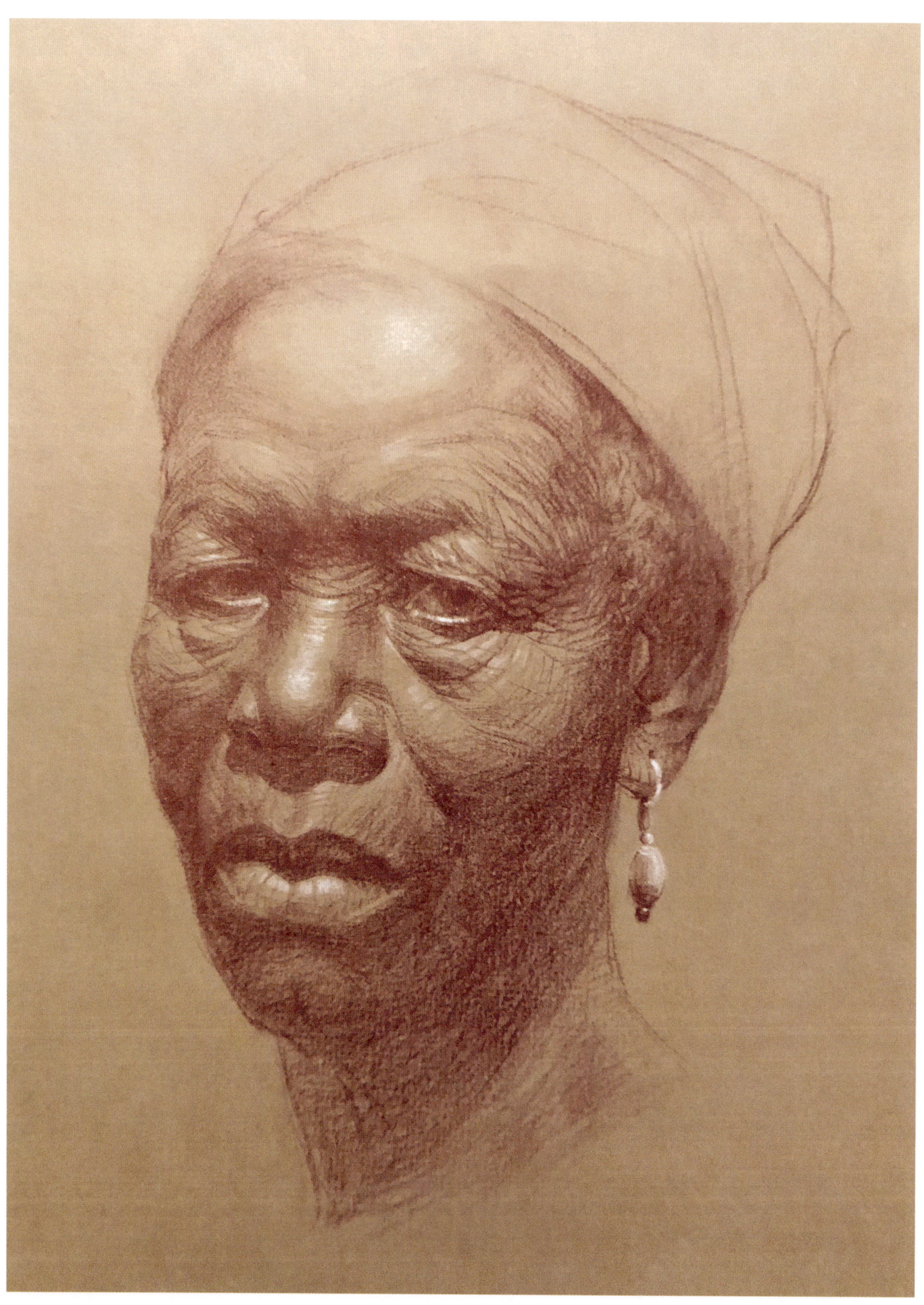

▲ ***Mediums:*** CarbOthello pastel pencils in Caput Mortuum Red (#645) and Titanium White (#100) for highlights

Surface: Strathmore 500 Series charcoal paper in Golden Brown

RESOURCES

Books

Sketch
by Zhaoming Wu

Henry Yan's Figure Drawing:
Techniques and Tips
by Henry Yan

Drawing People:
How to Portray the Clothed Figure
by Barbara Bradley

The Artist's Complete Guide to
Drawing the Head
by William Maughan

Drawing the Head and Hands
by Andrew Loomis

Materials Used in This Book

SURFACES
Canson Mi-Teintes drawing paper
Moleskin sketchbooks
Strathmore 500 Series charcoal paper
Strathmore 400 Series drawing paper
Strathmore 500 Series drawing paper

DRAWING TOOLS
CarbOthello pastel pencils
General's charcoal pencils
Grumbacher Matte Final Fixative
Prismacolor Kneaded Eraser
Winsor & Newton Vine Charcoal
Winsor & Newton Willow Charcoal

ACKNOWLEDGMENTS

From the bottom of my heart, I'd like to express my thanks to Academy of Art University, its administration staff, and the president, Dr. Elisa Stephens. Most of my drawings in this book were created in the studios of Academy of Art University. I would like to express my gratitude to the many faculty members at the Academy of Art University who have been so helpful and supportive and have encouraged me throughout the development of this book.

First to Zhao-Ming Wu and Henry Yan, artists whom I have admired for so long. They have been the greatest and kindest mentors under whom I have had the pleasure of studying since 2011. I have been sitting on these giants' shoulders and their keen guidance has opened me to new horizons. Another internationally acclaimed artist, Chien Chung-Wei, motivates me to create portrait drawings which aim at touching people's hearts and strive for excellence. Thanks to Tomutsu Takishima and Kazu Sano, who were my first mentors when I started to teach at Academy of Art University. My long-time friend Ivan Chan has always believed in me as an artist since college; her good sense and wise advice have stood by me faithfully during my journey in art. Tatsuya Kuroyanagi has put in so much enthusiasm professionally photographing and scanning hundreds of drawings for this book; his invaluable encouragement and unconditional love gave me confidence to complete this book. And Daniel Yen's Photoshop expertise helped to save me so much time and labor.

My special thanks go to the many professional models who posed for me in various guises. Their artistic creativity and remarkable presence pour life into the images in this book.

My further thanks go to Quarry Books acquiring editor, Joy Aquilino; editorial project manager, Meredith Quinn; and all of the staff who have aided and guided me through the long process of bringing this book to reality.

And last, but not least, my most heartfelt gratitude to my dear family, especially my brother Kelvin, who have always believed in my talents as an artist. I will walk tirelessly on my artistic journey, hoping that one day, I may be able to meet the expectations of all of my mentors, family, friends, students, and fans from social media. Thank you all!

ABOUT THE AUTHOR

OLIVER SIN graduated from the Academy of Art University in San Francisco with a bachelor of fine arts in illustration. He began his career as a computer games concept artist, including stints at LucasArts Entertainment Company and 3DO, and has been teaching for Academy of Art University's School of Animation and Visual Effects (2D Animation) and the School of Fine Art since 2001. His award-winning portrait art has been recognized by the Portrait Society of America, and featured in ArtistsNetwork.com, the quarterly journal *The Art of the Portrait*, *International Artist* and *Southwest Art* magazines, *Strokes of Genius 9*, *Strokes of Genius 11*, and *Creative Quarterly* magazines for more than a decade.

Born in Hong Kong, China, Sin has lived in San Francisco since 1990. Aside from teaching at AAU, he has also taught portrait drawing workshops at New Museum Los Gatos, Triton Museum of Art, and Pacific Art League.

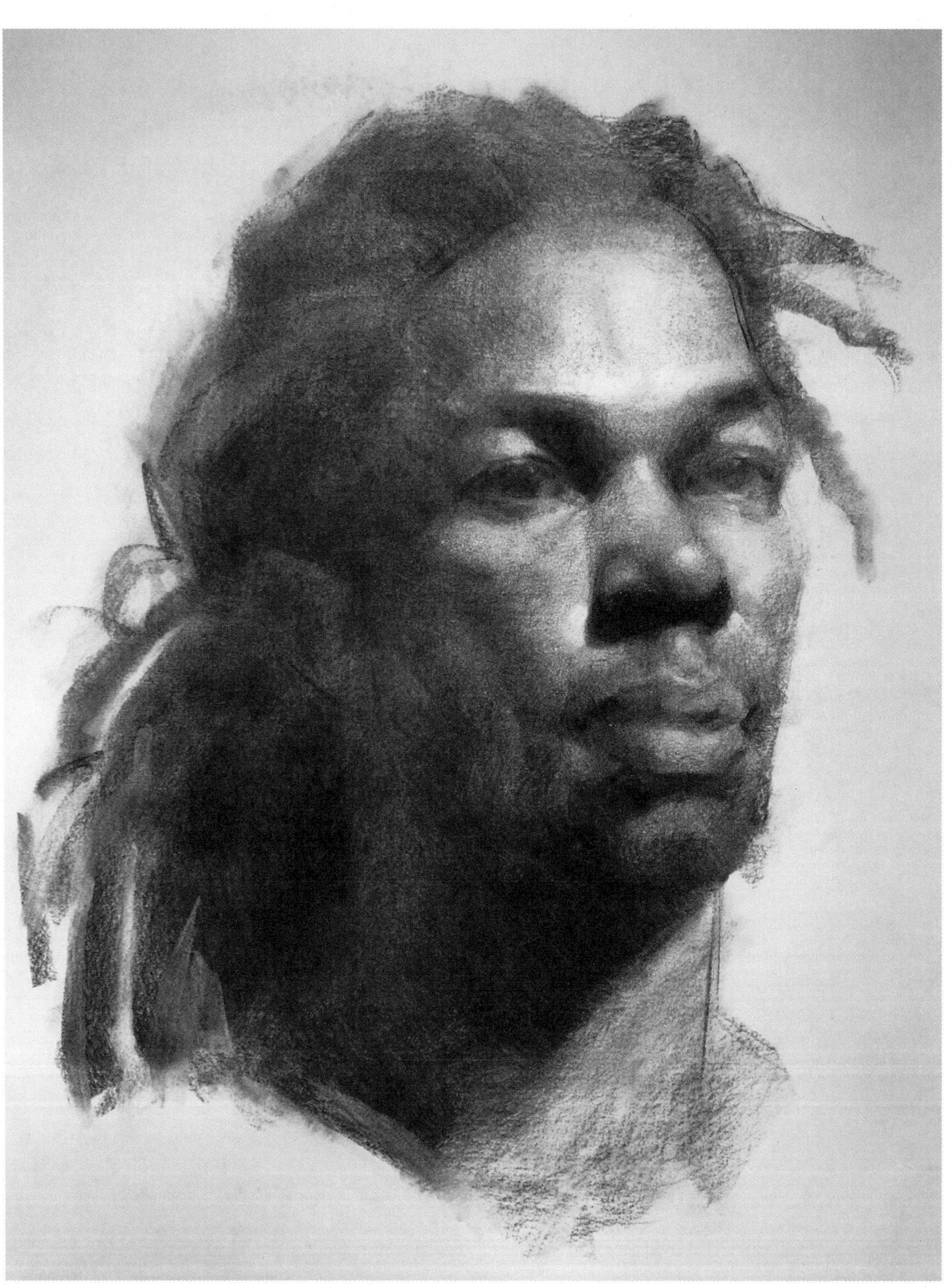